THE **J. PHILIP HOGAN** WORLD MISSIONS SERIES **2**

Alan R. Johnson

D1548181

APOSTOLIC
FUNCTION
IN 21ST CENTURY MISSIONS

ASSEMBLIES OF GOD THEOLOGICAL SEMINARY

Published by William Carey Library
1605 E. Elizabeth Street
Pasadena, CA 91104 | www.missionbooks.org

Naomi McSwain, editorial manager
Johanna Deming and Rosemary Lee-Norman, assistant editors
Hugh Pindur, graphic design

William Carey Library is a ministry of the
U.S. Center for World Mission
Pasadena, CA | www.uscwm.org

Printed in the United States of America
13 12 11 10 09   6 5 4 3 2 CH

Library of Congress Cataloging-in-Publication Data

Johnson, Alan R.
Apostolic function in 21st century missions / Alan R. Johnson.
  p. cm. -- (The J. Philip Hogan world missions series ; v. 2)
Includes bibliographical references (p.) and index.
ISBN 978-0-87808-011-3
1. Missions--Theory. I. Title. II. Series.

BV2063.J53 2009
266'.994--dc222

008052390

CONTENTS

GRATIS

131080

ABOUT THE AUTHOR

Alan R. Johnson, Ph.D.

Alan R. Johnson was born and raised in Seattle, Washington. He and his wife Lynette of 30 years, have lived primarily in Thailand for the past two decades under appointment of Assemblies of God World Missions. They have worked in church planting and various forms of formal and informal training with the Thailand Assemblies of God. In recent years they have begun pioneer work among the urban poor, developing a house church network and ministries to children in a series of slum communities in Bangkok.

In addition to his work with the urban poor, Alan has been involved in several functions at a broader level that coalesce around least-reached peoples. These ministries include the Strategic Church Planting Initiative in the Asia Pacific region, which focuses on developing new church planting teams among least-reached groups, the Institute for Buddhist Studies that trains people working among people groups influenced by Buddhist worldviews, and the Acts 1:8 Project which is an international committee focusing on emerging missions movements and unreached people groups in the Assemblies of God worldwide fellowship.

Alan is a graduate of Northwest University (B.A. in Pastoral Ministry), Assemblies of God Theological Seminary (M.A. in Biblical Studies), and Azusa Pacific University (M.A. in Social Sciences). His Ph.D. was awarded through the Oxford Centre for Mission Studies/University of

Wales. His dissertation was an ethnographic work on social influence processes in a slum community in Bangkok.

Alan and Lynette have two grown daughters, Laura and Rebecca, who are both alumni of Northwest University. Laura, and her husband Mark Snider live in Memphis, Tennessee, where he completed a pediatric residency and started a fellowship in hematology/oncology at St. Jude Children's Research Hospital in 2009. Laura is the real writer in the family and recently finished an M.F.A. in creative writing at the University of Memphis. Rebecca married Phillip Mefford in the spring of 2008 and they are working with an unreached people group in central Asia.

The Johnsons continue their work among slum dwellers in Bangkok, Thailand.

J. PHILIP HOGAN WORLD MISSIONS
SERIES INTRODUCTION

The J. Philip Hogan World Missions Series will be an effort by the Assemblies of God Theological Seminary to provide fresh missiological thinking in the Pentecostal tradition to the Assemblies of God and all Christian traditions committed to the mandate of the Great Commission.

The legacy of J. Philip Hogan calls us to pursue rigorous missiological reflection that wrestles well with our cultural context and commits itself to allow biblical revelation to critique our missionary efforts. Hogan counted among his closest friends the finest missiological minds of his day. He welcomed them as colleagues and, in turn, enriched their lives with his rich missionary statesmanship.

The J. Philip Hogan World Missions series will keep this rich dialogue with missions colleagues started by Hogan alive in the twenty-first century. Every annually appointed J. Philip Hogan professor will be asked to produce a monograph for publication in the Hogan World Missions Series. This will provide a global field-based pool of missiological thinking that can challenge the Pentecostal community and enrich the Christian communities committed to the redemptive mission of Jesus Christ.

PREFACE

The central idea of this monograph is a simple one: go where the church does not exist. If reading this helps any individual, group, pastor, church, or mission agency to bring to bear their energy and time upon a people group that does not have a strong movement of churches among it, then my purpose in writing will be fulfilled.

Looking back on the history that led to writing this monograph, I can see God's hand and grace very clearly. There are a series of relational connectors that made this possible; without these "door-openers" in my life, the ideas presented here would still be on scraps of paper and in fragments of different sizes and types in various notebooks and computers in my office in Bangkok.

Although the intellectual and relational history started long ago, the chain of events that led to this monograph can be traced back quite easily to what I literally thought was a joke or mistake at one point. Just prior to leaving his office as the Regional Director for Asia Pacific, Bob Houlihan named me to serve as our region's representative on a newly formed Commission on Strategy and Planning. In looking at the list of members, I was sure Bob must have been jet-lagged and hit a typo somewhere as they were a high powered group among whom I would clearly be the junior, least educated and experienced member.

This group, chaired by Doug Petersen, was excessively kind and good humored; from our first meeting they made me feel very welcome. In John York, one of the Commission members, I found a soul-mate in my passion for unreached peoples. John was known as the "apostle of *missio dei*" among the African church movements where he worked in theological education and casting the vision for African mission to unreached tribes and tongues. During a Commission meeting in an office in Springfield, Missouri, we were talking about pre-field training for missionary candidates and John, out of the blue, suggested that we include a lecture on current issues. Then, as a sidelight, he added, "And Al should present it." Doug agreed. The summer of 1999, I organized some notes and presented a brief lecture at our candidate school. Doug and John liked it and encouraged me to put it in writing. As that project grew, I was encouraged to submit it for presentation at the 2000 meeting of the Society for Pentecostal Studies (SPS).

Enter Byron Klaus. I had previously met Byron through the Commission group and he became the responder to my SPS paper in March 2000. My relationship with Byron and his awareness of my interest and writing on the theme of people group thinking led to the invitation to serve as the J. Philip Hogan Professor of World Missions at the Assemblies of God Theological Seminary (AGTS) for the 2006-2007 academic year. One of the main duties of the chair each year is to produce a missiological monograph, which brings us to this piece of writing here.

There is no way to explain or repay the debt of gratitude that I have to Bob, Doug, John, and Byron. They made this unique opportunity to focus time on writing about a topic near and dear to my heart possible. In addition, there are many others that I need to thank publicly for their part in bringing this piece to completion. I spent one semester at AGTS, and the staff and faculty there were incredibly gracious. I have benefited significantly from conversations about the subject matter with Joe Castleberry and DeLonn Rance. DeLonn was kind enough to sit in on my AGTS course in the fall of 2006 and read through a preliminary draft of the monograph. His insights have constantly sharpened my thinking in the process of work on this material.

Bill Prevette, an AGWM colleague who is currently finishing his Ph.D. dissertation with the Oxford Centre for Mission Studies, went the extra mile, when his own writing work was demanding all his energy, to read through the entire first draft and provide detailed and stimulating comments that were invaluable to me.

I spent the second half of the academic year in the Seattle area writing full-time, without any teaching duties. I need to thank my mother, Evelyn White, for the use of her congenial home, which provided a conducive atmosphere for writing. On my writing days, we would begin with a "breakfast club" talking about various things over our bowls of oatmeal; then I had the remainder of the day to write in the quiet of her home which affords a view of Mt. Rainier in good weather and a lovely garden in the back where more than one good idea came to me that made it into the monograph. Mark Rodli, who worked with us in Thailand for a year, came to the rescue time after time in hunting down books in libraries, doing internet searching, photocopying, and chauffeuring me around so I could get more writing time in. His extra energy helped push me forward when I was most weary. John Hoole, a long-time friend from our home church, New Life Church at Renton, gave me a most helpful tutorial on how to develop diagrams in the PowerPoint environment.

Thanks also goes to my children, Laura and Mark Snider and Rebecca and Phillip Mefford, for cheering me on in all my writing and academic pursuits. They have been ever-ready with listening ears as "monograph thinking" has bled over into our conversations during our all too short times together. Finally, to my best friend and wife of nearly 30 years, Lynette, I owe thanks, gratitude and appreciation that cannot be measured. She alone knows how little I would have accomplished without her constant encouragement, support and comforting presence.

1

INTRODUCTION

The Dangerous Chart

When people ask me why I became a missionary, the short answer is that I was driven out of my mind by a chart. Nearly thirty years of post-chart life later I remain bent by the experience, and there is no hope (or desire) for a return to my pre-chart days or view of the world. Since most people do not find diagrams of concentric circles so disturbing, let me back up and give some more details.

My experience of the chart was set up by two events that happened before and during my freshmen year of college. Just after high school graduation I began attending an Assemblies of God church and that summer I was baptized in the Holy Spirit. That experience brought a zeal and passion to share the Gospel. During the first quarter at the University of Washington I read a missionary biography and was deeply moved by this man's example. It birthed in me a desire to use my life in Christian service. These two events ultimately led to a decisive calling into full-time vocational ministry.

Then the chart happened. While working on staff at a local church, a missionary friend handed me a brochure about a group trying to found an organization called the U. S. Center for World Mission. I liked the idea because I thought missions was cool and sent them the $15.95

they were requesting. They sent me a receipt and inside the envelope was a chart. At the time I had a tiny youth pastor office without any decorations on the wall, so I thought this would be nice to lend a little color to the room. That was my mistake. The blue circles making up the diagram hung about five feet from my head where I sat at my desk working on youth pastorish kinds of things like answering phone messages, planning events, writing sermons, and talking with students. Day after day I would look at this simple set of circles depicting the five major blocks of unreached people. Looking turned into praying, which in turn lead to more reading and study until the Holy Spirit used that data to create an unshakable conviction that I personally had to work among an unreached people. I tell people jokingly that the receipt should have come with something akin to the surgeon general's warning on cigarette packages—WARNING THIS WILL MESS UP YOUR MIND AND SEND YOU TO PLACES FAR AWAY AND BEND YOUR THINKING BEYOND REPAIR.

The message of the chart (there are now much more sophisticated graphics and statistics) that so disturbed me was that there were people groups in the world without anybody in their setting to tell them about Jesus. This meant that somebody had to leave their own culture that had the Gospel to go to one that did not have it in order to proclaim it there and plant the church. The irony is that several years of listening to missionary speakers never made we want to become one. It was not because I did not think they were doing something great. Rather with my missiological naiveté and lack of context, the glowing reports I heard were so victorious and exciting they only confirmed my conviction that overseas the job was being finished and someone needed to stay in America to try to bring such revival here.

In my pre-chart life, I never had a sense of personal responsibility towards people in other parts of the world. My local church experience of hearing missionary reports had fanned the flame for evangelism, but it never pushed me toward the conclusion that I must be involved personally. The chart changed all of that. Suddenly I found myself in a world where some people had access to the Gospel and others did not—unless someone crossed a cultural frontier with the message. My heart had already been stirred to evangelism, but study of the chart moved me from a kind of monochrome conception where all evangelism was equal to a brilliant full color picture that showed some people having the potential for access to the Gospel with others having no access at all. Over time I realized that my own setting in North America was filled with potential for people to hear the Gospel through myriads of believers, while in other places there were no Christian near neighbors to tell the story, or so few that they still required help in reaching their people.

My own personal calling to involvement in missions came as the two streams of my experience converged. Baptism in the Spirit brought passion to reach the lost, while missiological data showed me the state of the world and where those with least access to the Gospel were located. I ended up in Thailand working among Buddhist people. My assumption was that everyone in cross-cultural work thought the same way about missions and that sharing the Gospel in places where the church did not exist or was very small was at the heart of things.

BEGINNING TO SEE THE "WHERE" QUESTION

Imagine my surprise when later in my career, through reading and meeting other people both within and outside of my organization, I found that not only did many missionaries not know much about unreached people groups, there was often even a feeling of antipathy towards the idea. As time went on I also began to notice confusion at the grassroots level of conceptions of mission. People were moving away from the idea of planting the church among people that had no church movement to going to places with many Christians to help them in varying ways. Sometimes when discussing people group thinking with other missionaries the objection will be raised that the insights that Ralph Winter had thirty years ago are now passé, that they have been left behind and that we have a more sophisticated view of missions today.

The difficulty with this view is that it is plainly not supported by the data. The increasingly sophisticated database about the status of global Christianity shows that nearly 40 percent of the world lives in a situation where there is either no near neighbor witness in their sociocultural setting or a very small one. It is precisely because of this reality that I think the insights that come from what is now known as the frontier mission movement are so relevant to the time in which we live. Recent reflection has led me to believe that the really important contribution of unreached people group thinking and the frontier missions movement to missiology will be its making explicit what has tended to be implicit in our thinking about missions for much of our two thousand year history.

Looking back over Christian mission history we see the variety of ways that mission has been carried out. From apostolic bands to monks and monasteries, the work of Pietists, Moravians, and since Carey, the voluntary missionary society; all found from Scripture their theology of mission that defines the why, what, and how of missions. In sketching the contours of a biblical theology of mission, Bosch notes that such a project seeks answers to these three basic questions—why mission, how mission, and what is mission?—in specific contexts.[1] I would suggest that these three questions are not enough; and that implicit within our two thousand years of mission theologizing are also understandings about *where* mission should take place as well.[2] This is the genius so to speak boiled out of all that frontier missions and unreached people thinking brings to us; without answering "among whom" and thus "where" mission is to be done in light of the witness of Scripture and God's intent for the world, we do not yet have a full blown missiology.

While ideally we would like to think that what we do and where we go as missionaries grows out of our understanding of the Bible and the leading of the Holy Spirit, in reality it is not that simple. At each time and place we have a history, there are commitments made, people have preceded us, and thus there is no isomorphic connection between what we believe about from the Bible and what we do. The "where" question of missions has always been present and is woven deeply into our understanding of God's mission and our role in it. While it has often been neglected in missiological thinking (witness Bosch writing in 1993 with no mention of this at all) the observation and growing empirical evidence of the great gulf between a world where church movements exist and where they do not, must put the "where" dimension as a priority focus for all who are concerned about God's mission.

The neglect of the "where" dimension of mission is a reminder that we are children of our age, and thus there are some things that we see

---

1   David J. Bosch, "Reflections on Biblical Models of Mission," in *Toward the Twenty-First Century in Christian Mission: Essays in Honor of Gerald H. Anderson*, ed. James M. Phillips and Robert T. Coote (Grand Rapids: Eerdmans, 1993), 179.

2   The "where" question actually addresses the issue of "among whom" will mission be conducted? Because it fits better with the interrogatives already used by Bosch, I will use "where" throughout the monograph to refer to not simply geography but to the people to whom cross-cultural workers are bringing the Gospel.

very clearly, and other things that are obscured by the trends, fashions and tastes of our era. Taber reminds us that:

> One must by no means underestimate the degree to which Christians in general and missionaries in particular are people of their age and culture, even with respect to their theology. The missionary movement has surely not been determined by the world in which missionaries grew up, but it has been definitely influenced; missionaries have to an astonishing degree followed the twists and turns of prevalent social attitudes and values, no less really because their conformity was so largely unwitting.[3]

There are forces afoot today that conspire against seeing the "where" issue clearly in Scripture; therefore, this monograph is devoted primarily to this theme.

THE MAIN ARGUMENTS IN BRIEF

My purpose in writing is to present three major arguments that are driven by a problematic. The problem is a lack of clarity about the nature and practice of cross-cultural missions. Over the scope of this monograph, I address this problematic in three major arguments, each of which makes up a part of the solution. The first is that *where* Christian redemptive activities take place is a critical issue for those who take the Bible seriously. While *what* we do and *how* we do it are of vast importance, those who take Scripture as an authoritative revelation have written and wrestled through these two dimensions of mission in great detail. While our practice is never perfect, and always a shadow of the example of our Lord, at this point in our history, collectively we do the *what* and *how* of mission well. In addition to this fact, there is vigorous and ongoing debate about these issues that continues to

---

3   Charles R. Taber, *The World Is Too Much with Us: "Culture" in Modern Protestant Missions*, ed. Wilbert R. Shenk, The Modern Missions Era, 1792-1992: An Appraisal (Macon, Georgia: Mercer University Press, 1991), 160.

refine and feed our understanding and practice along these dimensions. However, as Christians we can do all the right things for the right reasons, in the right way, but if we are not doing them in the right places and among the right people, we are missing something that is very close to the Father's heart for the world. Thus, one part of the solution to the problem of unclear mission thinking that I am advocating is to get the "where" question answered correctly.

My second point has to do with influencing how we practice mission. At least from a historical perspective, eloquent voices and movements have argued for and become identified with what, where, and how issues of mission. So much so, that entire frameworks or perspectives have grown up around them. While not mutually exclusive by any means, within the Evangelical, Pentecostal, and Charismatic (EPC) streams of missions,[4] which are based in a view of Scripture as an authoritative

---

4   Major streams of missions are categorized in various ways by different writers. Jongeneel and Van Engelen note that after New Delhi, Uppsala, and Vatican II three streams are discernible: Evangelical, Ecumenical, and Roman Catholic; J. A. B. Jongeneel and J. M. Van Engelen, "Contemporary Currents in Missiology," in *Missiology: An Ecumenical Introduction: Texts and Contexts of Global Christianity*, ed. A. Camps et al. (Grand Rapids: Eerdmans, 1995), 446. McGavran and Glasser break it into four streams: Ecumenical (conciliar), Evangelical, Roman Catholic, and Liberationist, noting that there are breakdowns between these and that some, such as Evangelicals, have numerous subgroups; Ibid.; also Donald Anderson McGavran and Arthur F. Glasser, *Contemporary Theologies of Mission* (Grand Rapids: Baker, 1983); see also James A. Scherer and Stephen B. Bevans, eds. *New Directions in Mission and Evangelization 1: Basic Statements 1974-1991*, ed. James A. Scherer and Stephen B. Bevans, New Directions in Mission and Evangelization, vol. 1 (Maryknoll, New York: Orbis Books, 1992); and Van Engen uses a five-fold categorization: Roman Catholic, Orthodox, Conciliar, Evangelical, and Pentecostal/Charismatic; Charles Van Engen, *Mission on the Way: Issues in Mission Theology*, (Grand Rapids: Baker Books, 1996), 17. Glasser sees the earmarks of Evangelicalism as unquestioned submission to the trustworthiness of authority of Scripture as the Word of God, the essentialness of the atonement of Christ to be made fit for the presence and fellowship of God, an existential saving encounter with the Holy Spirit, a concern for the proper scriptural use of the sacraments. He notes that most would add the obligation to evangelize non-Christians throughout the world; Arthur Glasser, "Evangelical Missions," in *Toward the Twenty-First Century in Christian Mission: Essays in Honor of Gerald H. Anderson*, ed. James M. Phillips

revelation from God, there are discernible frameworks represented both in the literature and in organizations around the planting and growing of churches, the expression of Christian social concern, and a focus on getting the Gospel to unreached people groups where no church movements currently exist. It is not too much of an over-generalization to say that on the whole cross-cultural workers, mission agencies, and church movements, while representing lots of interests, tend to find their emphasis in one of these areas. While there is no doubt that some configuration of all three of these frameworks will be found within a single organization (or person's ministry), it often is the case that actual practice is shaped around values and commitments that grow out of one of these major frames.

My second argument then is based in the idea that in the 21st century all the participants in global mission need to have their practice shaped by an integration of insights from these varying frames rather than seeing or treating them as competing ways of approaching the mission of the church. It is in paying attention to our operating frameworks, and drawing upon more of them that we insure that what we do and

---

and Robert T. Coote (Grand Rapids: Eerdmans Publishing Company, 1993), 11. Winter notes that the evangelical movement cannot be properly understood as an ecclesiastical phenomenon, but is "rather a new spirit, a new set of expectations about what a true Christian really was like" and that its most significant characteristic is "its emphasis upon the quite literal spiritual transformation of the individual"; Ralph Winter, "Introduction: Why an Evangelical Response to Bangkok?" In *The Evangelical Response to Bangkok*, ed. Ralph Winter (South Pasadena: William Carey Library, 1973), 7-8. Glasser notes that Webber sees 14 different Evangelical subcultures while he himself uses five: separatist fundamentalists, who are still caught up in the fundamentalist-liberal struggles of the 20s and 30s, low-key dispensational Evangelicals, who fill the ranks of the faith missions and smaller Evangelical denominations, Charismatic Evangelicals, from traditional Pentecostal to mainline Charismatics, Ecumenical Evangelical, and nonconciliar, traditionally orthodox communions such as Reformed, Lutheran, Mennonite, Plymouth Brethren; Ibid., 11-12. What I am designating as the E (Evangelical), P (Pentecostal) and C (Charismatic) missiologies and missions all fall under the broader categorization used by Glasser and would adhere to his five major earmarks and the emphasis on spiritual transformation noted by Winter.

where we go are being directed by the Scriptures and the Spirit and not the latest missions fad.

My final argument, and where the title for the monograph is drawn from, is that we can stay clear in our concept of missions, answer the "where" question, and best keep in step with the Scriptural witness to God's global plan when our conceptions of mission practice are drawn from the Pauline version of apostleship. When cross-cultural workers take their identity from apostolic function it ties them into the insights of the major mission paradigms, provides a clear answer to the "where" question, and results in a clear view of cross-cultural mission that invigorates the work of the church both within and outside of its own cultural borders.

OVERVIEW OF THE CHAPTERS

In the next chapter, I set the stage for the three major arguments by laying out the problematic of unclear thinking about missions. I show that there has been a shift in understanding away from the conception of missions as preaching the Gospel and planting the church in places where it does not exist and develop an account of how and why we are at a critical point in our understanding and practice. Chapter 3 then looks at the notion of paradigms as a tool for thinking about missions. In chapter 4, I argue for apostolic function as a paradigm of missionary identity and then, in chapters 5 and 6, I examine in detail the "where" question of missions in the frontier mission paradigm. Chapter 7 develops my argument for using mission paradigms in a comprehensive and integrative fashion and provides some illustrative material to show what this might look like. In the final chapter, I discuss issues that grow out of addressing the "where" question in missions.

2

THE GROWING LACK OF CLARITY
ABOUT MISSIONS

In the opening years of the twentieth century, a new thrust of missions began out of the conviction that the work of the Spirit they were experiencing heralded a restoration of the apostolic church and its practices. This movement was marked by urgency to reap a final harvest before the return of Christ and the expectation of signs and wonders to accompany the preaching of the Gospel. Now, nearly 100 years later, the efforts of these humble pioneers have been multiplied by the Holy Spirit till churches of the Pentecostal/Charismatic persuasion represent a stream of Christianity that is estimated by 2050 will number a billon people.[5]

The success of Pentecostal/Charismatic streams of missions is a part of what has turned out to be a massive global shift of Christianity from the north to the south.[6] It is precisely the reality of this success that raises critical questions in today's current mission setting. Listen to Lesslie Newbigin:

---

5   Michael Pocock, Gailyn Van Rheenen, and Douglas McConnell, *The Changing Face of World Missions: Engaging Contemporary Issues and Trends*, ed. A. Scott Moreau, Encountering Mission (Grand Rapids: Baker Academic, 2005), 58.

6   Philip Jenkins, *The Next Christendom: The Coming of Global Christianity* (Oxford: Oxford Press, 2002), 2-6.

The Christian church is now, for the first time in history, a truly global fellowship, present—in however humanly weak a form—in every part of the world, and including in its shared life a vast variety of human cultures, races, and languages. And that is our problem! ... It is no longer a matter of the simple command to go to the ends of the earth and preach the gospel where it has not been heard. In every nation there are already Christian believers. The church is already there, and its integrity must be honored.[7]

Newbigin's point that the church exists and must be honored by those who are going to work cross-culturally is well taken. However, while the successful expansion of Christianity may mean that it is no longer a "simple matter" to go where the Gospel has not been heard, it does not mean that the command to make disciples among the *ethne* of the world is completed. From one perspective, it makes a more stark contrast between those sociocultural settings that have existing church movements and the many peoples, tribes, and tongues where there are no church movements or very small ones.

While there are many issues in cross-cultural missions today, the critical one facing all those who take Scripture seriously is this issue of the existence of the church and its counterpart—all of the places remaining on earth where there are no church movements or very small ones.[8] When the Body of Christ worldwide should be marshalling all

---

7 Lesslie Newbigin, "Preface," in *Toward the Twenty-First Century in Christian Mission: Essays in Honor of Gerald H. Anderson*, ed. James M. Phillips and Robert T. Coote (Grand Rapids: Eerdmans Publishing Company, 1993), 2.

8 See the work of the Joshua Project at http://www.joshuaproject.net and their four-fold classification of the status of Christianity among all the people groups of the world at http://www.joshuaproject.net/definitions.php#jpscale. The Joshua Project Progress Scale represents an attempt to provide a consistent statistical framework for viewing, measuring, and tracking where in our world are the least numbers of Christians and church movements. By their definition of least-reached and unreached (all people groups with less than 2 percent Evangelical and less than 5 percent total Christian adherents of any kind) almost 40 percent of the world has either no or very limited near-neighbor witness of the Gospel.

its efforts to take the Gospel to those who have not heard, there are signs that current conceptions of missions are becoming confused. It is not erosion in understanding, but rather a proliferation of activity that threatens to choke the ability of the church to take the Gospel to the 40 percent who are least-reached and unreached. Here in the opening decades of the twenty-first century, when we need to be the most focused, the notion of missions is a contested idea.

The problematic that drives this study lies in the juxtaposition of the empirical reality of all the places where there are no church movements and the growing confusion about the nature of mission. The problematic is crystallized in these statements by Stephen Neill and Ralph Winter. In 1959, Neill wrote, "When everything is mission, nothing is mission."[9] Winter has also argued that the meaning of mission is universally misunderstood in Liberal, Conservative, Conciliar, and Independent circles.[10] He points out that practically everyone now seems to agree that Christian World Mission refers to "the redemptive activities of the church within the societies where the church is found (at home or abroad). But note, the phrase no longer needs point to the redemptive activity of the church within societies where the church is not found."[11]

Bosch points out that prior to the 1950s the meaning of the term "mission" had a "fairly circumscribed set of meanings" but that since the 1950s there has been an explosion of the use of the term and a broadening of the concept.[12] Generally, four main traditional defini-

---

9 Stephen Neill, *Creative Tension* (London: Edinburgh House Press, 1959), 81.

10 Ralph D. Winter, The Meaning of Mission: Understanding This Term Is Crucial to the Completion of the Missionary Task (*Mission Frontiers*, 1998, accessed 5 October 2006); available from www.missionfrontiers.org/1998/0304/ma9813.htm.

11 Ibid.

12 This included the sending of missionaries to designated territory, activities undertaken by missionaries, geographical area where missionaries are active, agency which sent the missionaries to the non-Christian world, the "mission

tions are used: a) propagation of the faith, b) expansion of the reign of God, c) conversion of the heathen, d) the founding of new churches.[13] Johannes Verkuyl points out that in the modern historical period of mission, six major definitions of mission have governed missionary practice.[14] Four of these would be identified with those that are commonly found among mission efforts of Evangelical background. These include the goals of converting the lost, planting churches, and developing indigenous church movements that support, propagate and govern themselves. Arguably the context in which these traditional conceptions of mission arose was one where there was a fairly sharp distinction between places where the church existed and where it did not, and these activities were implemented in order to plant the church where it did not previously exist. The growth of Christianity has passed by this kind of distinction and helped to initiate the shift in understanding that Winter has noted.

Part of the mission realities of our day include Newbigin's observation about the existence of the church, Neill's warning that there needs to be preserved some distinction between activities that are "missions" and others that are not, and Winter's point in the late 90s of the universal misunderstanding among the various streams of Christianity about the meaning of mission. The purpose of this monograph is to provide some conceptual tools to help mission practitioners at every level to navigate the complex relationships that have emerged in our world at the church/church and church/non-Christian world interface, to revitalize the conception of missions as planting the church where it

---

field," the center from which missionaries operated on the mission field; David Bosch, *Transforming Mission: Paradigm Shifts in Theology of Mission* (Maryknoll, New York: Orbis Books, 1991), 1, 511.

13   Ibid., 1.

14   Johannes Verkuyl, *Contemporary Missiology: An Introduction*, trans. Dale Cooper (Grand Rapids: Eerdmans, 1978), 180ff.

is not found, and to help clarify the role and contribution of all cross-cultural workers.

In the next three sections, I will examine current trends in missions that provide evidence that a shift of understanding has indeed happened, develop an account for why this has happened, and suggest the need for a new way of thinking about missions.

EVIDENCE FOR A SHIFT IN UNDERSTANDING OF THE IDEAS OF MISSIONS AND MISSIONARY

I begin with three caveats here. First, a thorough documenting of current mission trends as it relates to the conceptions of "missions" and "missionary" is a book length task that lies outside of the scope of this piece, and which waits to be done. Second, while my experience is limited to one particular Pentecostal organization and context, I believe that the issues I discuss here have a broader application to Evangelical and other Pentecostal/Charismatic streams of mission. Finally, some of the positions that I will deal with here are not internally consistent. They represent ideas and practices that are popular in nature, and precisely for that reason, are not nailed down to a point of conceptual consistency.

1. In many places, there is a conflation of the ideas of the evangelistic outreach of a local church or movement within its own sociocultural setting with the notion of missions. I first noticed this in my early years in Thailand where the Thai church movement we worked with raised funds for "missions." The term they used was *pantagit* (combining words for the ideas of obligation and activity) and sometimes they would pair with the English word for mission as *pantagit mitchan*. What they meant by this was going to other places in Thailand and planting churches. So the concept did not take into consideration at all the cultural

background of the group they were going to, or the status of Christianity among that group. In this sense it was "missions" because it was different. To preach the Gospel in one's own hometown was one thing, and to go somewhere else (often times it was an urban to rural flow) was thus *pantagit*. In America, my movement attempted to solve this difficulty by appending different adjectives to mission, with the resulting "home" for things happening on American soil and "foreign" for things done outside our borders.

My experiences in Thailand have led me to regularly ask the question of expatriates and local Christians from other places to define what mission is in their setting. The vast majority of the time people tell me that "mission" means preaching the Gospel in a different place. The problem with this is that any kind of outreach at all becomes missions, which has the deadening effect of equalizing all types of evangelism. Once all forms of evangelism are given identical footing there are no longer any criteria for making distinctions between people who have the potential for access to the Gospel in their setting and those who do not.[15] This actually leads to people going as cross-cultural workers out of a social setting with less Christians than the one they are going to, and giving their work the title "missionary" because it happens in a different place.

2. Another related, but somewhat different version of this conflation is found in the popular aphorism, "Everyone is a missionary." In this case, it is not just evangelism happening to the "other" that is missions, it is any outreach at all that becomes missionary. So people's neighbors become their mission field, and they become "missionaries" to their neighbors.

---

15   The issue of access is a subtle, but critical point that I will look at in detail at a later point.

3. Another very popular view of missions is that it relates to the crossing of geographic borders. This lies behind the "home" and "foreign" language that I noted above. This results in people being sent outside of their country to preach the Gospel to their own people who are living abroad, while ignoring within their own borders those groups of different religious, social, and linguistic background who do not have church movements at all. Such a view is very susceptible to the problems of "people blindness" where the person only sees their own, and their predisposition to dislike other groups, for a variety of reasons, hampers their ability to see them and thus reach out to them with the Gospel. Thus sociological considerations trump their theological understanding of God's love for all people and the whole world.

4. Another factor that is implicit in views of missions is that it must be conducted in a way that brings rapid results. Such a view is not simply a North American phenomenon. I was rather shocked when discussing with a Thai leader the need to bring the Gospel to a large minority group in the country. His response was that they would go to the already Christianized tribal groups because they could get fast results, and that they would leave resistant groups to us Westerners who had a lot of money to burn.[16] The tragedy here is that the remaining groups in the world that have the fewest or no Christians are also the most difficult to reach. The criterion of quick results means that their well-known resistance keeps decision-makers from ever allocating personnel and finances in their direction.

---

16 Pierson sees the expectation of quick results as a factor in the current missions scene that is rooted in contemporary American culture; Paul Pierson, "Local Churches in Mission: What's Behind the Impatience with Traditional Mission Agencies?," *International Bulletin of Missionary Research*, (1998): 147. In the case I have illustrated from Thailand, it is hard to know whether this need for instant results is something learned from association with western missionaries or is related to other factors in the Thai setting.

5. In some cases, a well-intentioned commitment to develop a strong national church has had the unintended consequence of modeling for local Christians a type of missionary service that inhibits their ability to do pioneer church planting. A person working in an African context told me that believers in the movement he is working with think that being a missionary means going to a Bible school. Years of seeing westerners work with an existing church movement has left this national church without any conception of pioneer work where there is no preexisting church movement. One result is that people repeatedly exposed to missionaries who work in Christian contexts in a supportive fashion begin to conceive of missions in these terms.

6. Growing affluence and the ease of travel has created the ability for people to get firsthand experience with cross-cultural work. One outgrowth of this convergence is the short-term missions movement, which not only espouses hands-on experience, but is increasingly seen as a viable methodology for missions.[17]

---

17 The October 2006 Special Edition of *Missiology: An International Review* is dedicated to the issue of short-term missions. Priest, et al., note that the short-term mission movement is "transforming the way North American Christians are engaging the world. But it is a grassroots and populist phenomenon almost completely divorced from scholarship, from missiology, and from seminary education"; Robert J. Priest and others, "Researching the Short-Term Mission Movement," *Missiology: An International Review* 34, no. 4 (2006): 434. They indicate that U. S. Christians involved in short-term missions vastly outnumber career missionaries and that is possible that more money now supports these short-term efforts than career missionaries as well; Ibid. See Priest, et al., for bibliographic data on the growing popular literature on short-term missions and for their research on the issue of short-term and support of career missionaries which calls into question the more positive results given by Paula Harris in "Calling Young People to Missionary Vocations in a 'Yahoo' World," *Missiology: An International Review* 30, no. 1 (2002). Missions is increasingly seen as a project rather than a long-term process done by career missionaries; Stan Guthrie, *Missions in the Third Millennium: 21 Key Trends for the 21st Century* (Carlisle, Cumbria, UK: Paternoster Press, 2000), 113. He notes that the tried and true approach of long-term commitment, translation, church planting, and training is no longer necessarily at the core of missions strategy in many corners. The new approach is characterized by bypassing traditional agencies, support of projects with defined

This is a worrisome trend for mission leaders who understand the complexity of planting and developing the church in any human society. Gary Corwin observes:

One of the great unfortunate shifts in our days is that many students, along with many of their elders, have unwittingly accepted the idea that embracing a call to the nations is primarily an instantaneous commitment having short-term consequences, resulting in a memorable experience. The accomplishment of long-term strategic Kingdom goals has, as a result, been too often replaced by the multiplication of 'mission experiences' as the chief end of outreach from North America. Thus 'been there, done that' comes to replace Isaiah's, 'Here am I, Lord, send me,' as the standard refrain in response to the needs of the world for the healing power of the gospel. The sacrifice is certainly far more manageable, but the significance of the impact doesn't even come close.[18]

Even more troubling than the truncated impact of short-term work is the potential for skewing missionary placement for those who are experiencing short-term missions as a major framework for understanding cross-cultural work. Because of limitations relating to language and cultural understanding, short-term trips are constructed experiences that almost by definition have to be designed and supported by someone who already has those skills, which is generally a long-term missionary. This means again, almost by definition, that the vast majority of short-term trips are going to take place where there are already existing churches. This creates two types of feedback loops, one positive and the other negative, that affect how people are influenced towards where they want to serve if they do move towards a long-term missions commitment.

---

short-term goals, using prayer to break down strongholds, and sending more short-termers.

18   Gary R. Corwin, "A Second Look: Student Heroes—Do It Again Lord!" *Evangelical Missions Quarterly*, (2003): 417.

FIGURE 1
Positive and Negative Feedback Loops
and Missions Calling

In figure 1, I illustrate this process in two pictures. The positive feedback loop shows how successful mission work generates news and reports in various means of communication, which leads to visits by people who then have a sense of calling to that place, which provides more workers and more success. In the negative loop, it is precisely the opposite; where the church does not exist there are no reports, no visits and, thus, people are less likely to develop a burden and calling to go.

7. No matter how people conceptualize the missionary task, the actual placement of cross-cultural workers around the globe is the strongest evidence for Winter's critique that missions is now seen as activities of the church were the church is found. Barrett and Johnson's map of what they call the great unevangelized belt shows clearly where the church does not exist and that the cross-cultural workforce of the global church is not located in force in these places.[19] Figure 2 illustrates this same evidence in

---

19 David B. Barrett and others, eds. *World Christian Trends AD 30-AD 2200: Interpreting the Annual Christian Megacensus* (Pasadena, California: William Carey Library, 2001), 53, 55. As with any statistical work, the reader always has to bear in mind the basis for the material presented, particularly how it was obtained and how terminology is used. Barrett divides the world into three major parts on the basis of a very specific measure of evangelization. By this measure, World A, the unevangelized world, has 38 countries and only 2.4 percent of the global foreign missionary force and 1.7 percent of foreign missionary money; Ibid., p. 52, 55. The unevangelized belt includes almost all the World A countries and

terms of the number of cross-cultural workers per million people among major cultural blocs.

FIGURE 2
Missionaries in Major Cultural Blocs

Number of Foreign Missionaries per Million in Major Cultural Blocs

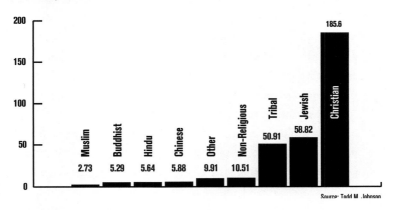

Source: Todd M. Johnson

This material is extracted from the third edition of the *Perspectives on the World Christian Movement Reader*, Pasadena, California: William Carey Library, 1999 and the Mission Frontiers June 2000 edition. © 2000 *Reprinted with permission.*

In his 2002 article on the statistical state of the world missionary enterprise, one of the questions Jaffarian asks is, "Where are missionaries needed?" He points out that the answer to this question depends on our missiology.[20] He illustrates it this way: if we think that missionaries are needed in circumstances of poverty, political repression, where the

some World B countries (what he calls the evangelized non-Christian world). While it is possible to disagree with Barrett's definitions regarding measures of evangelization, the overall picture of the world is hard to argue with as it shows clearly that the Christian movements and resources are overwhelmingly located in some places and not in others.

20 E. Michael Jaffarian, "The Statistical State of the Missionary Enterprise," *Missiology: An International Review* 30, no. 1 (2002): 28.

most non-Christians live, or where those who have not heard the Gospel reside, then there are logical choices of countries for missionaries to locate in that meet those criteria.[21] However, Jaffarian hits hard at the world Christian mission movement by pointing out that:

> Despite what we might say, or preach, or teach, it seems that great commission Christians of the world hold to none of those four positions. The statistical facts of the world missionary situation show that the churches of the world instead are following a missiology that says missionaries are most needed in circumstances not of poverty but of wealth, not of oppression but of freedom, not where non-Christians are, but where Christians are, and not where most have not heard the Gospel but where most have not only heard it but received it. Most of the largest missionary-receiving countries in the world are relatively wealthy, free, and Christian. The real, demonstrated sending priorities apparently emphasize helping Christians become better Christians rather than helping non-Christians consider Christ—or helping Christians of one kind (usually Catholic or Orthodox) become Christians of another kind (Evangelical or Catholic or Charismatic, and so on) rather than helping those who have not heard the gospel to hear it.[22]

The material I have briefly introduced here illustrates how at the level of understanding and practice, the formerly common understanding of missions and the role of the missionary has changed. Pierson calls our time a "new period in missions history" marked by the global shift of Christianity to the south, the internationalization of the mis-

---

21 Ibid.

22 Ibid. Although the material is not organized in a fashion to make this point, the prayer guide *Operation World: 21ˢᵗ Century Edition* by Patrick Johnstone and Jason Mandryk (Carlisle, United Kingdom: Paternoster Lifestyle, 2001), when seen in its totality at a country by country level, is striking in that, in general, the reader gets the strong impression that the largest numbers of missionaries are present where the church is the largest; there is a noticeably smaller missionary presence where the church is either very small or non-existent.

sionary movement, ease of communication and travel, the suspicion of institutional structures, the desire for personal contact and experience, and the multiplication of new churches, mission agencies, and methodologies.[23] In the next section, I will examine some reasons why these particular changes regarding missions have occurred.

AN ANALYSIS OF WHY VIEWS OF
MISSIONS HAVE CHANGED

The question that needs to be raised at this point is: How did we get to where we are today? While there are a number of possible reasons, I suggest that many people now view missions as supportive roles to already existing national churches as a result of the success of our cross-cultural endeavors on a scale unimaginable to those who did the first pioneer work. I will illustrate what I mean by this from my own context. In January 2006, Randy Hurst published an article on the growth of the Assemblies of God worldwide in *Today's Pentecostal Evangel*.[24] It includes an amazing graph that documents the number of Assemblies of God adherents starting with 300 pastors and their congregations in 1914 to some 53 million total adherents worldwide in 2005. That graph makes clear that growth started in the decade of the 1960s, but exploded from the 1970s and beyond.

With the first wave of missionaries, there was a pioneer ethos; people went to places where there were few Christians, preached the Gospel with the intention of creating an indigenous local movement capable of governing, supporting and propagating itself, and did the kind of generic work of evangelism, church planting, discipling, and training of ministers that built church movements capable of reaching their own people. The Pentecostal fire within these early pioneers was passed

---

23   Pierson, 150.

24   Randy Hurst, "The Secret of Accelerating and Lasting Growth," *Today's Pentecostal Evangel*, (2006): 24-25.

on into the spiritual DNA of the converts and leaders they trained by both teaching and modeling. Virtually anyone going out before 1970 went somewhere where the church movement was relatively small, and probably, by a rigorous definition of indigeneity, not yet fully capable of functioning without outside help to evangelize their sociocultural setting. In 1960, half of all the Assemblies of God adherents were still in America; by 1970, it was still 25 percent. In this sense, the pioneer generalist work of reaching, planting, and training was by definition going to be what these missionaries were involved in.

On the other hand, missionaries going out after 1970 were confronted with a new situation: national church movements that were increasingly large, robust and powerful. No longer needed in evangelism, church planting, and even first-tier Bible training, missionaries became advanced education specialists, managed (and helped finance) various institutions, became conduits to connect short-term teams from the west, supervised various construction efforts, and worked in various forms of media and communications.[25] This story could be repeated,

---

25 Within my own organizational context, I think that there has been an overall change in missionary practice and identity on one hand while retaining the sense of importance of a divine call to missions ministry. J. Philip Hogan, who served as the Executive Director of AG USA missions from 1959-1989, was very disturbed by the debate in the early 1960s where the recognition of the church in so many places that were formerly "mission fields" raised a question as to what to call cross-cultural workers who went to these existing churches to work with them, rather than to plant churches among cultural settings that had none. This issue came up at the World Council of Churches first Conference on World Mission and Evangelism at Mexico City in 1963 (Winter, The Meaning of Mission) and one suggestion was to split the terminology and call "fraternal workers" those going to work with already existing church movements, reserving the term missionary for those going to plant the Gospel among the non-Christian peoples of the world. Hogan's comment on this shows his perspective on the role of the missionary as one who proclaims the Gospel message, "Today, in some ecclesiastical circles, . . . The missionary that is needed now, they say, is really a worker in some technical or pedagogical skills; and, really a helper to the indigenous church. Instead of being called a 'missionary,' he is called a 'fraternal worker.' This emphasis would put the Great Commission in storage while the church adopts a kind of 'buddy' system, and the real heroes of the Cross are not men who confront heathen

substituting various levels of growth, with a variety of denominational and interdenominational mission organizations. It is the stated goal of many such groups to develop indigenous local churches and church movements. It seems that on one level everyone was somewhat caught off guard by their success. Although a goal was set, there was, in essence, no "missiology of success" to help decide when goals were reached and what to do when that happened. The result is that many mission organizations have no decision-making tools to help decide what needs to be done and how to respond to requests from national churches long after they are fully indigenous or as they are in last stages of the transition time moving towards it.

What follows naturally upon this first point is that success creates a machinery of mission and historical relationships with these new indigenous church movements. The reality is that all local church movements are inherently needy. There are two elements that are always at play among any given local church or movement of local churches. The first is that within their geographic sphere of ministry there are still many spiritually lost people. The second is that there will always be in these churches a shortage of workers. Thus, there is always justification for further work of evangelism and church planting and there are always ongoing needs for development and training. Over time it is not difficult to see how this situation can create the sense that mission is working among these movements that we (as a mission organization) have brought into being.

---

religions with the message of Calvary, but specialists who teach contour farming. The Assemblies of God does not believe this!"; Byron Klaus and Douglas Petersen, eds. *The Essential J. Philip Hogan*, The J. Philip Hogan World Missions Series, vol. 1 (Springfield, MO: Assemblies of God Theological Seminary, 2006), 100. I cannot help but think that Hogan and other like-minded mission leaders who value traditional conception of mission would be very disturbed today to see that the bulk of their missions staffs do indeed function as fraternal workers to very powerful indigenous churches.

This illustrates how systemic factors within organizations can override value commitments. Mission agencies have doctrinal positions regarding the nature of mission based on their understanding of Scripture. A standard belief among Evangelical and Pentecostal/Charismatic agencies is their commitment to taking the Gospel to non-Christian people. What we are seeing is a situation where agencies affirm this doctrinal position, while at the same time, the organizational system is weighted towards sending people to places where the church already exists because of long-standing commitments to church movements in such places. The forces within the organizational system itself drive practice more than the understanding of mission derived from Scripture.

Pentecostals and those influenced by the church growth movement value going where the Spirit is sovereignly working and bringing in the harvest.[26] With national churches springing into being all over the globe, and a value of being responsive to the work of the Spirit, it again seems natural that we did not foresee the resistant and those separated from the Gospel by barriers of language, religion, and social standing. There was a time, which Newbigin alludes to, when it was "simple" to obey the Great Commission in the sense that people were unreached all over the globe; there was no church and it took pioneers to reach the first generation. However, the success of going

---

26 Wilson in his biography of J. Philip Hogan, who served for 30 years as the executive director of the Assemblies of God missionary program, provides a number of illustrations from Hogan's thinking that show the sense of dependence on the guidance of the Spirit; *Strategy of the Spirit: J. Philip Hogan and the Growth of the Assemblies of God Worldwide 1960-1990* (Carlisle, Cumbria: Regnum Books International, 1997). It is the Spirit who leads laborers to strategic harvest opportunities (64, 136), and prepares peoples, communities, cities, and nations for sudden harvest (67, 136). Being strategic in this sense is going where God is pouring out his Spirit (72). McGavran argues that the New Testament church went where people responded, and that the Church won the winnable; *Understanding Church Growth*, Fully revised ed. (Grand Rapids, MI: Eerdmans, 1970), 37. He also notes that sudden ripenings for harvest are common (247) but in contrast to the Pentecostal ethos of following the leading of the Spirit, receptivity and response is discerned through sociological methods and observation (183, 245-65).

to responsive populations means that there are at the same time those who are non-responsive. It is no longer "simple" in that the cross-cultural worker must take into account the existence of the church in so many segments of the human societies of the world; it is also no longer "simple" because the most resistant people groups are left in the world. In the face of the incredible success experienced by many missions that have founded national churches, it is challenging to step up to the reality of years of hard labor with little fruit among resistant groups. The combination of the value of quick results that Pierson talks about with the mission machinery built around successful fields means that there is a natural tendency to continue to connect people to places that have the most Christians.

I have already cited Pierson with reference to values that influence missions. His article, which deals with the impatience that local churches feel when dealing with mission agencies, provides an interesting example of a point that I want to make. It is germane to what I am doing here because he documents a change in the way that people practice missions and then creates an account for why this happens.[27] What is of relevance to my argument is that, with one exception, none of the changes in the way that people practice missions have to do with changes in the way they understand or interpret Scripture. In the short run, from an anthropological or sociological perspective, the best explanation for people's behavior is their ideas; in the long-term, it is the environmental and material conditions that take precedence in

---

27 Pierson suggests a number of factors that are behind the impatience that local churches have with established missions agencies. He roots this change in the shift of values in contemporary American society. His list includes values resulting from being post-Western, post denominational, post-ideological, and post Christendom; anti-institutionalism; the expectation of quick results; postmodern theological relativism and universalism; a general suspicion and fear of long-term commitments, and individualistic ecclesiology; Pierson, 146-48.

creating change.[28] The primacy of adaptive change rests in the areas of technology, economy, and social organization linked to production,[29] not with what people think about.

In terms of technological and economic factors, revolutions in transportation, communications, and the economic affluence of the West and North have created a situation that allows for people to move and communicate across geographic and cultural boundaries in an unprecedented fashion. People who in the past would have been involved in supporting and praying for the efforts of cross-cultural missionaries are now traveling and participating for brief periods of time alongside these people. In a reverse flow, Christians from the non-western world are now able to connect directly with local churches and leaders in the West. While formal doctrinal understanding of missions has not yet radically changed, technological and economic factors have created the ability for the grassroots to interface with what was formerly the provenance of cross-cultural workers and their agencies, who acted as professionals who worked in isolation from their supporting constituency.

Pierson's point was that the culture change engendered by this new ability to access "mission fields" means that local churches are capable of by-passing the missions agencies in favor of doing their own work. My point is that the culture changes driven by technological and economic factors have already shaped many missions practices. This includes the shift towards a short-term focus, missions as project, the expectation of quick results, and the problem of amateurization driven in part by the need for personal involvement.[30] This process also includes

---

28 Michael Kearney, *World View* (Novato, CA: Chandler and Sharp Publishers, 1984), 4.

29 Roger Keesing, "Theories of Culture," *Annual Review of Anthropology* 3 (1974): 75-76.

30 On the problem of amateurization see my comments on page 160-161 and following; see Guthrie's discussion of the shift from missions as process to project, Guthrie, 112-16.

conceptual changes that will eventually follow the changes in practice that are driven by cultural changes. The result is a theology of missions and philosophies of missions held at one level while actual practice is driven by systemic, technological, and economic factors.[31] In other words, both systemic and technological/economic factors are pushing missions practice in the same direction—towards involvement with the already Christian world where church movements are the strongest.

THE NEED FOR NEW THINKING

In the previous two sections, I have attempted to document a shift in the conception of missions among the Evangelical, Pentecostal, and Charismatic (EPC) streams of missions and suggest an analysis for why this is happening. The issues at hand here are serious. When everything becomes mission and when the primary locus of the Christian world mission become places where the church already exists, there are tragic consequences for the 40 percent of the world with limited or no near-neighbor witness. I am aware that one of the problems of employing the kind of language I am using here is that it can be easily misconstrued by some as: a) denigrating or lessening in some fashion the importance of cross-cultural work where churches already exist, and b) advocating that missions and missionaries not be involved in places where the church already exists. I want to be very clear from the outset that I am doing neither.

What I am arguing is that our current unbalanced focus on the Christian world is tragic for the 40 percent because they are still waiting for wit-

---

31 Seel argues that American Evangelicals have treated modernity as a set of ideas rather than a social reality and thus have staunchly defended orthodox doctrine while accommodating to tools of modernity; John Seel, "Modernity and Evangelicals: American Evangelicalism as a Global Case Study," in *Faith and Modernity*, ed. Philip Sampson, Vinay Samuel, and Chris Sugden (Oxford: Regnum Books International, 1994), 295. This illustrates how easy it is to maintain a discourse of belief/values at one level while actually operating on completely different set of principles.

nesses of the Gospel to come and plant the church movements that will provide the best potential for their people group to have many people birthed into God's kingdom. I am against all language that pits one part of the world or people against another and which lifts up the spiritual needs of one by downgrading the needs of another. In chapter 7, I will seek to develop a comprehensive and integrated approach that values all cross-cultural labor, provides a framework for orienting it to the needs of the unreached, and recognizes the importance of long-term cross-cultural labor alongside emerging and growing national churches to their development and effectiveness.

So the question that we must all face is how should we respond to this moment we find ourselves in? I believe good thinking about missions that is grounded in Scripture and current realities is something that all of God's people need to engage in and bring to bear on their local churches regardless of their location in the world. Bosch reminds us that the Bible is not a storehouse of truths we draw on at random to find immutable laws of mission. Rather, there are different theologies of mission found in Scripture and the mission of the church always refers to "particular forms, related to specific time, places, or needs, of participation in the *missio Dei*."[32]

This engagement of Scripture and the current realities of our age and setting are at the heart of what is termed missiology. Escobar defines missiology as "an interdisciplinary approach to understand missionary action. It looks at missionary facts from the perspective of the Bible, theology, history and social sciences. Missiology is a critical reflection on praxis in light of God's word."[33] This means that missiology is by its

---

32 Bosch, 10.

33 Samuel Escobar, "Evangelical Missiology: Peering in the Future," in *Global Missiology for the 21st Century: The Iguassu Dialogue*, ed. William D. Taylor (Grand Rapids: Baker Academic, 2000), 101. Verkuyl is a good example of a classic definition of the term, "Missiology is the study of the salvation activities of the Father, Son and Holy Spirit throughout the world geared toward bringing

very nature something that is done on the fly; it requires a reflection on current context. Escobar's definition recognizes that the terrain of missions is in continual flux and new challenges and configurations in the world compel us to reflect them in the light of Scripture. The issues of one age are not the issues of the next. My argument in this monograph centers on our current reality of the imbalance at the global level in the location of cross-cultural workers. Many people groups remain unreached. I am aware that it is quite possible one day in the future we could find ourselves in the position where there *will* be robust church movements in every identifiable people group in our world and yet the Lord has not yet returned. Such a configuration would again require new reflection as to the critical issues and needs and the role of cross-cultural workers. However, until that happens we cannot neglect the reality of the 40 percent that are unreached and least-reached in our world and this issue must remain central to our missiological studies.

If God is indeed the God of mission and his people are a missionary people, then we will also believe that every person has a role to play in God's global mission.[34] In order to better clarify the various participants in this global mission and their interrelationships I have developed a 10 point continuum (figure 3) which stretches from the individual Christian in a given sociocultural setting all the way to the cross-cultural worker sent out by the newly formed church that results from the efforts of Christians in the original setting.

---

the Kingdom of God into existence"; 5; see Justice Anderson, "An Overview of Missiology," in *Missiology*, ed. John Mark Terry, Ebbie Smith, and Justice Anderson (Nashville: Broadmann & Holman, 1998), 1-9 for an overview of the etymology of the term missiology, suggestions for alternate terms over the years, a list of classic definitions, and its scope.

34 Paul Hiebert, "Foreword," in *Announcing the Kingdom: The Story of God's Mission in the Bible*, ed. Arthur F. Glasser et al. (Grand Rapids: Baker Academic, 2005), 8.

FIGURE 3
Participants in Global Mission

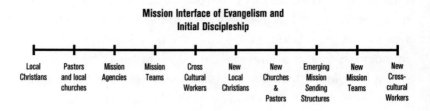

Mission Interface of Evangelism and
Initial Discipleship

| Local Christians | Pastors and local churches | Mission Agencies | Mission Teams | Cross Cultural Workers | New Local Christians | New Churches & Pastors | Emerging Mission Sending Structures | New Mission Teams | New Cross-cultural Workers |

The participants here include both individuals (as Christians and leaders in a local setting and as cross-cultural workers) and various aggregates whether in local churches, as mission agencies or mission teams. A few explanations are needed. First, this represents an ideal since in many places the newly planted churches do not yet have sending structures. Second, the primary interface between these two groups is the cross-cultural workers and teams and the new Christians and churches they have planted. Finally, the trends I have documented above affect people at every point of this continuum. While we are aware that mission agencies and their workers have a mission philosophy, we tend not to think of individual Christians, pastors, and local churches as having a "missiology." Everyone has a missiology, even if it is not formally expressed, but implicit; there are always values guiding decisions about where we will go, what we will do, and how we will do it. These are missiological decisions. This underscores the need for solid missiological thinking grounded in Scripture and current realities to guide new understandings and practice for the participants along every point in this continuum.

CHAPTER SUMMARY

In this chapter, I introduced the problematic that is central to this study. Inside of the EPC streams of missions there are no longer clear understandings about the meaning or practice of missions. The result is that there are increasingly sharp lines of demarcation between the world where the church exists and where it does not. Tragically, at the global level, the bulk of cross-cultural workers are located and laboring in the world where there are many Christians and church movements. I then provided evidence for this shift in understanding and developed a tentative analysis as to why this happened. Finally, I argued that our collective lack of clarity in our thinking about missions demands new missiological reflection so that all the participants in God's mission can sharpen their focus in the days ahead and insure that the Gospel is proclaimed and churches planted among the unreached and least-reached of our world. In the next chapter, I introduce the idea of thinking about missions paradigmatically and explore its power for helping us to sharpen our focus on the critical missions tasks that face us.

3

THE NOTION OF PARADIGMS AND MISSIONS

In the last chapter, I argued that in many missions circles there is a growing lack of clarity about the nature of Christian mission. In many instances, missions is now seen as Christian activities done cross-culturally among a group that already has Christians and church movements present. I now want to focus specifically on two specific manifestations of this loss of clarity: it impacts *where* people go and *what* they do, with the latter being a function of the former. In the first, the data tells us that the vast majority of cross-cultural workers are located in the world where many Christians, churches, and movements of churches already exist. I need to add here that I am not saying by this that I am advocating some kind of hard and fast rule that says where there are churches there should be no cross-cultural workers. In a later section, I will argue that one of the most strategic cross-cultural worker functions is precisely to work with existing Christians, churches, and movements; but the key point is the *kind of work* being done, and I will elaborate on this later.

In general, the problem of *what* cross-cultural workers do stems from the fact that they are working in places where there are many Christians and strong churches. This means that there is a greatly increased chance that they are doing things that local Christians can and are already doing or should be doing. Again, this is not to discount specific callings where God specially anoints some individuals to work cross-culturally in the capacity of evangelist or to revive or renew a church movement. However, in a broad sense, the missionary task should not be redundant with the work of local Christians, but rather focus on something that forwards the participation of those Christians and churches in God's global mission.

These two facts, location and type of work, are part of the missions realities of our day and highlight the critical need for a missiology that is capable of responding to this situation and mobilizing the body of Christ to carry the Gospel to where it has not yet been heard and where the church is not planted. Such a missiology will do two things in particular that are of vast strategic importance. First, it would serve as an instrument in God's hands to call forth a new generation of workers to pioneer the church among the unreached and least-reached. Second, it would ignite cross-cultural workers in every location to orient their efforts to catalyzing the church movements they are part of to make as many disciples as possible within their own people group and at the same time come full cycle to send their own people to the unreached as well.

SHAPING A MISSIOLOGY FOR OUR CURRENT CONTEXT: THINKING PARADIGMATICALLY ABOUT MISSIONS

The question becomes how, given our current realities, can we forge such a missiology? It is not simply a matter of starting all over again. Newbigin's observation about the presence of the church is just as appropriate for the presence of cross-cultural workers already on the ground in many parts of the world, working in conjunction with these Christians and churches. While theoretically it would be nice to call the church back to some kind of pristine New Testament missiology, Bosch reminds us that even there the mission of the church is always rooted in the local and particular. What this means is that the missiology that we develop must take into account not only the existence of the church and the places where Christ is not yet known, but also the presence of current cross-cultural workers in many of these places.

I do not think anyone would argue against the idea that the way towards a sharper focus in missions is to seek to bring more scriptural insights to bear on current understandings; the question is how to do that. We are all reading Scripture, there are many fine works written on biblical theology of mission, yet there is no simple and direct movement of all of this biblical material into our mission philosophies and practice. The relation of biblical principles to our contemporary practice of mission is much more complex and interwoven with our history, presuppositions about the Bible and mission, relationships outside our own organizational settings and with the younger churches in other cultural settings, and the current fashions and trends that make up our missions context.

I believe that one way to move forward is to start where we are at in terms of the frameworks of missions that are in operation today. Within the EPC stream of missions there are already existing frameworks that represent well-established insights into Scripture with a history of practice. Our orienting frameworks for mission have both strengths and weaknesses. The strength is in what the framework helps us to "see" clearly while the weakness is that these operational frameworks so define our conceptual world that things which lie outside of them are obscured, distorted, and even unseen. The result is that, within the EPC stream, the existing major frameworks are sometimes seen as competing approaches or "camps" that represent incompatible or at least radically different forms of mission practice.

Bosch notes that it was Kung, in his historico-theological subdivisions of the history of Christianity, who applied Kuhn's notion of paradigmatic thinking in science as a way of conceptualizing major eras of Christian thought.[35] Bosch points out that Kung's six divisions of Christian thought was not an original idea; the originality came in seeing these eras as "paradigms" and the change from one to another as a true "paradigm shift."[36] In this sense, each epoch "reflects a theological 'paradigm' profoundly different from any of its predecessors" so that "in each era the Christians of that period understood and experienced their faith in ways only partially commensurable with the understanding and experience of believers of other eras."[37] The word paradigm comes from the Greek *paradeigma* which means "pattern" or "example," and the noun *paradeiknunai* meaning "demonstrate." It was Kuhn, theorizing on work in the natural sciences, who argued that science functions with major models or theoretical structures that "define" what is true and shape what we know and how we know it.[38] He invoked the term "paradigm" as an accepted model, pattern, and locus of commitment to explain the kind of framework that comes to guide future practice. He notes that "paradigms gain their status because they are more successful than their competitors in solving a few problems that the group of practitioners has come to recognize as

---

35   Bosch, 181, 183.

36   Ibid.

37   Ibid., 183.

38   Kuhn calls "normal science" the "research firmly based upon one or more past scientific achievements" that are acknowledged to form the foundation for further practice; Thomas S. Kuhn, *The Structure of Scientific Revolutions*, ed. Otto Neurath, Rudolf Carnap, and Charles Morris, 2d ed., Enlarged ed., International Encyclopedia of Unified Science, Foundations of the Unity of Science, vol. II, Number 2 (Chicago, Illinois: The University of Chicago Press, 1970), 10. He asserts that coherent traditions of scientific research (represented, for instance, in astronomy by Ptolemaic and Copernican views or in optics by corpuscular and wave rubrics), are the loci of commitment that the study of which "prepares a student for membership in the particular scientific community with which he will later practice" and which lies prior to the concepts, laws, theories and points of view that can be abstracted from them; Ibid., 10-11.

acute."[39] In his view, normal science is not looking for major novelties[40] but is a "highly cumulative enterprise" seeking to advance the scope and precision of the paradigm.[41] Thus, science does not advance by small accumulations of knowledge, but rather through revolutions where "a few individuals begin to perceive reality in ways *qualitatively* different from their predecessors and contemporaries, who are practicing 'normal science.'"[42] "Discovery commences with the awareness of anomaly, i.e., the recognition that nature has somehow violated the paradigm-induced expectations that govern normal science."[43] Scientific revolutions are thus changes in worldview.[44] As old models and theoretical structures become less capable of explaining all of the data on hand, eventually some come to "see" things in a new light and a new model/structure emerges that is more capable of accounting for existing facts.

Macro-Paradigms

Bosch points out that Kuhn's use of paradigm is a rather slippery concept—Kuhn is charged with using it in at least 22 senses within his work.[45] What is germane to our discussion here is that Bosch took Kung's paradigmatic divisions of Christian history and thought and has applied the notion of paradigmatic thinking to missiology. The major

---

39   Ibid., 23.

40   Ibid., 35.

41   Ibid., 52.

42   Bosch, 184.

43   Kuhn, 52-53.

44   Ibid., 111.

45   Bosch, 185. Bosch acknowledges the criticisms that have been made of Kuhn's work and reminds us of the need for caution in applying the idea to theology; Ibid., 184.

divisions serve as macro-paradigms[46] that are frameworks or perspectives that reflect the historical setting and understandings from Scripture that frame and constrain the conduct of missions. Thus, they define what "normal missions" is within that particular orientation. The six macro-paradigms are: the Apocalyptic-early Christianity, Hellenistic-patristic period, Medieval-Roman Catholic, Protestant reformation, Enlightenment, and the Emerging Ecumenical. Bosch observes:

> In each of these eras, Christians, from within their own contexts, wrestled with the question of what the Christian faith and, by implication, the Christian mission meant for them. Needless to say, all of them believed and argued that their understanding of the faith and of the church's mission was faithful to God's intent. This did not, however, mean that they all thought alike and came to the same conclusions.[47]

Another approach that focuses on the macro-paradigm level is what Bevans and Schroeder do in proposing that there are six key questions that are always being worked out in Christian mission. The questions are:

1. Who is Jesus Christ and what is his meaning?

2. What is the nature of the Christian church?

3. How does the church regard its eschatological future?

4. What is the nature of the salvation it preaches?

5. How does the church value the human?

6. What is the value of human culture as the context in which the Gospel is preached?

---

46 Bosch observed that Kung's categorization is too broad and Kung himself called for distinctions between macro, mid-level and micro paradigms; Ibid., 188.

47 Ibid., 182.

They then show how these questions were answered historically in three major theological streams with roots that start in the early church fathers through to the present.[48] Schroeder and Bevans' observations about the importance of theological perspective in answering the six questions that are constants in mission remind us that mission paradigms are intimately tied to a particular view of Scripture.

As I have already noted, Bosch reminds us that Kuhn's idea of paradigm is a slippery concept; he warns us that it cannot be uncritically applied to theology or missiology.[49] Nevertheless, if we are careful to define how we are using the concept, there are a number of points at which the concept of paradigms can help us in our thinking about missions.[50] One of the most important things we can take from thinking about missions in terms of paradigms is that it helps us to step outside of ourselves for a moment and realize that our primary operating paradigm of missions defines for us what is "normal missions." It is the conceptual infrastructure that answers for us the questions of why we do missions, what the content of the message is, where it should be done, and how we carry it out in our particular historical and organizational context. With our paradigm, we know the questions and the answers and we

---

48 Stephen B. Bevans and Roger P. Schroeder, *Constants in Context: A Theology of Missions for Today* (Maryknoll, NY: Orbis, 2004), 35.

49 Bosch, 185.

50 It is critical, when using the notion of paradigm in missions, to establish in what sense and how broadly we are using the term. Kung's observation of macro, meso, and micro paradigms is helpful. I have noted the work of Bosch and Bevans and Schroeder as being macro-level paradigms, Hesselgrave, on the other hand, has written a book entitled, *Paradigms in Conflict: 10 Key Questions in Christian Missions Today* (Grand Rapids: Kregel Academic and Professional, 2005), where he looks at a set of ten issues where there is a continuum of views in the mission community. As such, they represent specific parts of missions, but are not in and of themselves complete orienting frameworks or macro-paradigms. They represent micro-level paradigms where, for instance, someone who adopts a spiritual warfare approach to missions would be deeply influenced at many points by this perspective, but they would fit more broadly into a macro or mid-level paradigm as well in keeping with their theological and historical commitments.

shape our practice around these understandings. Without a notion of paradigm, like the fish in water, we never "see" that we are in the water; but paradigmatic thinking gives us tools for starting to see how we are shaped and what structures our thought and praxis.

The Benefits of Mid-Level Mission Paradigms

While macro-paradigms are useful in certain ways, one of them being to help us place ourselves in the broader universe of missions practice, in general I think they are of limited use for practitioners. They cover so much ground that they lose the ability to help an individual, church movement, or mission agency shape their practice.[51] I find that Kung's

---

51 For instance, Bevans and Schroeder, using their mix of theological perspectives across the six questions, see three major frameworks for missions in operation in the late twentieth-century. Mission as participation in the Mission of the Triune God, Mission as liberating service for the reign of God, and Mission as proclamation of Jesus Christ as Universal Savior; Bevans and Schroeder, 283-84 and chapters 9-11. Within these three frameworks are Roman Catholicism, Orthodoxy, Conciliar Protestantism as represented in the World Council of Churches and Evangelicals/Pentecostals/Charismatics. Their suggestion for an integrated view is missions as prophetic dialogue with its combination of their three major streams and ten distinct components; Ibid., 348-95. Bosch's sixth historical paradigm, which he calls the "emerging ecumenical" represents both what is present today and his own view as to where things need to go. He lists 13 propositions that are interrelated and are part of the new paradigm: Mission as the church with others; Mission as *missio dei;* Mission as mediating salvation; Mission as the quest for justice; Mission as evangelism (with examples of 18 different views of evangelization, pp. 409-420), Mission as contextualization; Mission as liberation, which encompasses liberation theology; Mission as inculturation (a second important model of contextualization); Mission as common witness—the ecumenical vision; Mission as ministry by the whole people of God—mobilizing the laity; Mission as witness to people of other living faiths; Mission as theology; and Mission as action in hope; Bosch, 368-510. Both of these attempts at articulating a master macro-paradigm are of limited help to workers on the ground precisely because of their breadth. They incorporate too wide a range of ideas and positions, so at the end of the day practitioners are left with little to help them make decisions about what to do at the actual fieldwork or strategic planning level. To make this observation is not to diminish in any way the tremendous scholarship represented in both of these works and their value in understanding the theological and historical dimensions of Christian missions.

notion of macro, meso (mid), and micro-paradigms (see footnote 46) opens the door for using the paradigm concept at less comprehensive levels. I see mid-level paradigms as having the potential to be very useful tools for people engaged in making decisions about their missions practice. My focus in this study is on the stream of missions that flows from a commitment to the authority of Scripture and that is represented by EPC forms of missions. If you take the EPC streams as representative of a macro-perspective it is possible to identify distinct orienting frameworks or mid-level paradigms under that larger umbrella that both explicitly and implicitly answer questions regarding the why, what, where, and how of missions. These mid-level paradigms are composed of our biblical commitments and understandings and provide the interpretive mechanisms for the interplay between Scripture and our current mission realities.

The first is the framework that focuses primarily on the planting, growing, and multiplication of churches. The second is a framework that emphasizes the social implications of the Gospel in Christian social concern. Both of these paradigms are weighted towards "what" questions. A third paradigm in today's mission scene arose around the "where" question in missions. Its focus is on planting the church where it does not exist among unreached people groups. In general, this paradigm rests under the broader umbrella of the church planting and growth framework, but practically, it has emerged as its own paradigm as mission organizations have come into being with a predominate ethos concerning the "where" question. It has come to represent a stream of missiology known as "frontier missions" which proponents of this view contrast with the work of "regular missions" that strengthens the church where it already exists. Because these three paradigms will be central to my discussions throughout the rest of this study, I will refer to them in an abbreviated fashion as the paradigms of church planting/ growth, Christian social concern,[52] and frontier mission.

Before I move on to my next point, it is necessary to make some clarifying comments here at the outset about what I am identifying as three major paradigms within the EPC stream of missions. By asserting the paradigmatic status of these three frames, I am intentionally being reductionist for a purpose. I am aware that in real life you cannot reify these positions and that there are no individuals, church organizations, or missions agencies that fit neatly into one of these paradigms. There are no impermeable walls operating here. However, by asserting their paradigmatic status, I am arguing that for many of us they do indeed function as paradigms of how we view and practice missions. They do indeed represent identifiable groupings where the focus of work tends to be around the nexus of either church planting/church growth/leadership training or pioneer

---

52 I have chosen to use Christian social concern as a descriptor for this mission framework out of a wide field of terminologies that represent a large umbrella of values, biblical perspectives and commitments. Examples include holism and the idea of holistic mission as used in the Lausanne Covenant, see Chris Wright, *Re-Affirming Holistic Mission: A Cross-Centered Approach in All Areas of Life* (Lausanne World Pulse, 2005, accessed 6 October 2007), available from http://www.lausanneworldpulse.com/pdf/issues/LWP1005.pdf.); the idea of transformational mission which seeks to bring the Lordship of Jesus into every arena of life, Vinay Samuel and Chris Sugden, eds. *Mission as Transformation: A Theology of the Whole Gospel* (Irvine, CA: Regnum, 1999); social justice, Waldron Scott, *Bring Forth Justice: A Contemporary Perspective on Mission* (Grand Rapids: Eerdmans, 1980); social action, Ron Sider, *Evangelism and Social Action: Uniting the Church to Heal a Lost and Broken World* (London: Hodder and Stoughton, 1993); and transformational development, Bruce Bradshaw, *Bridging the Gap: Evangelism, Development and Shalom* (Monrovia: MARC, 1993); Bryant L. Myers, *Walking with the Poor* (Maryknoll: Orbis, 1999). I am using "Christian social concern" here as a generic way of talking about the implications of the coming of the Gospel to human societies in contrast to truncated views of evangelism that see the good news only dealing with the spiritual side of humanity and not their entire existence. See Sider's *Evangelism and Social Action* chapter two for a helpful overview of major models and sub-types concerning the nature of the Gospel and relationship between evangelism and social action.

church planting among an unreached people group, or Christian social concern and development. As paradigms, they are not impenetrable boxes, but more like conceptual orbits that influence understanding and practice for individuals, mission teams and agencies. In this sense, they define for us "normal missions" and within these frames we know what questions to ask and the proper answers.

I also acknowledge that for many standard mission agencies[53] within the EPC streams their purpose and goal statements reflect not just one, but sometimes two, or in some cases all three of the emphases represented in these paradigms.[54] This includes evangelism, planting of churches and church movements, training leaders and showing Christian compassion and social concern, and in some cases, a focus on doing these things where the church does not already exist. Historically, mission organizations start within one of these frames and their primary ethos and operations are defined by that frame.[55] They will have

---

53 Winter has a taxonomy of six types of missionary agencies; "Six Spheres of Mission Overseas," *Mission Frontiers*, (1998). Standard mission agencies are analogous to the general practitioner in medicine. Their primary base is in evangelism and church planting, but they do everything. They are represented by the denominational, interdenominational, and church planting missions. Service missions provide technical assistance to standard mission agencies and national churches. Relief and development missions focus on meeting human need, Indigenous missions work with "native missionaries," Short-Term Missions send out teams for short periods of time, and Congregational Direct missions, which tend to be in the mega-church category, develop their own mission activity.

54 For example, the Society for International Ministries (SIM) has four primary purposes: evangelize the unreached, minister to human need, disciple believers into churches, and equip churches to fulfill Christ's Commission. In my own organization, the Assemblies of God, there are four primary pillars: reaching people with the Gospel, planting churches, training leaders, and showing compassion in Jesus' name.

55 My own organization serves as an example of what I mean here. It could be argued that historically the emphasis on Jesus as Savior, Healer, Baptizer in the Holy Spirit, and Soon Coming King and our contemporary mission statement of four pillars, to evangelize, plant churches, train leaders, and show compassion in Jesus' name inherently carry within them the two paradigms of church growth and social concern. However, even though social concern has been evident from

some individuals within the organization that operate in one of the other paradigms. They also often adjust their purpose statements to reflect other paradigmatic emphases, while their major focus remains their original frame.

Why are mid-level paradigms helpful to us? It is because each one serves as a lens that has a powerful point of focus rooted in a key Scriptural theme. Each of these three major mission perspectives—church growth, social concern, and unreached peoples—are based in insights into Scripture at their point of emphasis. All three have generated a large amount of writing, critique, and ongoing vigorous academic and practitioner debate which leads to continued refinement for each frame. What this means for participants in God's mission is that when they view mission through that particular paradigmatic lens, they can see in very sharp focus the particular point of emphasis within Scripture of that paradigm. I use the illustration of a magnifying glass to try and get this point across. When you use a magnifying glass you can see very clearly in the middle of the glass. The power of these paradigms is that they serve as magnifying glasses to certain parts of Scripture. By learning to see outside of our preferred paradigm, we enrich ourselves by seeing what other light is shed on our understanding of missions by another paradigm.

The magnifying glass illustration also reveals another reason that these mid-level paradigms are helpful to us when we learn to think paradigmatically and to step outside of our own perspective. While the middle of the magnifying glass is clear, if you go to the edges the picture is fuzzy and distorted. In a similar fashion, these mission paradigms help us to see very clearly in their area of emphasis, but if we press too far we will find distortion. This distortion can come

---

the very beginning, the primary focus of Assemblies of God missions has been on the planting of indigenous church movements; see Gary B. McGee, "Saving Souls or Saving Lives?," *Paraclete* 28, no. 4 (1994).

from making the central theme of the paradigm everything so that it drowns out all other themes (*only* plant the church!, *only* do social action!) or through following a line of logic to the point of absurdity (all the tribes and tongues are to be represented around God's throne, so groups evangelized centuries ago no longer need to hear the Gospel because there are representatives around the throne already). Thus, thinking paradigmatically about missions at this mid-level becomes a warning to us that any given paradigm is incapable of representing all that Scripture has to say about God's mission and our participation in it. To focus on any one lens to the exclusion of another is to miss vital points in the Scripture witness about God's plan for the world.

This leads me to another point about the usefulness of paradigmatic thinking. Because of the complexity and fullness of Scripture, I am not sure that it is possible to have a single comprehensive paradigm that would serve as our guide in mission. At one point, I thought that with hard work we could arrive at one, single, unified, and integrated missions paradigm. Now I am more inclined to think that in our human limitedness, we are better served by seeking the best insights from the various paradigms (realizing that even these three major paradigms do not represent the last word on all that God wants to do) and seek to integrate their insights into our practice. This means that in any particular, specific, sociocultural setting, the participants in God's mission can use these paradigms to shine light on their situation in order to have a deeper biblical understanding of God's purposes in that place and time.

Practically speaking, how can we utilize these mid-level missions paradigms as we participate in God's mission? An illustration of how we can approach the use of paradigms of mission came to me while I was teaching a course one day. The class was doing an exercise where we listed on one side of the board all of the official pronouncements and writings that showed the missiology of a particular organization. On the other side of the board we made a list that was as comprehensive as possible about the kinds of things that missionaries in that organization actually do. We then spent some time comparing those two sides and reflecting on what they told us about our practice. One student made the observation that after looking at the missions philosophy in contrast to the actual practices, it appeared that the items on the practice side of the board, to use her terminology, "came out of our head." This observation grew out of the fact that one of the major tenets of the organization in question was the importance of building a national church organization that was fully indigenous. She noted that many of the things on the "practice" side of the board were not things that would facilitate the growth of an indigenous movement or be suggested or sanctioned by an indigenous national church if given a choice in the matter.

It was at that moment that I suddenly saw how a mission paradigm should stimulate us to ask questions. If we act in a way that is inconsistent with our ministry philosophy and values as expressed in our paradigm, then we are ignoring it, rather than allowing it to query and challenge what we do. This means that we can use multiple mission paradigms to let their particular focal point raise questions that will guide us in working out our actual practice of missions. This is not a mechanistic exercise where we go through a checklist, but rather it provides questions that are based in biblical convictions that we can bring before the Lord of the Harvest to ask for guidance in how to apply in our specific setting.

CHAPTER SUMMARY AND CONCLUSIONS

It is now time to return to the argument I started this chapter with and the question that I raised. The focal problem of this monograph is the lack of clarity in thinking about missions that has resulted in much activity of both the wrong kind (cross-cultural workers doing redundant work that local Christians can and should be doing) and in the wrong places (where there are many Christians and churches rather than where there are none). The question I raised is how we can shape a missiology that deals with these "where" and "what" issues? I am advocating that we learn to think paradigmatically about missions. This means that we first learn to "see" our own mid-level paradigm and to stand outside of it, and then to look through the lenses of other paradigms to incorporate their most powerful insights into our practice. One way to do this is to utilize the mission paradigms of church growth, social concern, and unreached peoples for their critical insights into Scripture, which in turn are used as question–generating devices to challenge and evaluate our practice and sharpen the focus of our missions activity. When the major insights of the three major paradigms of the EPC stream are taken in an integrative fashion, they provide a corrective to much current missions practice that is either trend-driven, faddish or too narrowly located in a single perspective.

To this point I have identified a problem and suggested a methodology that holds within it the ability to bring course correction for this problem. In chapter 7, I will explore in detail my idea of integrating paradigms. However, in order to set the stage for integrating missions paradigm insights I want to spend some time looking at two areas that I feel are underdeveloped in our thinking about missions and thus play a part in our current situation and are key to moving beyond our contemporary crisis. I believe that in order to properly address the problem of a lack of clarity in missions, we need to add a fourth paradigm, that of missionary identity. In the next chapter, I will look at the notion of apostolic function as a frame for understanding missionary identity; inherent in an apostolic identity is an intentional focus that is the opposite of the "everything is mission" problem.

With apostolic function as a master rubric for missionary action, I will then spend two chapters looking, in detail, at the insights from frontier mission missiology with its focus on unreached people groups. There are two reasons for my choice of frontier mission missiology as the paradigm for exploration. First, in terms of mission paradigms, both church planting/growth and social concern have a robust literature and are firmly established, if not often integrated, in the missions community. On the other hand, frontier mission missiology is new chronologically speaking, and has had the benefit/misfortune of becoming a major media thrust of missions in the decade of the 1990s. Thus, it has achieved buzzword status and all of the problems that accrue with that, rather than receiving the kind of serious critique and academic debate that has surrounded the other two paradigms. Second, frontier mission missiology is directly concerned with the problematic that I have identified in the current trend toward seeing Christian mission as redemptive activities where the church already exists. It stands as a challenge to the other mission paradigms by raising the status of the "where" question of missions as the critical question that must be answered before pursuing the content and practice issues.

4

APOSTOLIC FUNCTION: THE PARADIGM
OF MISSIONARY IDENTITY

In this chapter I argue that collectively we need a new sense of missionary identity. I am using identity here in the sense of "who we think we are" as cross-cultural workers, and "who others think we are" when they view us in the missionary role. Identity is that internal compass that gives direction to missionary work and provides the bigger picture into which the cross-cultural workers and teams fit. The rationale for a new identity is rooted in the problems associated with our current one. In broad brush strokes, this is how cross-cultural workers are often viewed and view themselves:

> The primary factor that makes a person a missionary is crossing a geographic boundary, and this often includes a cultural boundary as well. After crossing this border, the missionary does all kinds of good things (pan-missionism), which often includes what are seen as "spiritual" activities (like evangelism, planting churches, and training leaders) and "social" service (like helping the poor).

These first two points are explicit in our thinking, but a third is implicit and rarely brought into the level of discourse: missionaries need to produce tangible results in their work. This weights the work toward that which is countable, quantifiable, and reportable—whether it is souls won, buildings built, or orphans housed and fed.

In this identity there are two important concepts that are missing. The first is that there are no criteria to distinguish missionary activity from the activity of regular Christians except where it takes place culturally or geographically. Eventually this comes back to haunt the whole enterprise of missions because if there is indeed no difference between what I should be doing in my own local church in my own sociocultural setting and somewhere else, there is no compelling reason to cross geographic and cultural boundaries at all. Local need will always overwhelm the less visible and tangible need of those different than us and who are far removed via physical or cultural distance.[56]

The second is that there is nothing to galvanize the positive insights of this identity to mobilize Christians to go where the church does not exist. The configuration of missionary presence that Jaffarian noted is not accidental; it grows out of unwritten and unspoken values about what "counts" in the eyes of workers and those that send them. What we now require is a missionary identity that maintains a difference between the role of local Christians, not simply in location but in the kind of work they do, that takes into account the presence/absence and strength/weakness of Christian movements in the people among whom we are working, and which can make a compelling call to take the Gospel to those who have no near-neighbor witness.

I want to propose that missionary identity be rooted in the idea of apostolic function. I will define this term in detail below, but for a working sense, by apostolic function, I am focusing on how apostles

---

56 Newbigin's observation in 1953 is relevant here: even with churches that accept the obligation of world-wide missionary work, "it is taken for granted that the missionary obligation is one that has to be met after the needs of the home have been fully met; that existing gains have to be thoroughly consolidated before we go further afield"; Lesslie Newbigin, *The Household of God: Lectures on the Nature of the Church* (London: SCM Press, 1953), 144. He then contrasts this attitude with a variety of NT evidence that shows "a determination to stake out God's claim to the whole world at once, without expecting that one area should be fully worked out before the next is claimed"; Ibid., 144-45.

both conceived their task and what they actually did. In this view, functioning in an apostolic fashion becomes the template for self-understanding[57] that shapes all missionary activity and the reasons for that activity. The notion of apostolic function I am advocating also takes on paradigmatic status just like church planting/growth, frontier missions to the unreached, and Christian social concern. It becomes the umbrella rubric for all three of these because, as I will show in this chapter, these three perspectives are all contained within the apostolic role.

To set the stage for my concept of apostolic function, I will begin with a biblical overview of apostolic ministry in the New Testament. I will then discuss how apostolic function can serve as a heuristic for cross-cultural work and missionary identity, and conclude by looking at some broad themes related to this idea of apostolic function and how it relates to our current context.

BIBLICAL OVERVIEW

Betz notes that while the term "apostle" is well attested in the New Testament and early Christian writing, there are numerous unresolved problems associated with the term.[58] As with some other key New

---

57 The idea of a "template for self-understanding" was taken from Dana Robert in an essay about Luke as a mission historian; "Encounter with Christ: Luke as Mission Historian for the Twenty-First Century," in *Evangelical, Ecumenical, and Anabaptist Missiologies in Conversation: Essays in Honor of Wilbert Shenk*, ed. James R. Krabill, Walter Sawatsky, and Charles Van Engen (Maryknoll, New York: Orbis Books, 2006), 19. Robert points out that Luke's history provides the narrative that anchors the work of Paul and also the template for self-understanding of many branches of Christianity. That phrase concisely encompasses the idea that I am arguing for in the apostolic function concept; that Paul's understanding and practice of apostleship serve as a template for the way in which we understand ourselves in the missionary role.

58 Hans Dieter Betz, "Apostle," in *The Anchor Bible Dictionary*, ed. David Noel Freedman et al. (New York: Doubleday, 1992), 309. It is often noted by authors writing on this subject that it was Lightfoot's essay "The Name and Office of an Apostle"

Testament terms, it appears that the early Christians chose "an unfamiliar word, seldom used in the secular language, with little ready-made content, in order to fill it with one expressing its own conceptions."[59] Some of the issues include a variety of shades of definition,[60] the relationship between Christian apostleship and the Jewish institution of the *saliah*,[61] the relationship between Luke's identification of the disciples of Jesus during his earthly life with the apostles and the Twelve, Paul's

in his 1865 commentary on Galatians that laid out the fundamental problems that have occupied research on apostleship in the modern period; Joseph Barber Lightfoot, *The Epistle of St. Paul to the Galatians*, 3rd ed., Classic Commentary Library (Grand Rapids: Zondervan, 1962); also Rudolph Schnackenburg, "Apostles Before and During Paul's Time," in *Apostolic History and the Gospel*, ed. W. Ward Gasque and Ralph P. Martin (Grand Rapids: William B. Eerdmans, 1970), 287; Walter Schmithals, *The Office of Apostle in the Early Church*, trans. John E. Steely (Nashville: Abingdon Press, 1969), 19; Francis H. Agnew, "The Origin of the NT Apostle Concept: A Review of Research," *Journal of Biblical Literature* 105, no. 1 (1986): 76. Schutz cites Lightfoot's work as defining the problem and points out that the name and office of apostle is a vexing and intractable problem of New Testament studies. John Howard *Schutz, Paul and the Anatomy of Apostolic Authority* (Cambridge: Cambridge University Press, 1975), 4.

59   Dietrich Muller, "Apostle, Apostello (Part)," in *The New International Dictionary of New Testament Theology*, ed. Colin Brown et al. (Grand Rapids, MI: Zondervan, 1975), 135.

60   See Hans Dieter Betz, "Apostle," in *The Anchor Bible Dictionary*, ed. David Noel Freedman et al. (New York: Doubleday, 1992), 309.

61   The dominant view in scholarship has been that of Rengstorf (1964, 421, 424) who roots the idea of apostleship in history with the personal call of Jesus and connects it with the Jewish concept of *saliah* (427). However, this view has been argued against; see Muller (131-134) for a review of alternative positions on this issue. Muller offers the thought that the verb *apostello* should perhaps be seen as the starting point for a solution since in secular Greek it already carried the idea of divine authorization. Since the Hellenistic church would likely not have understood the idea of the *saliah*, Gentile Christians would have understood the idea of apostle already from the secular Greek concept as an authorized messenger; Ibid., 134. In Agnew's review of the literature on the origin of the NT apostle-concept, he concludes that older *saliah* theory does indeed provide a background for the concept when adjustments are made "by loosening dependence upon the rabbinic *saliah*-figure with a conjectured use of the nominal form *saliah* in the period contemporaneous with the NT period, and by showing the existence of the *slh/appostellein* sending-convention in the OT and NT with reference to figures of profound religious and theological significance"; Francis H. Agnew,

reinterpretation of the idea of apostleship,[62] and the lack of clarity as to who could be reckoned an apostle and how many there were.[63] There is an ongoing debate as to how to understand the office of apostle as it functioned in the early church and whether or not the office is thus limited to that first generation or continues as an ecclesiastical office or function.[64]

"The Origin of the NT Apostle-Concept: A Review Research," *Journal of Biblical Literature* 105, no. 1 (1985): 96.

62 Betz, 310-11. For good overviews of some of the main issues regarding origins of the apostolate see J. Andrew Kirk, "Apostleship Since Rengstorf: Towards a Synthesis," *New Testament Studies* 21, no. 2 (1975); Colin G. Kruse, "Apostle," in *Dictionary of Jesus and the Gospels*, ed. Joel B. Green, Scot McKnight, and I. Howard Marshall (Downers Grove, Illinois: InterVarsity Press, 1992); Schnackenburg; and Agnew. The major positions on the origins of apostles are views relating to the Jewish institution of the *saliah*, views that see it rooted in Christian sources, Gnostic influence, and modified views with all three of those playing a part to some degree.

63 See Muller, 130; Karl Heinrich Rengstorf, "Apostello, (Pempo), Exapostello, Apostolos, Pseudoapostolos, Apostole," in *Theological Dictionary of the New Testament*, ed. Gerhard Kittel (Grand Rapids: William B. Eerdmans, 1964), 431.

64 Ibid., 432. Schmithals sees the message and the office given by Jesus (31) and Hans von Campenhausen understands the rank and authority of the apostolate as restricted to the first apostolic generation "and can be neither continued nor renewed once this has come to an end"; Hans von Campenhausen, *Ecclesiastical Authority and Spiritual Power in the Church of the First Three Centuries* (Stanford, CA: Stanford University Press, 1969), 23. Jones argues that the "last of all" in I Corinthians 15:8 is indeed chronological and thus creates serious difficulties for all views of ongoing apostolic ministry whether Pentecostal/Charismatic or Roman Catholic; Peter R. Jones, "I Corinthians 15:8: Paul the Last Apostle," *Tyndale Bulletin* 36 (1985): 30-31. Kirk, however, argues that there is an underlying unity to all of the distinctions and discontinuities found in the New Testament; it is the special call of Christ and the one apostolic mission; "Apostleship," 262. He concludes that the continuity is rooted in the nature of the call and the specific task which is proclamation and church planting, while the discontinuity is in the differing historical circumstances and way in which that call comes; Ibid., 264. Therefore, it is not "contrary to the New Testament witness to consider that the same apostolic ministry in differing historical circumstances, exists to this day"; Ibid. Fee holds to a view that allows for ongoing function and first century uniqueness: "Can anything be said in our day about 'apostles'? Given the two criteria expressed here, one would have to allow that apostles do not exist in the sense that Paul defines his own ministry. But it should also be noted that this

Acknowledging the areas of debate, I now want to set forth my own positions that will stake out the parameters for my arguments about what I am calling "apostolic function." First, I make a distinction between apostle as an office and as a function. Part of our contemporary difficulty with the use and understanding of the term apostle has to do with the conceptual tangling of apostles as the initial founders of the church (Eph. 2:20), the unique position of the Twelve, and the fact that the term was applied to a wider group than those who were the original followers of Jesus.[65] Fee's comment is relevant here:

> Part of the problem with the term is that it has a sense of function as well as that of office or position. That is, it primarily had to do with some who were 'sent' by Christ to preach the gospel (cf. 1:17). But those who were so sent, and especially those who founded churches as a result of their evangelizing, came to be known as apostles, a designation that had inherent in it a sense of position as well (especially for those who were directly associated with Christ

---

might be too narrow a view, based strictly on Paul's own personal experience. His more functional understanding of apostleship (see on 1:1) would certainly have its modern counterparts in those who found and lead churches in unevangelized areas. Only when 'apostle' is used in a non-Pauline sense of 'guarantors of the traditions' would the usage be narrowed to the first century"; Gordon D. Fee, *The First Epistle to the Corinthians* (Grand Rapids: Eerdmans, 1987), 397. Fee interprets the "last of all" in I Cor. 15:8 as a final link in the enumerative chain so that it means, "finally"; Ibid., 732; see his overview of the debate on the term on 732 footnote 98.

65   Fee points out that the reference to "the Twelve" in I Cor. 15:5 shows that early on this was a title given to the special group that Jesus called to be with him. "This designation for Jesus' disciples, plus the fact that Paul will later refer to another appearance to 'all the apostles' (v. 7), suggest most strongly that the joining of these two terms into the title 'the twelve apostles' had not yet taken place in the church. That is, in Paul's view 'the Twelve' were a distinct entity, no doubt considered apostles, but the latter designation covered a much larger group of people"; Ibid., 729. The wider group where the term apostle is used includes I Cor. 15:7, (all the apostles and James the brother of the Lord), Andronicus and Junia in Rom. 16:7 (where it is likely that this is a husband and wife; Betz, "Apostle," 310; and Fee, 729 footnote 80), Barnabas (Acts 14:4, I Cor. 9:5-6) and Paul himself.

in his earthly ministry). In Paul the functional and positional usages nearly coalesce.[66]

By making a distinction between the office of apostle as those who played a special role in the initial founding of the church, who were commissioned personally by Jesus, and who were used by the Holy Spirit in the writing of Scripture from a wider group that functioned as "bearers of the NT message"[67] I am creating space for an ongoing apostolic role while holding a sense of the office as limited to the first generation.[68]

A second area concerns issues of authority and church organization, which are often tied together. There are some who would argue that the church is better served when it is organized around apostolic leadership and that those who lead are recognized and given authority as apostles.[69] What I find interesting is that such an approach seems to

---

66 Ibid., 30.

67 Rengstorf, 422.

68 Ibid. This is essentially Kirk's position that I have noted above in footnote 64 above.

69 See for instance, C. Peter Wagner, "The New Apostolic Reformation," in *The New Apostolic Churches*, ed. C. Peter Wagner (Ventura, California: Regal, 1998), 13-25. Starting in the mid to late 1990s, there has been a spate of writing looking at the restoration of apostolic ministry in one form or another; David Cannistraci, *Apostles and the Emerging Apostolic Movement* (Ventura, California: Renew, 1996); David Cartledge, *The Apostolic Revolution: The Restoration of Apostles and Prophets in the Assemblies of God in Australia* (Chester Hill, NSW, Australia: Paraclete Institute); John Eckhardt, *Moving in the Apostolic* (Ventura, California: Regal, 1999); Alan Hirsch, *The Forgotten Ways: Reactivating the Missional Church* (Grand Rapids: Brazos Press, 2006); Bryn Jones, *The Radical Church: Restoring the Apostolic Edge* (Shippensburg, Pennsylvania: Destiny Image Publishers, 1999); Bishop Claude E. Payne and Hamilton Beazley, *Reclaiming the Great Commission: A Practical Model for Transforming Denominations and Congregations* (San Francisco, California: Jossey-Bass, 2000); C. Peter Wagner, *Churchquake! How the New Apostolic Reformation Is Shaking up the Church as We Know It* (Ventura, California: Regal, 1999); C. Peter Wagner, ed. *The New Apostolic Churches: Rediscovering the New Testament Model of Leadership and Why It Is God's Desire for the Church Today* (Ventura, California: Regal, 1998). C. Peter Wagner, *Aftershock! How the*

assume that more authority equals more success in terms of church growth and thus can legitimize authoritarian cultural modes of leadership by wrapping it in the mantle of apostleship.[70] I think it is wise to keep two things in perspective when looking at issues of authority and church organization. The first is that in terms of the biblical data, Paul uses the term *exousia* (authority) "fewer than a dozen times in his writings, mostly as something he refuses to exercise even when it has the support of Jesus' express command."[71] Banks notes that Paul's relationship with his churches is for the most part expressed in the

---

Second Apostolic Age Is Changing the Church (Ventura, California: Regal Books, 2004). Synan notes the recent interest in Pentecostal circles on the restoration of the "fivefold ministries" of Eph. 4:11-13; Vinson Synan, "Apostolic Practice," in *He Gave Apostles: Apostolic Ministry in the 21st Century*, ed. Edgar R. Lee, Encounter: The Pentecostal Ministry Series (Springfield, Missouri: Assemblies of God Theological Seminary, 2005), 12. Pentecostals-Charismatics believe that the *charismata* (gifts of the Spirit) have been restored and thus the question is often asked as to why the offices of apostle and prophet have not been restored to the church; Ibid., 14. He reviews major church traditions and provides an excellent overview and critique of what is called the New Apostolic Reformation; Ibid., 16-23.

70 Heuser and Klaus note that Pentecostal-Charismatic ideology carries within it both a liberating belief system connected to the promises of encounter with God and divine assistance and the potential for abusive leaders to thrive; Roger Heuser and Byron Klaus, "Charismatic Leadership Theory: A Shadow Side Confessed," in *He Gave Apostles: Apostolic Ministry in the 21st Century*, ed. Edgar R. Lee, Encounter: The Pentecostal Ministry Series (Springfield, Missouri: Assemblies of God Theological Seminary, 2005), 121. It can produce "self-sacrificing, pioneering leadership that forges new frontiers under the 'fire and cloud' of an eschatological identity" but also "yields the possibility of non-accountable dynamic leaders who fashion a following with the 'sound-bites' of God-like utterances in the context of manipulative phenomenology, thus creating an image of powerful ministry leadership"; Ibid. They also point out that while Charismatic leadership can be potentially abusive, the routinized institutional leadership that follows "is implicitly controlling"; Ibid., 123. At the end of the day, it is the temptation of all forms of leadership to control and use power for its own benefits. Those who champion Charismatic leadership often conceive of it as the exercise of apostleship and as the cure for the abuses and control of institutionalism. It is naïve to assume that such leaders will either eliminate the problems of abuse of power or stave off the eventual appearance of status quo, pragmatic, institutional forms.

71 Robert Banks, *Paul's Idea of Community: The Early House Churches in Their Cultural Setting*, rev. ed. (Peabody, Massachusetts: Hendrickson, 1994), 174.

terminology of family life (father, mother, nurse) "rather than through the analogies from the legal, administrative, political, or even religious sphere," he uses "exhortation and appeal rather than command or decree," and "never employs the very strong term of command, *epitage*, for his own instructions."[72] The second is that merely changing leadership terminology away from business language or traditional church language, in favor of "apostle" and the idea of networking, while the basic substructure is rooted in church growth theory and highly gifted CEO type leaders of large churches does little to address the malaise of the church in the West. Hirsch's comments are relevant here: church growth concepts do not work for most of churches and nearly forty years of church growth thinking has not halted the decline of the church in the Western world.[73]

For those who are tempted to baptize authoritarian and hierarchical forms of leadership and church organization under the notion of apostleship as presented in the New Testament, Ritva Williams offers an analysis of the data that must be reckoned with.[74] Focusing on the household as the social setting of where churches met, Williams develops how both Jesus and Paul see groups that center around Jesus functioning as surrogate families or fictive kinship groups.[75] She then examines the role of patrons and patronage networks and the role of intermediaries and brokers in those relationships. She concludes:

> The organization of the early churches as fictive kinship groups simultaneously restricted patriarchal status to God and the role of

---

72 Ibid., 175-76.

73 Hirsch, 36, see also footnote 7.

74 Ritva H. Williams, *Stewards, Prophets, Keepers of the Word* (Peabody, Massachusetts: Hendrickson Publishers, 2006).

75 See Ibid., 184-92 for the summary of her work on Jesus and Paul and the functions of steward, prophet, and keepers of the word.

patron to the heavenly Father, and cast Jesus, the disciples, and later church leaders most frequently in the role of brokers.[76]

Williams work that shows Jesus and his early followers, by both critiquing and reordering the patriarchal household to put God the Father at the center of the new family of faith, renders problematic hierarchical, authoritarian and benevolent patron models that dominate human societies.[77]

While issues of authority and organization are not irrelevant in cross-cultural church planting, I think there are bigger issues at stake for missions in the arena of apostolic identity and activity. While scholarship continues to explore a number of issues related to apostleship, when it comes to what apostles actually do, there is a great deal of agreement. The verb *apostello* in classical Greek means to send and was used in contexts of delegation where an envoy had the full power to act as personal representative of the one sending.[78] It was used in the LXX to translate *salah*, which does not describe so much the sending as it does the authorization of the messenger not to an office, but to a particular function or task.[79] *Apostolos* was originally an adjective derived from the verb and as a noun has the basic concept of the sending of messengers or envoys.[80]

---

76 Ibid.

77 Ibid., 3-4. She says, "Paul uses steward and stewardship language in relation to his own claims to status and authority within and over the churches that he has established. As we shall see, Paul's strategy offers a subversive critique of the dominant Greco-Roman ideology of benevolent patriarchalism endorsed by his critics"; Ibid., 4.

78 Erich Von Eicken and Helgo Lindner, "Apostle, Apostello (Part)," in *The New International Dictionary of New Testament Theology*, ed. Colin Brown et al. (Grand Rapids: Zondervan, 1975), 127; and Rengstorf, 400.

79 Von Eicken and Lindner, 127.

80 Betz, 309.

While there is a wide range of use of the term in the New Testament,[81] Betz points out that chronologically the earliest use in the New Testament is "as an administrative designation for envoys, delegates, and representatives" (II Cor. 8:23, Phil. 2:25); it also has a more religious sense of a preacher of the Gospel (Acts 1:21-26, 13:1-3); then there is Luke's identification of the disciples of Jesus with the apostles and the Twelve, and Paul's reinterpretation which is different than that of Luke-Acts.[82] What is quite clear is that *apostolos* is used, as Rengstorf puts it more generically, as the comprehensive term for "the bearers of the New Testament message."[83] Others use a term more familiar to modern Christians, but of more recent coinage in saying that the apostles were missionaries whose work was "centered in the proclamation of the Gospel and the founding and administering of new churches (see I Cor. 9:5, 12:28; Eph. 2:20; 3:5; 4:11; Rev. 18:20; Did. 11:3-6)."[84] Apostleship was bound with the duty of mission to the Gentiles[85] and that "we may take it as incontrovertible that the missionary commission was an essential part of the primitive Christian apostolate."[86]

One of the problems with writers' use of the term "missionary" to describe apostolic work is that we tend to read our current ideas about missions and missionaries back into these texts. Bosch reminds us that the term "missions" is of fairly recent origin. Prior to the sixteenth century, *missio* (sending) was used as a theological term for the send-

---

81   Ibid.

82   Ibid., 309-310.

83   Rengstorf, 422.

84   Betz, 309-310.

85   Muller, 129.

86   Ibid., 134. Schmithals, 35; Schnackenburg, 298, 30; and von Campenhausen, 22; all use the term "missionary" to describe apostolic work although they see apostleship as embracing more than our modern notion of missionary covers. Schutz says that nothing comes closer to suggest the central missionary nature of apostolic activity than the verb "evangelize" (*euanggelizomai*); 36.

ing of the Son by the Father and the Holy Spirit by the Father and the Son. In the 1700s, the Jesuits began to use the term for the spreading of the Christian faith.[87]

In order to attempt to gain something of a fresh look at this biblical material, I want to avoid the use of the term "missionary" and try to focus specifically on what apostles did and then move from there to think about how it applies to our current situation and what light it sheds on our contemporary understandings of the terms "missionary" and "missions."[88]

THE WORK OF APOSTLES

Proclaiming the Kingdom, Bearing Witness to Jesus, and Planting Churches

Those who were called to be with Jesus were sent out to proclaim the coming of the Kingdom (Mark 3:14, 6:6-12; Matt. 10:5-9; Luke 9:1-6). Jesus then commissioned his followers to make disciples of the *ethne* and to be his witnesses moving from Jerusalem outward to the uttermost parts of the earth (Acts 1:8). In the book of Acts, Luke follows the program of Acts 1:8 as the good news moves from Jerusalem

---

87 Bosch, *Transforming Mission*, 1.

88 In doing this, I am trying to follow Kostenberger's encouragement to let the New Testament speak to us on its own terms, rather than finding "what we have already determined to find there on other grounds"; Andreas J. Kostenberger, "The Place of Mission in New Testament Theology: An Attempt to Determine the Significance of Mission within the Scope of the New Testament's Message as a Whole," *Missiology: An International Review* 27, no. 3 (1999): 349. I also am aware that to synthetically draw together material across various biblical sources cuts against the grain of scholarship that would see varying strains and ideas of apostleship across these writings. In this exercise, I am taking the broadest view of apostleship as including those who were called by Jesus in the Gospels to be with him, and who are designated in Acts and from the writings of Paul. For reviews that include what apostles do, see von Campenhausen, 12-29; and Schmithals' discussion of the apostolate of Paul; 21-57.

and Judea with the establishment of the church there (the believers in Jerusalem are called collectively the church in Acts 5:11, 8:1, 3, and 11:22; more broadly there is reference to the "church in Judea" Acts 9:31) into Samaria through the ministry of Philip (8:4-8) and Peter and John as they preach in Samaritan villages on their return to Jerusalem (Acts 8:25), and then crosses into Gentile communities with Peter (Acts 10:27-48) and unnamed disciples from Cyrus and Cyrene who plant the church among Greeks at Antioch in Acts 11:19-21. Luke then traces the work of Paul as he moves out from the Antioch church to make disciples and establish them as local churches (see Acts 16:40-41 for churches in Syria and Cilicia; Acts 14:23 for churches formed on his first missionary journey out of Antioch in Galatia and Phrygia; and Acts 16, Philippi; Acts 17, Thessalonica and Berea; Acts 18, Corinth; and Acts 19-20 for Ephesus).

Ministry With Power, Signs, and Wonders

It is inherent in the call to follow Jesus that the disciple takes on the task of Jesus and is given power and authority to fulfill that task. Jesus makes the disciples fishers of men (Matthew 4:19), those called to be with him are sent out to preach and have authority to cast out demons (Mark 3:14-15), when the 12 and 70 are sent out, they are given power and authority to drive out demons, cure diseases and proclaim the coming of God's rule (Luke 9:1-6, 10:1-12). They are called to be in intimate relationship with Jesus and bear fruit (John 15:1-8) and to do his works (John 14:12). Acts 1:1 serves as a theological bridge between Luke and Acts by showing that in the Gospel, Luke wrote about what Jesus began to do and teach. The book of Acts continues the works of Jesus, even after He is ascended as the Holy Spirit gives power to His disciples. In the opening presentations of Acts, the Church is founded in Jerusalem and the apostles bear witness to the resurrection with great power (4:33) and signs and wonders (5:12). Miracles, signs and wonders are not just the province of the apostles, but happen through others as well (Stephen, Acts 6:8; Philip, Acts 8:4-8). In the ministry of Paul, both in Luke's record and in his writings, healings and works of power play a significant role in the advancement of the Gospel (see Acts 13:9-11; a generic report of signs and wonders in 14:3; a report of extraordinary miracles through Paul 14:8-10, 19:11; 20:10; and Paul's own reflections Rom. 15:19; I Cor. 2:1-4; II Cor. 12:12).

Ministry Led by the Holy Spirit

Bruce, in his commentary on Acts, notes that a leading theological theme of Luke is the leading of the Spirit.[89] While the record focuses on a few of the leading personalities, Luke shows that it is the entire community of followers that is constituted by the Spirit. Bruce summarizes in this way:

> The Christian community is Spirit-filled and Spirit-led, so much so that its voice is the voice of the Spirit (cf., e.g., 5:3, 15:28) and the whole evangelistic enterprise from Jerusalem to Rome, is directed by the Spirit (cf., e.g., 16:6-10).[90]

Bruce points out that it is part of Luke's plan in writing to show that the progress of the faith "was no mere product of human planning, it was directed by divine agency."[91] These "bearers of the New Testament message" were led and empowered by the Spirit to proclaim the good news and demonstrate it with miraculous signs, wonders, and healings. Carter, summarizing apostolic methods that were used to make Christ known, includes personal witness, miracles, oral preaching, itineration, charities, church organization and supervision, training of promising

---

89 Frederick Fyvie Bruce, *The Book of Acts*, ed. Gordon D. Fee, rev. ed., The New International Commentary on the New Testament (Grand Rapids: William B. Eerdmans, 1988), 13; see also Williams, 6.

90 Bruce, 13, note 48.

91 Ibid., 13.

converts, planting the Gospel in strategic centers and writing and circulating Christian letters.[92] He points out that this was not simply the work of a few, but that in the early church there was a sense that the responsibility of universal witness was upon every believer.[93] "Whatever social, economic, political, or other implications the Gospel may have had, the primary and distinctive aim of the first century Christians was to make Christ known to all the world as Savior and Lord."[94]

Suffering

The ministry of the apostles was marked by opposition, persecution, and suffering. In Jerusalem, Peter and John were apprehended after the healing of the crippled man at the temple gate (Acts 4:3-22). At that point they were commanded not to speak or teach in Jesus' name. Later the apostles, as a group, were arrested (Acts 5:18), miraculously freed by an angel of the Lord (5:19), then retaken without force (5:26), flogged and released (5:40). After Paul's conversion, his testimony in Damascus leads the Jews to attempt to kill him (Acts 9:23) and, when he comes to Jerusalem, the same thing happens and he is sent off to Tarsus for his safety (9:29-30). At a later period, James was martyred by Herod (Acts 12:2) and then Peter was taken with the same intent, but again miraculously delivered (12:6-11). Luke's record of Paul's missionary journeys in Acts are laced with abuse and violence as he proclaims the message of Jesus (there is abusive talk against the preaching 13:44, 14:2, 17:13; persecution 13:50; stoning 14:19; jail and flogging 16:19-24; rioting 17:5, 19:23-41; bringing Paul to court 18:12-13; and finally his arrest in Jerusalem, imprisonment and trip to Rome in the final

---

92 C. W. Carter, "Apostolic Age," in *Zondervan Pictorial Encyclopedia of the Bible*, ed. Merrill C. Tenney (Grand Rapids: Zondervan, 1975), 223.

93 Ibid.

94 Ibid. See Kostenberger, 353 for a series of citations from N. T. Wright and others on the centrality of missionary activity to the Christian faith of the first century and Wright's conclusion that that world mission is the most obvious feature of Christian praxis.

chapters of Acts). Paul's own letters shed more light on the sufferings he faced (Rom. 15:31; I Cor. 2:1-4, 16:8; II Cor. 1:8-11; his long list of hardships in II Cor. 6:3-10 and 11:21b-29; I Thess. 2:1-2; II Tim. 2:9) and his view that apostles are like men condemned to death, who are the scum of the earth and refuse of the world (I Cor. 4:8-13).

Caring for the Weak

It is a telling sign of our tendency in the West to split the "spiritual" and "physical/social" domains that our images of apostolic ministry rarely include images of caring for the weak and marginalized.[95] Our earliest records of the church is that it devoted itself to apostolic doctrine (Acts 2:42); note the concern that no one lack in the new community constituted by the Spirit. While the apostles see their focus of ministry as the preaching of the Word and prayer, they provide the impetus for the mechanism that cared for the Greek widows. Paul says to the Ephesian elders in Acts 20:34-35:

---

[95] It is interesting that the intense debate found among Christians who believe in the authority of Scripture regarding the relationship between evangelism and social responsibility was not problematic for either Jesus or Paul. You cannot pick up a book on missions without having to deal with the issue of evangelism and social action. McGee notes that, "Missionaries and church leaders have long struggled with the tension between preaching the gospel and establishing charitable ministries (schools, orphanages, and hospitals) overseas. Should the missionary focus on saving souls or saving lives? Can one be done without "lionizing" the importance of the other?"; McGee, "Saving Souls," 11. There are three views that I personally find unsatisfactory that represent common attempts to explain the relationship between evangelism and social action. The first is to say that our only concern is to preach the Gospel, which treats people as if they were disembodied spirits with only souls that need to be saved. The second asserts that we do good deeds in order to preach the Gospel which makes us appear to be dangling a carrot on a stick before needy people. The third is the expression "no distinction between word and deed" which logically leads to "deeds" without words since they are equivalent, and thus in reverse compartmentalizes deeds away from the words that bring the interpretation of those very deeds.

You yourselves know that these hands of mine have supplied my own needs and the needs of my companions. In everything I did, I showed you that by this kind of hard work we must help the weak, remembering the words the Lord Jesus himself said: "It is more blessed to give than to receive."

Paul and the apostles in Jerusalem shared a concern for the poor believers there (Gal. 2:10). His work on collecting an offering for them (I Cor. 16:1-4), his concern that widows be cared for by the local church (I Tim. 5:3-16), and his admonition to help the weak (*asthenes*—the same word as in the Acts passage which can refer to economic weakness and poverty in both contexts) shows that he did not conduct himself in an either/or fashion. The experience of being reconciled to God, and living as a community under the rule of God, meant that these things were the natural expressions and implications worked out in human relationships of the message that he preached.

MINISTRY AS AN APOSTOLIC TEAM

Both from Luke's account of Paul's work in Acts and from his own writings, we know that Paul did not work as an individual but in a team.[96] Bank's work on the early house churches shows that there were distinct differences between how Paul conceived of the churches he was planting versus his church planting group. In the *ekklesia*, the "body" metaphor is dominant, with its focus on the participation in a common life. With those who traveled and labored with him Paul used the term *ergon* (work) to describe it, where the focus was the sharing of a common task.[97] He notes that in terms of the apparatus

---

96 Roger S. Greenway and Timothy M. Monsma, *Cities: Missions' New Frontier* (Grand Rapids: Baker Book House, 1989), 14. He points out that while much of what happened in the New Testament about missionary outreach is not recorded, what is clear is that it was not the work of a few individuals, but an extended group of apostolic associates.

97 Banks, 160-61. See Gal. 6:4; I Cor. 3:8-15, 9:1, 16:10, Phil. 2:30

for planting churches and the network of relationships built around it, there are no parallels in the religious propagation of that period.[98] He summarizes that nature of Paul's church planting band as a grouping of specialists identified by their gifts, backed by sponsoring families and communities, with a specific function and structure focused on preaching the Gospel, founding churches and helping them to mature.[99] Winter draws on sociological language to help describe this two-fold structure of local church and missionary band,[100] arguing that across church history there have been comparable indigenous structures that have the same function.[101] In order to compare differing formal structures with similar function, he employs the terms modality and sodality. A modality "is a structured fellowship in which there is no distinction of sex or age," like local churches, and a sodality "is a structured fellowship in which membership involves an adult second decision beyond modality membership" like the missionary band.[102] As modalities, local congregations are "admirably suited to carry out the task of mission in the local context"[103] while the mission sodality was a mobile team dedicated to "surmounting all the geographic, cultural,

---

98 Ibid., 167.

99 Ibid., 169. See Glasser's detailed treatment of the apostolic team; Arthur F. Glasser and others, *Announcing the Kingdom: The Story of God's Mission in the Bible* (Grand Rapids: Baker Academic, 2005), 300-304; and Joseph C. and Michele C., "Field-Governed Mission Structures Part I: In the New Testament," *International Journal of Frontier Missions* 18, no. 2 (2001): 60-64. For an overview on the origins of mission structures, see Brian Stanley, "Where Have Our Mission Structures Come From?," *Transformation* 20, no. 1 (2003); and for a look at structures of the past and where they are heading in the future, see Stanley Skreslet, "Impending Transformation: Mission Structures for a New Century," *International Bulletin of Missionary Research* 23, no. 1 (1999): 2-6.

100 Ralph Winter, "The Two Structures of God's Redemptive Mission," in *Perspectives on the World Christian Movement: A Reader*, ed. Ralph D. Winter and Steven C. Hawthorne (Pasadena: William Carey Library, 1999), 220.

101 Ibid., 222.

102 Ibid., 224.

103 Glasser and others, 300.

and linguistic barriers keeping tribes, tongues and nations from the knowledge of Christ."[104]

WHERE APOSTOLIC MINISTRY TOOK PLACE

While the work of preaching the Gospel by apostolic teams is recognized, the issue of where they went and how they made those decisions has not traditionally been a focus in studies dealing with apostleship. However, I think that it is precisely at these points that the issues of apostolic identity are most clearly revealed. Looking broadly at the biblical material, there are four elements to bring into consideration.

Pioneer Church Planting

The first is that from the starting point of the early church, their commission, which had the soteriological focus of proclaiming the Gospel message of God's gracious salvation to be appropriated by faith,[105] was carried out in what we would today describe as pioneer settings. Meaning by this that literally everywhere these early witnesses went they were planting the first churches and communities of Christ followers. This is an important point because in our setting, 2000 years later, with the vast expansion of Christianity, it is easy for us to think of "proclaiming the Gospel" and planting communities of faith as an activity that happens in the context of many various (and sometimes competing) expressions of Christianity, rather than winning the first generation of disciples in places where there were none before.

Thus, Kostenberger makes the right observation, that while in contemporary use "missions" generally refers to cross-cultural ministry, the biblical terminology does not require this. He points out that mission in the New Testament centers around a person or group's commission

---

104 Ibid., 301.

105 Kostenberger, 348.

to a particular task, one which is soteriological in nature.[106] However, he then jumps to a conclusion that is not warranted: that "the cross-cultural aspect of Christian mission is not a necessary part of mission" even after noting that Acts 1:8 shows that "mission may, and frequently will, involve the crossing of ethnic, cultural, or other boundaries."[107] I think that what happens here is again the confusion that results from taking the word "mission" with all of its history and trying to find it in the New Testament. In the paragraph in question, Kostenberger wants to avoid a too narrow definition of missions as well as a too broad one. At the end of the day, this attempt to walk the terminological middle falls short because it misses the "pioneer" nature of the New Testament setting and tries to locate a fixed meaning for mission in regard to the crossing of cultural boundaries when the situation is dynamic and not static.

Specific Callings and Specific Guidance

A second piece of evidence is that it becomes apparent that in the New Testament there is a sense of both fluidity and specificity to the commissioning to proclaim the Gospel. Paul sees himself as apostle to the Gentiles (I Tim. 2:7, Gal. 2:7-8, Rom. 15:16) while Peter is an apostle to the Jews (Gal. 2:7-8). Thus, there appears to be a general sense of the overall direction that they pursued in their work of preaching the Gospel. Peter worked primarily within his own cultural background and Paul worked primarily outside of his own. There is also fluidity that can come from the sovereign work and specific guidance of the Holy Spirit. Peter's vision and the direction of the Spirit (Acts 10:9-20) means that he becomes the vessel by God's choice from whose lips the Gentiles would first hear the Gospel (Acts 15:7).[108] Paul, on the

---

106 Ibid.

107 Ibid.

108 See Bruce, 289, footnote 36 for the reading on this verse that shows how God chose the apostles that through one of them, Peter as their representative, the Gentiles

other hand, carries a tremendous personal burden for his own people (Rom. 9:1-4) and shares the Gospel with them at every opportunity, yet spends the bulk of his time planting churches among majority Gentile populations.

What we see here is a natural outgrowth of the commission to make disciples of the *ethne* (Matt. 28:18-20). The pursuit of this commission carries people across cultural and ethnic boundaries (Acts 1:8). At the same time, the Holy Spirit calls some witnesses to share the Good News primarily in their own sociocultural setting while others work cross-culturally. However, these broader "callings" do not negate specific guidance from the Spirit that will lead people to do something temporarily outside their normal long-term focus.

Paul's Zeal to Preach Where Christ Was Not Known

This leads to a third factor that has to do with Paul's sense of identity as an apostle.

> Romans 15:20: "It has always been my ambition to preach the gospel where Christ was not known, so that I would not be building on someone else's foundation."

> Romans 15:23: "But now that there is no more place for me to work in these regions, . . ."

---

might hear the Gospel. Interestingly, Bruce notes that Peter's action with Gentiles "may have been one reason for the speed with which James the Just was henceforth acknowledged as the undisputed leaders of the mother-church: James at least enjoyed a public reputation which was unspotted by any suspicion of fraternizing with Gentiles"; Ibid., 223. Acts 21:20-26 illustrates how the understanding of the fellow apostles about the principle of evangelizing Gentiles was not shared widely by Jewish background believers.

> II Corinthians 10:16: ". . . so that we can preach the gospel in the regions beyond you. For we do not want to boast about work already done in another man's territory. . . ."

What this material introduces here is that, at least for Paul, his sense of apostleship included the notion that his work of church planting was to be focused in areas where there were no Christians or existing churches. These verses do not imply that everyone in these places was a Christ follower, but rather that in Paul's understanding of his commission, the presence of churches in a setting meant that he could move on to do his work preaching the good news in a place where Christ was not known and the church not yet planted.

The Holy Spirit Guided Their Work

Finally, the record also makes it apparent that Paul's desire to go where the church did not exist was not simply carried out in a mechanistic fashion. Luke shows us that Paul was moved out of Jerusalem through divine direction (Acts 22:17-21). Acts 16:6-10 shows how Paul is directed by the Spirit not to preach in Asia or Bithynia, but instead moved to Troas where he received the vision calling him to Macedonia. Bruce notes that "Paul's missionary journeys display an extraordinary combination of strategic planning and keen sensitiveness to the guidance of the Spirit of God, however that was conveyed—by prophetic utterance, inward prompting, or the overruling of external circumstances."[109]

APOSTLES AND MISSIONARIES: THE CHALLENGE OF TERMINOLOGY

The purpose of this biblical overview was to examine what apostles did and how they viewed their work. Noting the way that scholars tend to use the term "missionary" in their definition of apostle, I intentionally

---

109 Ibid., 306.

set that aside in this exercise. The biblical data shows that they served, and here I borrowed a phrase from Rengstorf, as the "bearers of the New Testament message." They proclaimed the Good News about Jesus through the power of the Spirit; were led by the Spirit, with miracles, signs, wonders, and healings confirming this proclamation; and organized those they won into local churches. They taught and modeled to these churches a concern for the weak, and in carrying out their ministry they suffered for the sake of Jesus' name. I also made four observations about where apostolic work was carried out and how these decisions were made. They were pioneer church planters, making initial breakthroughs in places where Christ was not known. Within a fluidity where the Spirit could bring immediate guidance, they could see their work as being primarily located among a certain type of people. Paul's sense of apostleship explicitly included going where Christ was not named and not building on another person's foundation, and finally, his choices of ministry location were guided supernaturally by the Spirit.

The question now becomes, does the term "missionary" with its contemporary conception of crossing geographic and cultural boundaries fit well with the work of apostles in the New Testament? Let me make a few observations on this issue. First, in my estimation there is no perfect terminology. Because of the contextual nature of language, terms will always derive their meaning from current use. It is impossible for us in the twenty-first century to completely eliminate the history of usage and constellation of meanings that are associated with either apostle or missionary. It is incumbent on whoever would use these terms to establish the ground rules for their use in advance and to clarify precisely what one means by the term.[110]

---

110 In the final chapter in the section on terminological issues I will show how this problem with the terminology relating to "missionary" is bound up in three different kinds of Christian work that need to be kept conceptually distinct.

Second, if we take the verbal root of apostle and missionary (*apostello* and *missio*) as sending and the nouns as those who are sent with a commission, you still have to fill in the content of what "sent ones" do and work around the historical content that each of these terms have picked up over the years.

Third, where you land on the emphasis of the work of apostles/missionaries seems to be more a matter of preference in understanding the text than in the actual biblical data. If you take apostle in its most generic sense as someone commissioned with a message (as Kostenberger does), then you can see the crossing of cultural boundaries to plant the church among people who have not heard as somewhat incidental to the concept. If, however, the Pauline notion of going where Christ is not named is foregrounded, then the crossing of cultural boundaries inherent in discipling the *ethne* and being witnesses to the ends of the earth becomes a central concept in the idea of apostleship.

What this means is that the term "missionary" then takes its meaning from the definition of apostleship in use. If you take the most generic sense of apostle, then the missionary is a church planter and there is no essential difference between this work within one's own cultural setting and without. If, however, the cross-cultural and pioneer aspects of apostle are taken as primary, then there is a distinction between evangelism and cross-cultural evangelism. The work of a local church or apostle within his or her own sociocultural setting is evangelism while the pioneer work of planting the church in cultures where Christ is not known becomes cross-cultural evangelism or missionary work.

APOSTOLIC FUNCTION IS A HEURISTIC THAT DEFINES FOR US WHAT, WHY, AND HOW WE WORK

The terminology problem is not something easily solved. While theologians continue to grapple with the biblical texts, mission practitioners can benefit greatly from what we do know about apostolic ministry. I began this presentation by pointing out that our current understanding of missionary identity was inadequate to the challenges of our mission realities and that we need a more sophisticated and nuanced view of missions that can differentiate between places where the church exists and where it does not and mobilize the church to proclaim Christ where He is not yet known.

I believe that our current understandings about missions and the role of the missionary can be invigorated by rooting our sense of identity in the notion of apostleship.[111] This does not mean that I am suggesting there is some kind of one-to-one mapping of the biblical data to our practice now. Rather, it is taking how apostles function in a heuristic fashion and infusing our work with that same vision. I am using "heuristic" here in the sense of an interpretive rubric for helping us to understand what we do, why we do it, and how we operate. By apostolic function I mean that at both the level of the individual cross-cultural worker, the mission team, and the sending agency, there is a focus on the apostolic task of preaching the Gospel where it has not been heard, planting the church where it does not exist, and leading people to the obedience of faith so that they, too, will express Jesus Christ in their social worlds and participate in God's global mission. It is a catalytic and comprehensive function that shapes cross-cultural work so that whatever local expression it may take, the ultimate goal is to see the

---

111 Within the frontier mission movement there have been occasional uses of the idea of apostolic ministry focused on church planting where Christ is not named. See Harold Dollar, "The Twelve Apostles: Models for Frontier Missions?," *International Journal of Frontier Missions* 10, no. 2 (1993); Dan Greene, *Dusting Off the Apostolic Function* (International Journal of Frontier Missions, 1984, accessed 5 October 2007), available from http:www.ijfm.org/PDFs_IJFM/01_3_PDFs/greene.pdf; Dick Scoggins, "Nurturing a New Generation of "Pauline" and "Petrine" Apostles," *Mission Frontiers* July-August (2006). Sinclair has recently issued a call for Apostolic Networks or "apostolic service providers" that serve apostolic church planting teams in various areas of expertise link together to facilitate their work; Dan Sinclair and Dick Scoggins, "Introducing the Apnet: A 21st Century Approach to Apostolic Ministry," *Mission Frontiers* November-December (2006): 14.

church planted where it does not exist and to see local bodies of believers become fully obedient to Christ and missional themselves. Note that I am not saying we are apostles; that is not something we choose, for it is God who gives apostles to the body of Christ.[112] What I am advocating is that the role and work of an apostle in the Pauline fashion serve as the template for self-understanding of the missionary task. It is functioning in an apostolic fashion, embracing individually and corporately the vision of performing the Pauline task of missiological breakthrough whether by doing it themselves, doing it in conjunction with a national church movement, or equipping a national church movement to do it on their own.

Missionary identity rooted in the idea of apostolic function rescues cross-cultural work from becoming redundant because it reorients the entire purpose of the enterprise to God's passion to be worshiped by all the peoples, tribes, and tongues of His world. There is always an edge, an ear turned to the Spirit to seek out those who have never heard. No job can be done in a perfunctory manner and no task is insignificant because when we are functioning apostolically it embeds all work in the larger picture of bringing good news to social settings where it is not known.

---

112 Earlier I noted that, in the view I am taking, the function of an apostle is something ongoing in the body of Christ. The theological rationale for this idea is found in Kirk who sees a unity in all the New Testament distinctions about apostleship in the special call of Christ and the apostolic mission of proclamation and church planting; Kirk "Apostleship," 262. Both Schmithals and Schnackenburg hold views of apostleship that allow for either a missionary function without seeing an ongoing apostolic office; Schmithals, "The Office of Apostle," 35; or apostleship based in the idea of "successful missionary activity, which was possibly confirmed by 'signs of an apostle,' powerful preaching and proof of authority"; Schnackenburg, "Apostles Before and During Paul's Time," 301. I believe that God does still commission people to be apostles as a function and which approaches the sense of office that we see "coalescing in Paul," to use Fee's phrase. My point here is that I also think it is possible for cross-cultural workers and their teams to conceive of their work as to function apostolically even when they may not have the same type of commissioning and gifting as some do.

Apostolic function as missionary identity takes on paradigmatic status because it acts as a master rubric for all that we do. It covers why we do missions (for the sake of His name), where we do it (where Christ is not known), what we do (proclaim Christ and plant churches that live under God's rule), and how we do it (by the leading and power of the Spirit, with signs and wonders confirming the Word). In the section that follows, I will explain the idea of apostolic function in further detail and examine its impact on missionary endeavors.

Apostolic Function Means there are Some Things We Choose Not to Do

Apostolic function directly assails the problem observed by Neill that when everything is missions, nothing is missions. It is an intentionally narrow view of missions. Listen to Paul in I Corinthians 1:17: "For Christ did not send me to baptize, but to preach the gospel—not with words of human wisdom, lest the cross of Christ be emptied of its power." This verse lies near the beginning of a very complex section running from 1:10 to 4:21 where division is merely a symptom and the underlying problem has to do with the nature of the Gospel, the church, and apostolic ministry.[113] Fee points out that Paul is not denigrating in any way baptism, but rather the expression of his calling in a negative fashion is dictated by the nature of the argument he is making.[114] Fee reconstructs the setting for this section as most likely being a situation where Christian teachers are seen as purveyors of divine wisdom and the Christian faith is seen as an expression of wisdom (*sophia*). Corinthian presuppositions about both baptism and the use of "words of human wisdom" led them to call attention to the agency and status

---

113 Fee, 50. See pages 46-66 for Fee's reconstruction and exegesis of this section and specifically 1:10-25.

114 Ibid., 63. "Paul does not by any means depreciate baptism as such, as is shown in numerous passages in his epistles where he speaks of the significance of baptism, but only leaves it for his fellow workers to perform"; Schmithals, 55.

of the minister[115] and thus, as Fee points out, looking at leaders from this human perspective made both Paul and the Gospel look poorly.[116] Paul argues from being an apostle—a sent one of Christ—that what he was sent to do was proclaim the Good News, which draws attention to God and not the agent.[117]

What I want to highlight here is Paul's understanding of the work of an apostle as focused on "gospelizing;" it carries the sense of being very narrow and focused. He does not do everything, there are priorities that drive him as an apostle. I have already noted Romans 15:20, 23 and II Corinthians 10:16 that illustrate Paul's understanding of the apostolic task was not simply to proclaim the Good News, and plant local churches, but to actively seek out neglected regions where Christ was not yet known. My question is, if Paul were with us today, where the Church exists so powerfully in so many settings and is so weak or non-existent in other settings, is it not possible that he might develop another ad hoc argument like he did in I Corinthians presentation 1? In Corinth it concerned the nature of the Gospel, the church, and apostolic ministry,[118] but today it concerns the very nature of what missions and the missionary task is all about. I can see Paul arguing again that he does not do certain things and does not go certain places because that is not what he was sent to do. Paul's letters to his churches are filled with exhortations based in our new relationship with Christ about what believers are to do both within and without their own fellowship. Yet the overall picture we see is that Paul left the Christians

---

115 Anthony C. Thiselton, *The First Epistle to the Corinthians: A Commentary on the Greek Text* (Grand Rapids: Eerdmans, 2000), 142-45.

116 Fee, 49.

117 See also Frederic Louis Godet, *Commentary of First Corinthians* (Grand Rapids: Kregel, 1977) and David E. Garland, *1 Corinthians*, ed. Robert W. Yarbrough and Robert H. Stein, *Baker Exegetical Commentary on the New Testament* (Grand Rapids: Baker Academic, 2003) on this verse.

118 Fee, 50.

within their own social setting to lead the charge while he himself got on with the task of preaching Christ where He is unknown.

Apostolic Function Means that all Evangelism is Not Equal

One of the weaknesses of the "everything is mission" view is that there becomes no way to differentiate between people who are not Christians and their relative need to hear the Gospel.[119] Immediately this kind of "prioritizing" language raises red flags and an extreme sense of discomfort to all who affirm John 3:16 that God so loved the world. We know that God is not willing that any should perish (II Pet. 3:9) and that He desires all to be saved and come to a knowledge of the truth (I Tim. 2:4-5). At the same time, all have sinned and all are justified freely by His grace through the redemption that came by Christ Jesus (Rom. 3:23-24). Theologically, we affirm that all people are spiritually lost in an equal sense, regardless of geographic location or religious adherence. When a person is not reconciled to God through Jesus Christ, he/she is in a state of lostness. A person cannot be more lost spiritually than another person. In this sense, all evangelism is equal and there is equal priority and urgency.

Yet, I want to argue that there is another sense in which people are "lost" in different ways. I illustrate it in this fashion. "Why are the non-Christians Irem, A Turk, Ahmet, a Banjar, and Tin Sau, a Bama, lost in a way that the non-Christians John in Springfield, Missouri, José in Costa Rica, and Sun Yung in South Korea are not lost?" If all six of these people are equally lost theologically, what other perspective is there to consider? Before I provide an answer, let me review a Pauline

---

119 In my own context in North America it is a very common experience for people within our mission organization to have church members and family argue against working cross-culturally because of all the spiritual need that we are surrounded with at home. This illustrates my point exactly because if there are non-Christians here and non-Christians somewhere else, then the argument is, why go somewhere else, just work here.

perspective that is important to my notion of apostolic function. I have already noted the statements Paul makes in Romans 15:19, 20, and 23. In light of contemporary missionary practice, they are really quite remarkable. He says that he has fully proclaimed the Gospel of Christ from Jerusalem to Illyricum and that there is no longer any work for him in these regions. It becomes quite obvious that for Paul to "fully proclaim" the Gospel is something less than either personally preaching to every single person or seeing every single person become a follower of Christ. His argument is that because he has fully proclaimed Christ and there are others who have laid a foundation as well, it is now time for him to go on to Spain.

In this scenario, Paul is very clearly and explicitly showing that in his apostolic work all evangelism is not equal and that there are priorities for him that mean moving from one setting where there are spiritually lost people to another setting. Paul's sense of calling to preach Christ where He was not known (Rom. 15:20) is based on the fact that there were already local churches in existence. What this strongly implies is that in Paul's mind there is a distinction between the ongoing evange-listic mandate of local congregations who are to reach those proximate to them both geographically and culturally and the apostolic work of crossing geographic and cultural boundaries to go where Christ is not yet known. Thus, it is not a matter of every person in a place having yet heard the Gospel or becoming a believer, but rather that the potential exists for them to meet Christ through near-neighbor witness.

The answer then to the question I posed above is that Irem, Ahmet, and Tin Sau live in sociocultural settings where there are no Christians or very few, thus there is not even the potential for hearing the Gospel. By way of contrast, for John, José, and Sun Yung, although they are lost as well, there is potential for them to hear the Gospel because powerful indigenous church movement exists in their culture. It becomes an issue of access; while all people are equally lost, not all people have equal access to the Gospel. This idea of there being some basis for a differentiation between the evangelistic work of local congregations and the apostolic band fits well and is actually an extension of the distinction that is observed in the New Testament between church structures, which are "admirably suited to carry out the task of mission in the local context" and what we see in Acts 13-28 where "the expansion of the Christian movement was achieved through a strikingly different structure—the apostolic team or mission structure."[120]

Apostolic function means there is a different priority for the mission band. It does not mean that some people are less important or more important in terms of evangelism, rather each structure, local church and mission team, has its own sphere of work that must be pursued. This concept is helpful because it addresses the access issue for the unreached in our contemporary situation without pitting the spiritual need of non-Christians where there are church movements against those who live where there are no such near-neighbor witnesses. All non-Christians equally need to hear the message of Christ, but it is the priority of local church structures to reach those in their sphere and the unique contribution of the mission team, functioning in apostolic fashion, to seek out, by the guidance of the Holy Spirit, those who do not yet have access to the Gospel. Again, I think Paul's statements about going where Christ is not known and not building on another's foundation means that, were he assessing the missiological terrain today, he would rejoice in the powerful indigenous churches that exist in many settings and focus his efforts on going to sociocultural settings where the church is non-existent or a tiny, enclaved minority.

---

120 Glasser, et al., 300.

Apostolic Function Does Not Limit God's Sovereignty in Calling

The distinction between evangelism in a mono-cultural setting through the work of a local church and the apostolic function of crossing a cultural boundary to preach Christ where no church movement exists does not mean that there is a concretized taxonomy that must be rigidly followed and mechanistically applied to all ministry. Although Scripture can say that Peter was apostle to the Jews and Paul to the Gentiles, Peter is replaced as head of the Jerusalem church by James, the brother of Jesus, and disappears from the record in Acts after presentation 12 except for his defense of Paul in chapter 15. He is in Antioch (Gal. 2:11), possibly Corinth (I Cor. 1:12) and is associated with the church in Rome. It appears that Peter worked in situations with mixed congregations of both Jew and Gentile and in places where the church already existed. Paul, on the other hand, deliberately sought out situations to pioneer churches.

In our thinking about missions, we must submit to the sovereign guidance of God. We need to continually keep in our perspective that "the Spirit is the primary agent of mission, and human beings are secondary."[121] It is clear that God calls people to apostolic ministry to work among their own people group, and calls others to work cross-culturally. There will also be times when the Spirit calls people to work in a cross-cultural setting in an apostolic fashion to awaken an already existing church movement. The Lord of the Harvest will also place workers in cross-cultural settings to serve the body of Christ with their unique gifts in that particular place. What always needs to be kept in mind is that God works through the whole church in extending His rule and this involves many dimensions and a plurality of giftings that He distributes as He wills. God, who placed the capacity for culture

---

121 Ibid., 262.

inside of us as humans, is not bound by any system when it comes to placing his servants.

With that as background, what then is the benefit of the notion of apostolic function? It serves as a reminder to cross-cultural workers that they must be very clear in their role. If they are working in a role that a local Christian can do, the idea of apostolic function will query that decision. Apostolic ministry to an already existing church body naturally makes itself known through the fruit of the ministry in converts, churches planted and signs and wonders. For those who assert they are called cross-culturally to serve a local church movement and are doing ministry that is redundant to that of local believers, an apostolic function viewpoint will want to test that calling or help such a worker reorient themselves to a catalytic role as part of an apostolic team.

Apostolic Function Requires Teams with a Multiplicity of Giftings

One of the biggest objections to a view of missionary identity based in apostolic function is that it problematizes the labors of cross-cultural workers whose ministry is among strong indigenous church movements. I have already noted that the vast majority of cross-cultural workers are located in places where the church already exists and are in supportive not pioneering church planting type roles. The whole notion of apostolic function can be very unsettling to individual cross-cultural workers and their agencies. They often feel as if their work is devalued by such thinking. While apostolic function does challenge all cross-cultural workers and their agencies and has the potential to reorient their work, it actually is supportive of currently deployed workers and sees their labors as having the potential to be very strategic. In this section, I will expand upon some key ideas relating to apostolic function as it relates to those who are already working cross-culturally.

First, in keeping with the nature of the apostolic bands of the New Testament, apostolic function is best seen as operating corporately in a group rather than as the work of a single individual. What follows immediately upon this is the reality that the extremely difficult and complex work of proclaiming the Gospel, gathering disciples into churches, and training leadership so that an indigenous church movement can be formed where one did not previously exist is a work that demands all the gifts in the body. The body metaphor used by Paul in I Corinthians 12:12-26 is just as true for the mission team as it is for the local church. Apostolic function does not mean that everyone has the same giftings, but rather, as a heuristic, it shapes the identity of the entire team. The team's work has apostolic goals and values while at the same time the individual members are operating in their variety of gifts.

In a practical sense, when a mission team is working with apostolic function as its identity, what each worker actually does may continue to be the same—printing, media, teacher training, Bible school teaching, curriculum development, children's ministry, training youth leaders— but the reason for each activity is radically altered. Each worker shapes their labor around the ultimate apostolic goal of bringing the believers, local churches, and the entire national church movement they are working with and among to embrace the vision of reaching not only every person in their sociocultural setting, but of taking the Gospel to places where it has never been. Not only is the reason behind the work changed, how it is accomplished is also fundamentally reordered. In apostolic function, each worker is in a catalytic role of making sure that cross-cultural evangelism takes place among the least-reached, as all their efforts are bent in this direction and with this ultimate goal. Thus, the missionary team working where an initial Pauline breakthrough has already happened can embody apostolic function by challenging and modeling for the national church how to step out into settings where such breakthroughs are needed through teaching and training the national church to send their own cross-cultural workers to places where no church movements exist.

Apostolic Function Does Not Require Redeployment

Following right on the heels of my last point about the problematizing of cross-cultural work where the church exists is the jump to the wrong conclusion that apostolic function requires the redeployment of veteran workers to places where the church is not planted. Stirring up apostolic function does not mean redeploying already existing cross-cultural workers, but rather bending their expertise, giftings, and passion so that a church movement in all of its parts can be mobilized for both evangelism in its sociocultural setting and cross-cultural evangelism. In his presentation to the Evangelical Mission Society in 1991, Winter is adamant that the most strategic thing in reaching the unreached is not mass redeployment of existing missionaries or mass diversion of new missionaries going out from the West.[122] The most strategic work is for the existing missionary force to gain a new perspective, that which comes from people group thinking, so that they are:

> Making sure that prayed into and breathed into everything they do is a new vision for the so-called younger churches to get involved in their own mission sending. That means national churches sending out evangelists not only to their own people but training up pioneer missionaries with the special skills to go to truly frontier people groups.[123]

It is my observation that for local Christians and leaders their vision of those who need the Gospel is so constrained by those who are close to them geographically and culturally that when they finally do grasp

---

122 Ralph Winter, "Are 90% of Our Missionaries Serving in the Wrong Places?," *Mission Frontiers*, (1991): 35.

123 Ibid.

a peoples lens it is very common to have a strong reaction to the reality that most cross-cultural workers are present among groups with large numbers of Christians. Unfortunately, they often move from this new concept to policy by dropping support for workers in such areas and advocating redeployment of such workers. Winter's comment is appropriate here: "I actually believe that the achievement of a true missiological breakthrough into a new culture is often grossly underestimated as to its complexity."[124] This thought cuts both ways in that veteran cross-cultural workers are best suited towards continuing to work in their area of expertise to bring the churches they work with full cycle into mission vision and sending. On the other hand, the complex work of bringing breakthrough in a new culture is better taken on at the front end of a career so that there is adequate time after the initial learning curve to labor. It is unrealistic to think that people who have learned one cultural setting can simply jump to another and suddenly be effective in the complex circumstances of planting the church where it does not exist.

Apostolic Function Solves the Problem of Redundancy

The previous two points both deal with the issue of the reason for, the type, and method of accomplishment of cross-cultural workers who labor among already existing church movements. What apostolic function does is to problematize all three of these and challenge such workers to align their work with the vision of seeing disciples made among all the *ethne*. The question that I want to address here expands upon my last point: "If apostolic function does not call for the massive redeployment of cross-cultural workers from places where the churches exists to where it does not, what are those workers to do in the current locations?"

---

124 Ralph Winter, "Advancing Strategies of Closure: From Mission to Evangelism to Mission," *International Journal of Frontier Missions* 19, no. 4 (2002): 7.

Let me start by reiterating what the focus of apostolic function is for participants in God's mission. It is the continual impulse, under the guidance of the Holy Spirit, to take the message of Christ from where the faith is rooted into places and peoples where it is unknown and plant churches that are obedient to Jesus Christ in their social setting. When a missions movement (by movement I mean all of the participants from local Christians, churches, the agency and its workers) has its identity shaped by this idea of apostolic function all of their work is rooted in the larger goal of bringing glory to God through developing worshipping communities among the *ethne.* What is implicit here and which has been often neglected by mission agencies is that the churches developed also must share this same sense of apostolic identity and embrace their role in the mission of God to also take the Gospel across the frontiers of faith to those who have never heard.[125]

This means that every single effort and all giftings of all the participants are bent towards this task; there is an intentional focus upon passing on the spiritual heritage of Scriptural understanding, sensitivity to the Spirit, and apostolic vision. Cross-cultural work done in such a fashion is purposeful and conducted in a way to move towards these ultimate goals, rather than the good, but subordinate concerns of establishing a group of Christians in a particular social setting. Alan Hirsch has coined the term "apostolic genius" that comes very close to the heart of the idea that I am calling apostolic function. His comparison is from the fields of biology and genetics where DNA codes for genetic information pass on traits and are a self-replicating material. His notation for the spiritual concept is mDNA (where m stands for missional and thus is the spiritual analog of the biological version). He uses it "to explain

---

125 "Protestant missions, being modality-minded, have tended to assume that merely modalities, e.g., churches, need to be established. In most cases where mission work is being pursued by essentially semi-autonomous mission sodalities, it is the planting of modalities, not sodalities, that is the only goal"; Winter, "The Two Structures of God's Redemptive Mission," 228.

why the presence of a simple, intrinsic, reproducible, central guiding mechanism is necessary for the reproduction and sustainability of genuine missional movements."[126] In his metaphor, it is mDNA that codes for Apostolic Genius into the believing community, which is "the life force that pulsated through the New Testament church."[127] He defines it in this way:

> Apostolic Genius, to my mind, is the total phenomenon resulting from a complex of multiform and real experiences of God, types of expression, organizational structures, leadership ethos, spiritual power, mode of belief, etc. And it is the active presence, or lack of it, that makes all the difference to our experience of Jesus community, mission, and spiritual power.[128]

It is a constellation of six elements which includes the lordship of Jesus at its heart, the missional-incarnational impulse, disciple making, a sense of comradeship and communality he calls *communitas*, organic systems, and apostolic environment.[129]

Hirsch notes that apostolic ministry is a function not an office and has at its core being the "custodian of Apostolic Genius and of the gospel itself."[130] For Hirsch, the three primary functions of apostolic ministry are advancing the Gospel into new contexts and embedding the spiritual DNA into the new churches, ensuring these new churches remain true to the Gospel and its ethos through applying and integrating apostolic theology, and creating an environment where other ministries emerge.[131]

---

126 Hirsch, 76.

127 Ibid., 76-77.

128 Ibid., 78.

129 Ibid., 78-9. The bulk of his book, *The Forgotten Ways*, examines in detail each of these six elements.

130 Ibid., 153.

131 Ibid., 155-59.

Hirsch's work with the idea of Apostolic Genius catches both the sense of the ethos to take the Gospel to those who have never heard and the transmission of that ethos or spirit to the new emerging churches and movements that is inherent in what I am calling apostolic function for cross-cultural workers.[132]

This discussion now makes it quite clear that there is a world of difference between the work done by a Christian from one social setting who crosses a cultural boundary and does something that a local Christian in the new social setting is doing, can do, or should be doing, and the labor embodied in transmitting Apostolic Genius to a church movement. Crossing geographic/cultural boundaries and in essence functioning as a local Christian, is, from the perspective of apostolic

---

132 The difference between what I am developing as apostolic function and Hirsch's work lies in my more specific emphasis on cross-cultural workers and their application of the apostolic spirit which seeks out not simply non-Christians, but those who have no near-neighbor witness in their social setting. That element is in my mind the vital link to retaining a New Testament view of mission and is a key criterion for evaluating a given missiology. If there is no ability in a missiology to deal with the issue of access and if it does not explicitly help those who hold it to seek out those who do not have access to the Gospel, then it misses not just an element but what is the driving force behind apostolic ministry. Lord's development of a holistic Charismatic missiology is an excellent example of wonderful work that provides a clear and compelling framework for mission; Andrew Lord, *Spirit-Shaped Mission: A Holistic Charismatic Missiology* (Milton Keynes, United Kingdom: Paternoster, 2005). He summarizes it as being holistic in terms of content, outworkings, agency and life; Ibid., 135. "The content of mission includes evangelism, healing, and social reconciling and ecological action" carried out by individuals and communities "as they embrace a spirituality for mission that affects the whole of life"; Ibid. The problem with the book and the proposed missiology itself is that it never explicitly deals with where or among whom this mission is carried out and, thus, it misses a critical part of the apostolic heart. Hirsch's work is focused on developing missional churches in the Western setting; he does broach the subject of cultural distance and the need for reaching those who are truly outside the faith; Hirsch, 56-63. However, with his primary framework being the church in Western cultural settings, he does not explicitly probe the implications of Apostolic Genius for planting the church in sociocultural settings where it does not exist at all. It is clear, though, that the logic of his notion of Apostolic Genius requires the planting of churches where Christ is not known.

function, redundant work. I need to repeat here that I am not saying this is a bad thing, or that it is not a valuable contribution, or that it is not something that local Christians are very glad they do not have to do and are getting done for free. I also am not implying that the Holy Spirit would never call and equip people to serve in such a way. With all of those caveats in place, what I am saying is that from the perspective of apostolic function, there is a unique role to be played by cross-cultural workers who see their primary identity and function tied to planting churches and church movements that have apostolic spiritual DNA that transcends doing what local Christians can do.

An identity based in apostolic function may change the actual work a person does, it may alter the content to a degree in what they do, or it may change the reason why they are doing it. In order to make this more concrete, I want to illustrate with one specific point that is a major part of cross-cultural work, the teaching role. Many missionaries among existing church movements are involved in some kind of teaching of the Bible at a variety of levels ranging from small groups, to local churches, to lower-level ministerial training up to the graduate level. What happens when we look at the teaching role through the lens of apostolic function? Because in this frame the issue is developing churches that share the same vision, the role of the cross-cultural worker is cast as one who catalyzes, facilitates and transmits this kind of spiritual DNA. The first question then becomes whether or not the teaching is redundant? Could a local Christian do this same work?

Let me run through two scenarios. In the first, suppose that the answer to this question is no. This means that there is a vital role for the cross-cultural worker to fulfill by teaching and training to bring this church movement to maturity, obedience to the commands of Jesus, and participation in God's mission. This would form the explicit context of whatever the particular teaching content was, and should be communicated to the recipients so they in turn can pass this on to others.

In the second scenario, suppose that the answer to the question is yes, this work is indeed redundant. Does this necessarily mean that I, as a missionary, need to stop teaching? Absolutely not! It does mean that there are further questions to ask of the situation. The question that the idea of apostolic function raises for any existing church movement is where are they at in terms of their own understanding and practice of apostolic function? If a church movement lacks Hirsch's notion of "apostolic genius" then the critical role for cross-cultural workers is to teach, train, and model so that this happens. Particular content needs to be wrapped in the broader context of the *missio Dei* and the goal of making disciples among all the peoples of the earth.

Ultimately, determining whether work is redundant or not is an issue that the primary participants in the mission (which would include the sending agency, the worker and team and the local churches and leadership of the receiving body) need to ascertain through the guidance of the Holy Spirit. If a person's calling is confirmed by all these parties as being important to that body and they sense the leading of the Holy Spirit in this matter, it is not an issue. However, the vision of apostolic function and the role of passing on that kind of spiritual reproductive material to the receiving church are never going to have a negative impact on a church movement. It is a stance that will continually challenge the cross-cultural worker to evaluate their labor and maintain a humble posture of seeking the Spirit's guidance about when that spiritual DNA is rooted and to step back and let local people take the lead at a given point.

In practical terms in a world where churches exist, cross-cultural workers are already in place, and at the same time there may be people groups geographically near who do not have a viable and culturally relevant witnessing church in their society, what does apostolic function look like for the mission agency and team?

FIGURE 4
Possible Models of Apostolic Function

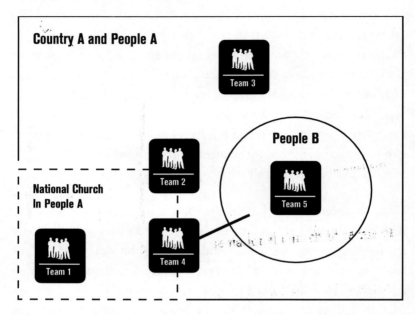

There are three major ways in which a team that seeks to function in an apostolic role could approach their work, which are graphically illustrated in figure 4. The first (team 1) would be to work within the context of the existing national church to help implant apostolic genius and missional DNA so that those churches and believers would become the laborers that would cross into the unreached people group. A second style (teams 2 and 4), particularly appropriate if there is some natural resistance or prejudice on the part of the national church to the unreached group, would be to work both with the national church and the unreached group, living in both worlds. In this approach, the mission team shows its solidarity and interest with the goals of the national church and yet maintains its own role as a mission sodality to proclaim Christ among the unreached. The style here is not to move out unilaterally, but to attempt to build bridges for evangelism into the unreached people and to the national church in terms of their own mission responsibility and to endeavor to bring along local Christians into ministry with them among the unreached group. Team 2 illustrates this process in trying to bridge Christians in the national church to do innovative outreach to their own people group, while team 4 illustrates the process of trying to bridge local Christians to work in unreached people B. The third approach (teams 3 and 5) is for the expatriate team to, by design, work independently from the national church to do pioneer planting among the unreached group. With team 3 this is happening in the people group A among which a small church movement already exists, and with team 5 it is happening in people B which has no church movement at all. The circumstances may require an outside group to work on the initial breakthrough, or the national church may completely refuse involvement. Depending on the situation, it could be possible for a mission agency to have all three of these approaches happening at the same time.

This discussion of how apostolic function can play out at the agency and team level illustrates an important point for all the participants in global mission: there are many ways to accomplish preaching the Gospel and planting the church among unreached people groups, and the participants at every level can have a part in it. It has been an unfortunate unintended consequence of the promotion of the needs of the unreached that it has come to be associated with the idea that a) all existing personnel and resources should be immediately moved into unreached groups, and b) any team or mission remaining working in a place where the church is established is somehow missing God's will. The primary questions of the apostolic team center on how best to accomplish the pioneer task and determining one's calling and giftings. Asking these questions means a wide variety of paths could provide satisfactory answers, but such answers should always have the role of existing church movements in mind. All the participants in God's global mission have a vital and strategic role to play.

Apostolic Function Provides a Way to Link the Planting of the Church With the Demonstration of Christian Social Concern

I have no doubt that if the Lord delays His return that within a few more decades Christians who take the Bible seriously will look back upon the vast amount of energy expended on writing and debating the issue of the relationship between evangelism and social responsibility as a bump in the road of church history. The days of solid conceptual walls between church planting and Christian social concern, as if they in some way embraced two separate worlds that thus had to be sorted out as to their priority and relationship, is now mercifully nearly behind us. The amount of quality theological writing on the subject of God's concern for humans as wholes has laid to rest, at least in scholarly levels, the need to argue for some kind of bifurcation between caring for people spiritually and physically.[133] God loves people, and people

---

133 The following works provide an overview of some of the theological and practical work on Christian social concern. Miriam Adeney, *God's Foreign Policy* (Grand Rapids: Eerdmans, 1984); Bruce Bradshaw, *Bridging the Gap: Evangelism, Development and Shalom* (Monrovia: MARC, 1993); Donald P. Brandt, "The Poor and the Lost: A Holistic View of Poverty," *Missiology: An International Review* 23, no. 3 (1995); Robert McAfee Brown, *Unexpected News: Reading the Bible with Third World Eyes* (Philadelphia: Westminster, 1984); Jayakumar Christian, "The Powerlessness of the Poor: Toward an Alternative Kingdom of God Based Paradigm for Response" (PhD, Fuller Theological Seminary, 1994); Jayakumar Christian, *God of the Empty-Handed: Poverty, Power and the Kingdom of God* (Monrovia: MARC Publications, 1999); Graham Cray, "A Theology of the Kingdom," in *Mission as Transformation: A Theology of the Whole Gospel*, ed. Vinay Samuel and Chris Sugden (Irvine: Regnum, 1999); Murray W. Dempster, "Evangelism, Social Concern and the Kingdom of God," in *Called and Empowered: Global Mission in Pentecostal Perspective*, ed. Murray W. Dempster, Byron D. Klaus, and Douglas Petersen (Peabody: Hendrickson Publishers, 1991); Murray W. Dempster, "Christian Social Concern in Pentecostal Perspective: Reformulating Pentecostal Eschatology," *Journal for Pentecostal Theology* 2 (1993); Murray W. Dempster, "A Theology of the Kingdom—A Pentecostal Contribution," in *Mission as Transformation: A Theology of the Whole Gospel*, ed. Vinay Samuel and Chris Sugden (Irvine: Regnum, 1999); Gary A. Haugen, *Good News About Injustice: A Witness of Courage in a Hurting World* (Downers Grove: InterVarsity Press, 1999); Paul Hertig, "The Jubilee Mission of Jesus in the Gospel of Luke: Reversals of Fortunes," *Missiology: An International Review* 26, no. 2 (1998); Veli-Matti Karkkainen, "Are Pentecostals

have stomachs, and children they love, and are entwined in economic and power relationships; they need shelter and care when they are sick. At its coarsest form, (which thankfully most missionaries happily ignored) the Gnostic split between spirit and body that legitimized saving the soul while completely ignoring the physical realities people live in is now seen in its proper historical context as reflecting issues in the intellectual world of the west at a certain period that were never a problem for everyone else.

In 1981, Jim Wallis wrote, "The goal of biblical conversion is not to save souls apart from history but to bring the Kingdom of God into the world with explosive force; it begins with individuals but is for the sake of the world"[134] He contrasted the segments of the church, which generally cohere around the issue of biblical authority, where some want to see conversion while forgetting the ultimate goal, and others do

---

Oblivious to Social Justice? Theological and Ecumenical Perspectives," *Missiology: An International Review* 29, no. 4 (2001); Craig Keener, "God Cares About People: A Pentecostal Perspective from Luke/Acts," *Enrichment*, (2004); Peter Kuzmic, "The Church and the Kingdom of God: A Theological Reflection," in *The Church: God's Agent for Change* (Exeter, UK: Paternoster, 1986); Robert C. Linthicum, *Empowering the Poor: Community Organizing Among City's 'Rag, Tag, and Bob Tail'* (Monrovia: MARC, 1991); Robert C. Linthicum, *Transforming Power: Biblical Strategies for Making a Difference in Your Community* (Downers Grove: InterVarsity Press, 2003); Darrow Miller, *Discipling Nations* (Seattle: YWAM, 1998); Bryant L. Myers, *Walking with the Poor* (Maryknoll: Orbis, 1999); Douglas Petersen, *Not by Might nor by Power: A Pentecostal Theology of Social Concern* (Oxford/ Irvine: Regnum Books International, 1996); Vinay Samuel and Chris Sugden, eds. *Mission as Transformation: A Theology of the Whole Gospel* (Irvine: Regnum, 1999); Ron Sider, *Good News and Good Works: A Theology of the Whole Gospel* (Grand Rapids: Baker Books, 1999); Ron Sider, *Just Generosity* (Grand Rapids: Baker, 1999); Tom Sine, *Mustard Seed Vs. Mcworld: Reinventing Life and Faith for the Future* (Grand Rapids: Baker, 1999); Valdir R. Steuernagel, "Social Concern and Evangelization: The Journey of the Lausanne Movement," *International Bulletin of Missionary Research*, (1991); Chris Sugden, *Gospel, Culture and Transformation* (Oxford: Regnum Books, 2000); Howard Synder, *The Community of the King* (Downers Grove: InterVarsity, 1977); Adeyemo Tokunboh, "Conflicting Options for Evangelicals," in *In Word and Deed*, ed. Bruce J. Nichols (Grand Rapids: Eerdmans, 1985).

134 Jim Wallis, *The Call to Conversion* (San Francisco: Harper and Row, 1981), 8.

Christian social action while forgetting the necessity of conversion.[135] He reminds both sides that they must recover the biblical meaning of conversion to Jesus Christ. Chris Wright points out that inherent in the notion of holistic mission is that it "includes the whole of what God calls and sends us to do. Evangelism without social action is not holistic mission. Likewise, social action without evangelism cannot be holistic mission either."[136] In the Evangelical, Pentecostal, Christmatic (EPC) streams of Christianity, this kind of recovery of the broader notion of conversion and salvation as encompassing human individuals, but having impact on all human social relations and the entire creation is well under way.[137] The issues that remain concern the way in which we should work out the will of God as it regards bringing reconciliation to people and seeing His rule extended in social relationships.

In my estimation, the two most critical issues in missions lie in addressing the two massive imbalances that exist in our world in light of the commission that our Lord gave us to make obedient disciples

135 Ibid. I like Wallis' phrasing here because it avoids separating what should be inseparable. Sometimes among Evangelicals the importance of the social impact of the Gospel has been phrased as "no distinction between word and deed." However, I find this to be just as bifurcating as those who would separate evangelism from social responsibility because it logically leads to "deeds" without words since this phrasing makes them appear separate rather than being intimately tied together. Thus, in reverse it compartmentalizes deeds away from the words that bring the interpretation of those very deeds. Shenk says that "the flaw in the 'word and deed' paradigm is that it has encouraged us to focus attention on the parts rather than on the whole, which is God's new order. Once this partial way of looking at Christian witness was accepted, it was impossible to arrive at the whole. We live in the constant frustration of trying to achieve balance and defend priorities. But the whole—that is, God's new order—is always greater than the way we add up the parts. Such arithmetic does not correspond with God's new order;" Wilbert R. Shenk, *Changing Frontiers of Mission* (Maryknoll: Orbis, 2001), 28-9.

136 Wright, "Reaffirming".

137 For examples of this kind of awareness see McGee, "Saving Souls"; in his work on developing a Charismatic missiology Lord includes ecological concerns; see Glasser's section on Jesus and the poor where the coming of the Kingdom "is to provide a tangible manifestation of God's attitude toward poverty and injustice"; Glasser and others, 216.

among the *ethne*. The first is the imbalance that exists in where the church is planted and the nearly 40 percent of humanity that lacks adequate near-neighbor witness. This calls us to labor to root the Gospel in human societies that have either no church planting movements or very small ones. The second is the imbalance that exists in material wealth, with a small minority of societies and segments of social systems enjoying personal affluence while the majority of the world struggles for literal survival across all the physical indicators that measure quality of life. This calls us to labor for the extension of God's rule to bring justice, peace, and provision through His new community to bless entire social systems.

While those in the EPC stream now increasingly recognize the comprehensiveness and unity of the mandate to labor for reconciliation and God's rule at the individual and societal levels, there is still the tendency to split this kind of work structurally into organizations that plant churches and organizations that do compassion, development, and work for justice. In some standard mission agencies, with broader concerns and commitments, Christian social action is present, but has an uneasy relationship to what is seen as the primary work of planting the church.[138] I have no difficulty with specialist organizations that band together around a single purpose. Those organizations have an important role in the body of Christ, but in this section I want to look at how the idea of apostolic function relates to standard mission agencies where Christian social action is part of a larger constellation of things that they do.

I believe that apostolic function as I have developed it in this presentation links together these two parts, planting the church and Christian

---

138 Sometimes this uneasy relationship is expressed in the necessity of framing all social activities in terms of how it either brought about conversions or set the stage in some way to prepare people for conversion. There is often a lack of theological integration as to how caring for people and working for justice relates to the coming of God's rule, conversion and the establishment of communities of faith.

social action, which get separated either into distinct organizations, or in the case of standard mission agencies, within the organization itself. We know from Scripture that God's concern holistically embraces the whole person—both individuals and social systems, personal and structural sin—yet, on the ground level of practice, we struggle with how to address these issues. Expressions of Christian social concern can end up being a kind of unwanted stepchild that is viewed suspiciously for eating up precious resources, or in its crassest form, becomes the "carrot on the stick" that draws people in so that we can get them properly converted. The fear becomes that evangelism will be eroded and overrun by the press of caring for physical needs.[139] However, the linkage that apostolic function brings provides a real-life ministry context that protects the proclamation of the Gospel and requires God's people to act. This linkage rejects any kind of bifurcation of the spiritual and physical and the manipulative use of the material to pull in converts. Apostolic function is about planting the church; in the book of Acts we see the preaching of the good news resulting in a new community. This is what Jesus intended and is what occupied the time and attention of the apostles. It was not just any church and we need to be careful not to read into the text our contemporary notion of a disparate group of individuals who gather once on Sunday. They planted churches with apostolic DNA, apostolic theology, and woven into that, as I have noted above, was a deep concern for those who were marginalized and physically impoverished. It is a church where Jesus is Lord and that works to extend that lordship in all of life and to make

---

139 McGee, "Saving Souls," 11. In my opinion, this fear is based on our penchant for constructing institutional answers that makes us fear pragmatism and money as the answer. As a missions agency, we need to remain wary of institutionalism and a naive view that simply throwing money from the West at the complex problems of poverty fulfills our duty and will solve the problem. Drive-by compassion, just as with drive-by evangelism, is a truncated version of the real thing, treating people as objects and imposing answers to problems generated from an outside perspective rather than from the perspective of the people purportedly being served.

that confession bind people "to participate in the new social reality that the Holy Spirit was sending forth into the world."[140]

Planting communities of redeemed people, rooted in apostolic theology, living under and expressing the Lordship of Jesus Christ, and committed to seeing His rule extend into their social setting, brings us face-to-face with the poor and social realities. It is in these relationships between and among God's new people and His people as they interact with the world that shatters our ability to compartmentalize. The predication of an ongoing relationship makes the temporal relations of preaching and caring a moot point because in a relationship viewed as a whole you can be doing both all of the time, even though chronologically there are moments where you are proclaiming and moments where you are helping people. As Winter put it so memorably, when it is a case of family, you never would even think about choosing between evangelism and social action.[141] In a relationship, you do not have to make choices because you are there face-to-face over time and there is no fear that either caring or proclamation will be diminished, nor does one have to "set-up" the other. The relationship provides the context for the interpretation of any given deed. Where there is relationship, there is the ability to explain the "why" of the deed or for the deed to illuminate the proclaimed word.

One of the objections that could be leveled at the idea of apostolic function is that in a similar way that the emphasis on planting the church

---

140 Glasser and others, 265.

141 "In English, the word blessing implies merely a benefit—not also a relationship, as in the Hebrew *barak*. Americans—even American missionaries—typically do not understand the full significance of the privileges, obligations, and permanent benefits of the family relationship. Yet, a relationship of just this significance is implied in the Hebrew *barak*. The implications here are profound and exceed the normal intent of evangelistic appeals. For example, in a family relationship you do not choose between evangelism and social action"; Ralph D. Winter, "Mission in the 1990's: Two Views I. Ralph D. Winter," *International Bulletin of Missionary Research* July (1990): 99.

where it does not exist problematizes the function of missionaries working with already existing churches, the apparently narrow emphasis on planting the church versus doing many other things problematizes those who feel called to work primarily in Christian social action. I will begin by repeating what I have already stated above. Apostolic function is not a ministry framework that is applied mechanistically across all times and circumstances. It is the sovereign God who places his laborers where He wills and there is no doubt that He calls people to express His compassion and work for His justice in settings other than their birth culture. We never want to limit the work of the Holy Spirit in directing His servants into fields of labor.

However, having said that, I feel that apostolic function and its corporate sense of working as a team towards apostolic goals draws together in the team context what is often separated into the different functions of church planting and social concern. In a pioneer setting, the role of transmitting Apostolic Genius, to use Hirsch's term, needs those with a social concern vision and theological underpinning to help teach and model that so it is an integral part of the identity of the new movement. The apostolic band needs all the giftings, and those who are called to care, show compassion, and work for justice should be intimately connected with those planting the church. This kind of collaboration reminds church planters of the DNA issues in making sure that caring for the weak is part of the soul of the new community. It also reminds workers in social action that it is not enough to develop institutional and programmatic answers, but rather that the rule of God must be lived out in and through the new community and flow to the broader society.

Finally, the catalytic and mobilizing role of apostolic function means that when an existing local church movement is missing any of the components of a true New Testament church, that apostolic DNA so to speak, then it is apostolic ministry to work among them to teach, model, demonstrate, and advocate for that element to become part of that movement. When church movements no longer reach people in their own sociocultural setting, when they have no vision and mechanism to do cross-cultural evangelism, when they do not care for the weak and marginalized, these conditions beg for a team functioning apostolically to come alongside and lovingly seek to bring them into the fullness of the experience of the church in the New Testament. Thus, while there may be people called to use their spiritual gifts in the area of Christian social concern cross-culturally, there will also be people called to fulfill an apostolic function in this regard by laboring to put the vision and practice of Christian social concern into the spiritual genetic material of a church movement.

A Practical Objection: What If I Do Not Feel Very Apostolic?

Even with a theology that is open to the ongoing function of apostles in the body of Christ, the practical issue is that most of us do not "feel" very apostolic. The job description can be rather daunting, whether you look at Paul as a model or think in terms of Charismatic leadership and fields of influence as Hirsch does.[142] The elegance and simplicity of the concept of apostolic function as I have explained it here is that you get to be yourself. It is God who makes apostles and graciously grants the gift mix to be able to bring that intangible atmosphere of influence Hirsch calls the matrix of apostolicity that leads to the emergence of missional churches.[143] Thus, it would always be wise to pray that the Lord of the Harvest would call and equip true apostles for His work. However, in the sense in which I am using the idea of "functioning" as an apostle in a cross-cultural context, the key factor

---

142 "Apostolic ministry, based as it is on inspirational-spiritual leadership, involves an organic, relational style of leadership that evokes purpose, movement, and response from those who come into its orbit. This is done on the basis of the apostolic person's discernible calling, spiritual gifting, and spiritual authority"; Hirsch, 161.

143 Ibid., 162.

is the burden and willingness to do the hard pioneer labor of reaching the first generation of converts. The reality is that there are not long lines of people waiting to do the backbreaking and mind-bending work of bringing the Gospel to a place where the Christian faith is small or non-existent. Therefore, I think that an appropriate response on our part should be to lay our lives before the Lord of the Harvest and ask Him to use those of us who are willing to attempt to function in an apostolic way, while at the same time continuing to pray that He will also raise up those who are truly gifted and called as apostles to or from within that particular society. I believe that with such offerings God is well pleased. Apostolic function does not require us to be something that we are not; it has its roots in the burden that the Holy Spirit gives some to preach Christ where He is not named.

CONCLUSION AND SUMMARY

I began this chapter by arguing that we need a new sense of missionary identity in order to combat the fuzziness of pan-missionism and to galvanize the church to take the Gospel to places where church movements do not exist. My proposal is that this new identity should be formed around the notion of apostolic function. By this term, I mean that cross-cultural work should be framed around the understanding that apostles had of their work and the actual kind of work they did. After reviewing the biblical material on apostleship, I argued that apostolic function—focus on the apostolic task of preaching the Gospel where it has not been heard, planting the church where it does not exist, and leading people to the obedience of faith so that they, too, will express Jesus Christ in their social worlds and participate in God's global mission—should form the heuristic that defines our identity and practice. In the remainder of the chapter, I developed eight themes where apostolic function relates to the contemporary practice of missions.

5

INSIGHTS FROM FRONTIER MISSION
MISSIOLOGY

Before I provide a detailed explanation of what is known as frontier mission missiology, I want to make a connection to the previous chapters and give direction for where we are going. The issues and line of argument I have followed to this point can be expressed in four main points:

1. At the current time in history there is a lack of clarity about our understanding and practice of missions.

2. This lack of clarity is manifest at the conceptual level in that virtually any activity is now seen as missions and, at the level of praxis, the bulk of cross-cultural workers are located in places where the majority of Christians and church movements exist.

3. I proposed that one way to help us restore clarity and focus to our understanding and practice of missions is to seek insight from three major paradigms of missions in the Evangelical, Penetecostal, Charismatic (EPC) streams and then integrate those perspectives. Each of these paradigms or orienting frames represent key biblical commitments regarding the mission of God. These three frames are church planting/growth, frontier mission to unreached people groups, and Christian social concern.

4. I then proposed the notion of apostolic function as a master rubric and heuristic for the self-identity of cross-cultural workers and teams. Apostolic function encompasses all three of the major paradigms and infuses cross-cultural work with a purpose and intentionality to plant and develop church movements that are fully missional and that seek to obey Jesus Christ and advance His kingdom rule in their social worlds and beyond.

In chapter 7, I will look at how integrating missions paradigms can help us with our practice. Before that, I want to examine in detail the paradigm of frontier mission missiology which has its focus on planting churches among what are known as unreached peoples. There are several reasons why I think that it is important to focus on this particular framework rather than church planting/growth or Christian social action. At the scholarly level, there is more extensive treatment of the other two paradigms than that of frontier missions. In terms of practical application to contemporary missions work, it is a current need; our situation requires that we deal with the empirical reality of many people groups that have no near-neighbor witness.

However, in my mind the most important reasons are because of the way frontier mission missiology has been co-opted, misunderstood and ignored. As the insights of this paradigm came into print they were such fertile ground that they gave birth to a wide variety of concepts, groups, and movements. One of the downsides of this popularity was that some of the solid missiology at its core that had to do with "where" issues of mission were co-opted by western media-driven hype concerned with finishing the task by the year 2000. Some of the technical terms that were foundational to its concepts had the misfortune of achieving buzzword status, with the corresponding erosion of clarity that process involves. Ideas of "people group," "reached," "unreached," and the "10/40 window" achieved iconic status and became the key to gaining support for any mission endeavor. The frenetic push to have a church for every people by the year 2000 obscured some of the truly powerful insights and concepts and alienated some missions organizations and teams that would have benefited from an application of those ideas to their missions practice.

The year 2000 came and went, Jesus did not come back, there are still unreached people, and the Christian world continues to shuttle workers back and forth to the already Christian world. Now, more than ever, the concepts of frontier mission missiology are needed to help us collectively regain our sense of who we are and what we are to be about. However, in many ways, these concepts that have such focusing power have been misunderstood and ignored. At times they are dismissed without ever having been considered and their implications grappled with in real-life settings. The more I talk with pastors, local church leaders, local Christians, mission leaders and cross-cultural workers, the more I am convinced of the utility and relevance of these ideas to our current setting in missions. The "people's lens" perspective remains novel and unsettling to both local Christians, their leaders, and to people working as missionaries with existing church movements.

In this chapter, I am going to use the major ideas of Ralph Winter's plenary paper presented at the International Congress on World Evangelization held in Lausanne, Switzerland in 1974 as the central themes to discuss the foundational concepts of this missions paradigm.[144] Although there were antecedents to unreached people group

---

144 This congress grew out of the vision of a number of leaders who met in Montreux Switzerland in 1960 to discuss and pray about the task of world evangelization; Billy Graham, "Let the Earth Hear His Voice," in *Let the Earth Hear His Voice: International Congress on World Evangelization Lausanne, Switzerland*, ed. J. D. Douglas (Minneapolis: World Wide Publications, 1975), 16. The first outgrowth of that small gathering was the Berlin Congress on evangelization in 1966 where Dr. Carl Henry served as the chairman. Between Berlin and Lausanne there was a building momentum towards a larger world level meeting through a number of regional congresses and Billy Graham noted that in the eight year period between Berlin and Lausanne nearly all the major countries of the world had

thinking,[145] the importance of Ralph Winter's paper as catalyst to the formation of a broader movement cannot be understated.

WINTER'S PRESENTATION AT LAUSANNE 1974

Winter's paper entitled, "The Highest Priority: Cross-Cultural Evangelism," became both a culmination and starting point in terms of missionary thinking. This presentation marked the end of an era of missions and the beginning of another that focused on peoples rather than countries. Corwin summarizes its impact this way:

> When in 1974 Dr. Ralph Winter gave his famous speech, . . .at the first Lausanne Congress on World Evangelization, a new era in mission history was begun. It was not really so much that a new

---

held congresses on evangelism; Ibid. In preparing for the Lausanne Congress it was intended from the beginning that the meeting itself not be a single event, but rather a continuing process; A. J. Dain, "International Congress on World Evangelization," in *In Let the Earth Hear His Voice: International Congress on World Evangelization Lausanne, Switzerland*, ed. Douglas J. D. (Minneapolis: World Wide Publications, 1975), 11. Those who attended were considered participants rather than delegates as it was not to be a legislative body, but rather a convening of Evangelical leaders and practitioners from around the world to, in the words of Billy Graham, "seek how we can work together to fulfill Christ's last commission as quickly and thoroughly as possible"; Billy Graham, "Why Lausanne?," in *In Let the Earth Hear His Voice: International Congress on World Evangelization Lausanne, Switzerland*, ed. J. D. Douglas (Minneapolis: World Wide Publications, 1975), 22. It was also intended that one of the results of the Congress would be a statement, known as the Lausanne Covenant, that would be produced and serve as a theological rallying point for the ongoing movement.

145 I briefly summarize a number of the pre-Lausanne roots to thinking about missions in terms of people groups in Alan R. Johnson, "Analyzing the Frontier Mission Movement and Unreached People Group Thinking Part I: The Frontier Mission Movement's Understanding of the Modern Mission Era," *International Journal of Frontier Missions* 18, no. 2 (2001): 85-86. I trace the background of how the Edinburgh 1980 meeting came to focus on reaching what were then called hidden people groups in, "Analyzing the Frontier Mission Movement and Unreached People Group Thinking Part II: Major Concepts of the Frontier Mission Movement," *International Journal of Frontier Missions* 18, no. 2 (2001): 89-90.

vision was born, but that a new way of looking at an old vision was provided. . . .What was new at Lausanne was that for the first time in the modern period the task was now couched primarily in terms of *ethne* or peoples and religious blocks, rather than in geographic or geo-political terms. Over the last two decades since that speech an astounding shift has taken place. The concept of unreached peoples (in contrast to unreached people) is on the lips of virtually everyone concerned with the mission of Christ's church.[146]

Winter started his address by pointing out a misunderstanding that he saw rising in the thinking of many Evangelicals. It was based on the incredible success of the Christian mission so that it was possible at that time to say that the Great Commission had been fulfilled at least in a geographical sense. In the light of this success, many had come to believe that the job was nearly completed and the task could be turned over to national churches that engaged in local evangelism.[147] He said, "Many Christian organizations, ranging widely from the World Council of Churches to many U. S. denominations, even some Evangelical groups, have rushed to the conclusion that we may now abandon traditional missionary strategy and count on local Christians everywhere to finish the job."[148] Winter conceded at this point that it is true that most conversions are going to come from near neighbor evangelism, but there is an additional truth "that most non-Christians in the world today are not culturally near neighbors of any Christians,

---

146 Gary Corwin, "Sociology and Missiology: Reflection on Mission Research," in *Missiology and the Social Sciences: Contributions, Cautions and Conclusions*, ed. Edward Rommen and Gary Corwin (Pasadena: William Carey Library, 1996), 20-21.

147 Ralph Winter, "The Highest Priority: Cross-Cultural Evangelism," in *Let the Earth Hear His Voice*, J. D. Douglas ed. (Minneapolis: World Wide Publications, 1975), 213.

148 Ibid.

and that it will take a special kind of 'cross-cultural' evangelism to reach them."[149]

This then is the critical thesis of what has become the frontier mission movement and is at the heart of unreached people group thinking. This insight is what I call the "sociology trumps the Bible" reality. Christians affirm that God loves the whole world and does not want anyone to perish, yet for a variety of reasons they are unable to "see" those who are different from them. What this means, and what is clearly documented in Christian mission history, is that the presence of Christians and churches in a place does not automatically mean that the good news will flow from them to those who are different from them (meaning those who are not near neighbors culturally to them). This is precisely why Winter first called these groups "hidden peoples;" not because they were necessarily far removed geographically from Christians and churches, but they were culturally distant and thus invisible. This means that we are all prone to having our approach to ministry heavily constrained by our social understandings as well as how we read Scripture.

Winter made three major points in this paper. The first is that evangelism changes and grows in complexity the farther the Gospel messenger is removed from the hearers in terms of cultural distance. The work of cross-cultural evangelism is of a different nature than evangelism done from within a sociocultural setting. Monocultural evangelism is the most powerful form, but the urgency stems from the fact that so many sociocultural systems lack near-neighbor witness and thus require a cross-cultural effort to root the Gospel so that this can take place. His second point was that the Bible supports this view of crossing cultural boundaries. Acts 1:8 shows that the Gospel must not only cross geographic, but cultural boundaries as well. Finally,

---

149 Ibid.

he made the observation that on the basis of this difference between monocultural evangelism and cross-cultural evangelism, the highest priority in missions is the complex work of cross-cultural evangelism among thousands of peoples who have no church movements. In the remainder of this chapter, I will use each of these three ideas as the starting point for the examination of major concepts that comprise what is now known as frontier mission missiology.

THE SIGNIFICANCE OF THE E-SCALE: ALL EVANGELISM IS NOT EQUAL

His first point focused on the need for cross-cultural evangelism and takes the perspective of what I call "missiological reality." What I mean by this term is the state of the world in light of the completion of the Great Commission. It is the assessment of the status of the Christian faith in the varying peoples of the earth among whom we have been commanded by our Lord to make disciples. Winter begins with four illustrations (from Pakistan, the Church of South India, the Bataks of north Sumatra and the Nagas of east India) which show how existing Christian movements can be effective in reaching their own people and at the same time cut off from other populations that are geographically nearby due to religious, caste, language and other cultural barriers. This led him to develop a continuum of evangelism that is the single most important concept that underlies his thesis (see figure 5). Using illustrations from contemporary experience, he shows how it is crucial to understand evangelism in terms of the cultural distance of the evangelist from the hearer.

FIGURE 5
The E Scale

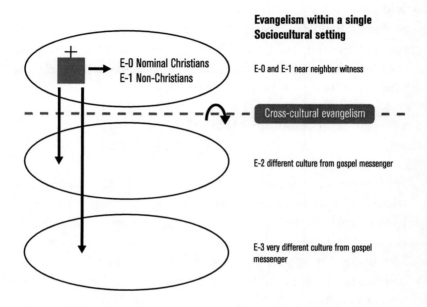

Evangelism within a single Sociocultural setting

E-0 Nominal Christians
E-1 Non-Christians

E-0 and E-1 near neighbor witness

Cross-cultural evangelism

E-2 different culture from gospel messenger

E-3 very different culture from gospel messenger

Rather than seeing all evangelism as equal, he devises a scale from E-1 to E-3 (E here is for evangelism) with the following definitions: E-1 is evangelism done among one's own cultural group, which is also called "near neighbor" evangelism. It is absolutely central to his thesis that we understand the ideas inherent in the term "near neighbor." This is more than just being close in terms of geographic location, but has to do with the cultural and worldview similarities that allow for both ease of communication and the development of trust and credibility. Evangelism of non-Christians within a person's own social sphere, although generally easier, is not necessarily so. People can be rather far from the assumptions and values of Christians and still be within the same cultural sphere. It is a mistake for people to assume that the task will be simple at the spiritual level. However, at the communication level it is much simpler, due to the amount of interpersonally shared cultural material, than when you begin to cross larger cultural distances.

E-2 occurs when evangelism crosses a boundary of what he calls "significant (but not monumental) differences of language and culture."[150] Finally, E-3 is evangelism at even farther cultural distance from the hearer. "The people needing to be reached in this third sphere live, work, talk, and think in languages and cultural patterns utterly different from those native to the evangelist."[151] The examples that he presents in this section are all based in language differences, but he notes that, "for the purpose of defining evangelistic strategy, any kind of obstacle, any kind of communication barrier affecting evangelism is significant."[152] Winter's conclusion is worth quoting in its entirety:

> The master pattern of the expansion of the Christian movement is first for special E-2 and E-3 efforts to cross cultural barriers into new communities and to establish strong, on-going, vigorously evangelizing denominations, and then for that national church to carry the work forward on the really high-powered E-1 level. We are thus forced to believe that until every tribe and tongue has a strong, powerfully evangelizing church in it, and thus an E-1 witness with

---

150 Winter, "The Highest Priority: Cross-Cultural Evangelism," 218.

151 Ibid.

152 Ibid., 215. It is important to note that this argument is moving from a biblical idea, that God wants to reach not just discrete individuals but people in their "groupness," to the sociological observation that the good news travels most easily and fastest among people who are the same. While in theory it is a wonderful thought to believe that Christians of one social group will naturally and willingly tell people of another social group about Jesus, history tells us otherwise. Winter's plea was based on the reality that for people groups living without culturally near neighbors in church movements capable of sharing the Gospel in a relevant fashion they would not be able to gain an adequate hearing of the Gospel, even if there were Christians living geographically proximate to them. Winter quotes Arthur Glasser's summary of the situation as this: "If every congregation in the world were to undergo a great revival and reach out to every person within their own people—that is, to everyone in the cultural spheres represented by each congregation—over half of all remaining non-Christians would still not be reached"; Ralph Winter, "The Story of the Frontier Mission Movement," *Mission Frontiers*, (1995): 48.

it, E-2 and E-3 efforts coming from the outside are still essential and highly urgent.[153]

A Distinction Between Frontier and Regular Missions

Five key points flow from this distinction between evangelism within a sociocultural setting and cross-cultural evangelism where the church does not exist. The first is that it not only sets up a distinction between monocultural and cross-cultural evangelism, but it differentiates between cross-cultural evangelism done by workers where church movements already exist and where there are none. What this means is that when mission agencies send cross-cultural workers to plant the church where it already exists, and not to places where it does not exist to establish pioneer beachheads, the agency becomes in essence a "foreign evangelism" agency.[154] Because the term "missions" had become so associated with crossing a geographic boundary and ignored the status of Christianity in this new (to the worker) location, Winter felt the need to find a way of explaining this critical distinction. However, because of the fact that the terms "mission" and "missionary" were used in different ways that were firmly entrenched, Winter found it necessary in his advocating for cross-cultural evangelism to develop a new set of terms to help bring clarification to the issues. Winter decided to add the adjective "frontier" to missions to separate this activity from what he then calls "regular" missions. Regular missions involves the very important work of assisting national church movements, doing works of compassion, training leaders and discipling new believers.[155] Frontier missions, then, "is the activity intended to accomplish the Pauline

---

153 Winter, "The Highest Priority: Cross-Cultural Evangelism," 220.

154 Ralph Winter, "Advancing Strategies of Closure: From Mission to Evangelism to Mission, " *International Journal of Frontier Missions* 19, no. 4 (2002): 7.

155 Ralph Winter, "Frontier Mission Perspectives," in *Seeds of Promise: World Consultation on Frontier Missions, Edinburgh '80*, Allan Starling, ed. (Pasadena: William Carey Library, 1981), 65.

kind of missiological breakthrough to a Hidden People Group."[156] The important thing to remember here is that making this distinction does not imply that one is "better" than the other. What it does stress is that our current missiological reality requires that we bring more focus, personnel, prayer, and resources to bear on true mission frontiers.

Defining Missiological Breakthrough

The second key idea flows out of the notion of frontier mission. When you cross a frontier from faith to non-faith, where there is no potential for access to the Gospel message because no church movement exists, then the first priority is missiological breakthrough. This is defined as the process "whereby a church in a new tradition is born within the indigenous culture (not borrowed and patched in from another country or cultural tradition). . . . Such a breakthrough classically was Paul's concern, that is, to produce a truly Gentile synagogue."[157] The goal of such a breakthrough is a viable church, which is a concept very important to the missiology and strategy of the frontier mission movement. Winter notes that the viable church is:

---

156 Ibid. Winter used the term "hidden" and it was after the 1982 work on definitions that "unreached" took on a technical status in missiology. The idea of people groups being hidden relates to what he describes as "people blindness." I will excerpt here from Winter to show his understanding of this problem: "I'm afraid that all our exultation about the fact that every *country* of the world has been penetrated has allowed many to suppose that every *culture* has now been penetrated. This misunderstanding is a malady so widespread that it deserves a special name. Let us call it 'people blindness—that is, blindness to the existence of separate *peoples within countries* . . . The little ethnic and cultural pieces of the complex mosaic which is human society are the very subdivisions which isolate four out of five non-Christians in the world today from an E-1 contact by existing Christians"; Ralph Winter, "The New Macedonia: A Revolutionary New Era in Mission Begins," in *Perspectives on the World Christian Movement: A Reader*, Ralph D. Winter and Steven C. Hawthorne, eds. (Pasadena: William Carey Library, 1999), 346.

157 Winter, "Frontier Mission Perspectives," 64-65.

not just anything someone may call a church, and this emphasis then corresponds to the previous statement: at least that minimum yet sufficiently developed indigenous Christian tradition to be capable of evangelizing its own people without E-2-or E-3 help. A barely viable church must be understood as a minimal goal. Nothing here should imply that nay such church anywhere should be considered totally independent of the world family of Christian, nor that it cannot both minister through and profit from continued cross-cultural contacts and expatriate help. All it means is that the missiological breakthrough has been made. This would seem to require at least a cluster of indigenous evangelizing congregations and a significant part of the Bible translated by the people themselves.[158]

The significance of this point is that it reminds us of how complex the task of cross-cultural evangelism is and how it may require the long-term presence of culturally skilled and sensitive cross-cultural workers who come alongside these movements and use their gifts to help them become truly indigenous and not simply foreign looking implants that can support, propagate, and govern themselves as small minorities that are irrelevant to the bulk of their societies. The robustness of this concept of viability serves as a corrective to the kind of naïve and short-sighted thinking that wants to pull out all cross-cultural workers where the church exists to redeploy them among the unreached. It is not nearly so simple as that and the powerful ideas of missiological breakthrough and viability help to focus cross-cultural efforts in the most strategic direction.

---

158 Ibid., 65-66.

Sociological Difference in Evangelism

In the chapter on apostolic function, I made the argument that for a mission sodality all evangelism is not equal because of the unique apostolic vision that seeks out places where Christ is not named. Thus, going where the church does not exist is a great priority for mission sodalities, even while theologically holding to the equal lostness of all people. The third key point that flows out of Winter's E-1 to E-3 concept is closely related to this and adds the sociological dimension to this argument that all evangelism is not equal. For mission sodalities it is a matter of access, and from this perspective it is a matter of difficulty and complexity. To hold the equality of evangelism in the sociological sense is to affirm that you can do the same things no matter what sociocultural setting you are in. Thus, sharing the Gospel with someone in Tibet or Toledo, Ohio are absolutely the same in every respect. However, this is not true. In a theological sense, it is true because the supracultural message of the Gospel does not change, but from a methodological perspective you must change. Winter reminds us that the greater the sociocultural distance between the Gospel messenger and the listener, the more difficult and complex the task. This is a very powerful concept that has many points of application and helps to clarify what needs to be done in a given locale. It anticipates the idea that there will be instances where cultural distances become large enough to warrant an entirely new church planting effort.

The Significance of the P-Scale: Connecting Cross-Cultural Workers to the Greatest Need

The fourth major idea that grows out of the E-Scale has to do with the second component of the definition of frontier missions—the concept of a "hidden" people group. Winter introduces another continuum to help illustrate why some people groups are hidden from already existing church movements. This continuum mirrors the one on evangelism with its E-0 to E-3 distinctions of cultural distance from the hearer. The P-Scale "helps compare the different cultural distances that potential converts need to move in order to join the nearest church."[159] The P-0 to P-3 continuum refers to individuals in people groups that are either very similar to that of the evangelist (P-0 meaning nominal and not born again; P-.5 meaning those on the fringe of the church but having a church within their people; P-1 referring to those who do not identify themselves as Christians, but have an indigenous evangelizing church within their group) or who are increasingly dissimilar (P-2 and P-2.5) or who do not have any Christian movement close to them culturally (P-3).[160]

The critical missiological point that Winter strives to make here is that even though there are many missionaries crossing E-2 and E-3 boundaries, they are most often doing so to work among a people that is P-1, meaning that they have an evangelizing church within their own cultural group. He points out that when the E number is larger than the P number "there is an inherent waste of effort, even though for other purposes such activity may be justified."[161] Thus "regular" missions takes place when cross-cultural missionaries work among a people that already can do near-neighbor evangelism. As a missionary, it is E-2 or E-3 work for them, but to the local people it is an E-1 situation. Winter is not denigrating such work, which has importance in leadership training and development of missionary activity from that group to other groups. Rather, he is pleading for the necessity of a proliferation of work by E-2 and E-3 missionaries among P-2 and P-3 groups, which is the special and complex work of missiological breakthrough and true "frontier" missions. These P-2 and P-3 groups are "hidden" because there is no church culturally close enough to

---

159 Ralph Winter and Bruce A. Koch, "Finishing the Task: The Unreached People Challenge," *International Journal of Frontier Missions* 19, no. 4 (2002): 16.

160 Winter, "Frontier Mission Perspectives," 62-64.

161 Ibid., 64.

reach out to them and they require a cross-cultural effort. These are precisely the type of groups and situations where existing churches manifest "people blindness," being unable to see past their own cultural walls and prejudices in order to reach out to a group that is different than them.

Missiological Reality Changes Over Time

The final point does not properly flow from the E-Scale as much as it is a perspective that forms the core ethos of frontier mission missiology. In my opinion, the prime distinguishing feature in this kind of missions thinking is the specificity and narrowness with which they define the terms "mission" and "missionary." Christian World Mission is the redemptive activities of the church in societies where the church is not found.[162] Thus, a missionary is one who crosses out of a society that has an existing church movement over cultural boundaries to bring the Gospel to a society that does not have the church. The perspective that undergirds this view, which I have noted above, is the sharp distinction between evangelism, which is the work of the church among its own people in the same cultural group, and mission, which means crossing a cultural boundary to bring an initial penetration of the Gospel among a cultural group.

I believe that this perspective, which in turn drives the definition of mission and missionary, is founded upon a certain interpretational viewpoint of the modern missionary movement. The key article that establishes this viewpoint is Winter's *Four Men, Three Eras*.[163] In these three overlapping eras, Winter sees fresh initiatives to fulfill the Great Commission generated from the faith and vision of four key men. During this period of time, the late 1700s to the present, we see that

---

162 Ralph Winter, "The Meaning of Mission: Understanding This Term Is Crucial to the Completion of the Missionary Task," *Mission Frontiers*, (1998): 15.

163 Ralph Winter, "Four Men, Three Eras," *Mission Frontiers*, (1997): 18-23.

although the task of preaching the Gospel remains the same, the dimensions of that task, in terms of what remains to be done in light of the Great Commission, changes. This viewpoint is the foundational assumption that sustains the argument of frontier mission missiology that missiological reality changes over time. I will briefly overview this article and then discuss its major implications.

The first era

The first era extends from the late 1700s till about 1865 and was initiated by the work of William Carey. Although his ideas were unpopular at first, his book, "An Enquiry Into the Obligations of Christians to Use Means for the Conversion of the Heathen" led some of his friends to form a small mission agency. Although Carey was not the first Protestant missionary, "his little book, in combination with the Evangelical Awakening, quickened vision and changed lives on both sides of the Atlantic."[164] Within a few short years, numerous agencies had sprung up both in Europe and America and there was an outpouring of dedicated people who were literally sacrificing their lives to move into new lands with the Gospel. This initial movement focused on the coastlands of Africa and Asia and by 1865 footholds were established throughout these regions.[165]

The second era

The second era was initiated by Hudson Taylor and covers 1865 to the present. Taylor stirred up controversy in his day by suggesting that the inland peoples of China needed to be reached with the Gospel. The question was asked as to why more agencies were needed when there were already many in existence, and why one should go to the interior

---

164 Ibid., 19.
165 Ibid.

when the jobs on the coastlands were not yet finished.[166] Taylor himself formed the China Inland Mission and, as a result of his influence, over forty new agencies sprang forth dedicated to reaching new peoples in the interiors of Africa and Asia.[167] Winter notes that the result of this movement, which continues to this day, is that "by 1967, over 90 percent of all missionaries from North America were working with strong national churches that had been in existence for some time."[168]

The third era

While the first era reached the coastlands and the second began thrusts to the inland territories, the third era moves away from geography to an emphasis on socio-cultural and ethnolinguistic groups. The roots of this era extend back to the 1930s in the work of Cameron Townsend in Central America and Donald McGavran in India. Both of these men went to the field as second era missionaries, part of the Student Volunteer movement. Like Carey and Taylor, who saw the need of initial penetration and penetration of the inland areas, these two men encountered barriers that helped them to see new unreached frontiers for mission.

Cameron Townsend in his work among indigenous Indian populations in Guatemala began to realize that people needed to be reached in their own language. His recognition of linguistic barriers led him to found Wycliffe Bible Translators, dedicated to translating God's Word into every existing language on earth. McGavran, laboring in the diversity of India's social groups, discovered the concept of homogeneous units of people that need to be penetrated with the Gospel message. Winter summarizes this viewpoint:

---

166 Ibid., 21.

167 Ibid.

168 Ibid., 22.

Once such a group is penetrated, diligently taking advantage of that missiological breakthrough along group lines, the strategic "bridge of God" to that people is established. The corollary of this truth is that fact that until such a breakthrough is made, normal evangelism and church planting cannot take place.[169]

McGavran then became the father of both the church growth movement and the frontier mission movement, "the one devoted to expanding within already penetrated groups, and the other devoted to deliberate approaches to the remaining unreached people groups."[170]

If you take this same historical data, and remove the assumption that missiological reality, meaning the state of the world through the lens of mission in terms of the level of completion of the Great Commission, changes over time, you arrive at completely different conclusions. If you can never get closer to completing the Great Commission over time because of the sheer weight of needing to evangelize every new generation, then there is nothing significant or unusual about the work of Carey, Taylor, McGavran and Townsend. Traditional Evangelical missiology sees a world of discrete individuals, and operates on the assumption that wherever people do not know Christ personally they are eternally lost and therefore, no matter where they are, they are the object of mission. Since there are always lost people in every generation, this means that, for the most part, missiological reality changes very little. The world may well have more and more Christians, but for practical purposes in terms of the Great Commission, the task remaining is still huge.

However, if you make the assumption that missiological reality can change over time because people in their "groupness" are "reached" by virtue of having existing church movements that create the potential for

169 Ibid.
170 Ibid.

them bringing the Gospel to their own people, then you open a special role for those who will cross cultural and geographic boundaries to plant the church where Christ is not known. From this perspective, the work of near neighbor evangelism within a sociocultural setting and cross-cultural pioneer work where there are no existing church movements are both critical. When Winter invoked the phrasing "highest priority" he did not mean in any way that the latter was better in some way than the former. He was merely responding to the empirical realities of a world where the majority of people have no access to near neighbor witness and thus their spiritual need must become central for God's missionary people if we are to take seriously His mission.

THE NEED BASED IN BIBLICAL REALITY

In his second point, Winter developed what I call the theme of "biblical reality." He draws upon Acts 1:8 to show that the mandate there contains not only the call to cross-geographical boundaries but cultural ones as well. He then applies his E-1 to E-3 evangelistic continuum to the work of Peter and Paul in reaching Gentiles. We see from the account in Acts 10, where the Lord had to help Peter overcome his cultural prejudice against Gentiles in order to go to the home of Cornelius, that reaching out to Gentiles was an E-3 task for him. For Paul, on the other hand, as a Jew with a familiarity with the Greek world, reaching Gentiles was an E-2 task to Paul.

John Piper asks the question, "Is the emphasis that has dominated mission discussion since 1974 a biblical teaching, or is it simply a strategic development that gives mission a sharper focus?"[171] Specifically, he wants to see if the missionary mandate is to reach as many individuals as possible, all the "fields" of the world, or people groups as the Bible defines

---

171 John Piper, "The Supremacy of God among 'All the Nations'" *International Journal of Frontier Missions* 13, no. 1 (1996): 16.

them.[172] The crux of the matter concerns the interpretation of the terms *mishpahot* (families, peoples) in Genesis 12:3 and *panta ta ethne* (all the nations) in Matthew 28:19. Richard Showalter, after an extensive review of the Hebrew terms *mishpahot* (clans) and *goyim* (peoples), concludes that, as used in the Genesis commission, they are "particular, yet inclusive, references to humanity in all its subdivisions. We find this underscored in both the meanings and usage of the words. In general, the *goyim* are larger subdivisions and the *mishpahot* are smaller. A free, but not misleading, sociological translation might be "cultures" (*goyim, mishpahot*) and "subcultures" (*mishpahot*).[173] Commenting on the meaning of *mishpahot*, Stanley Horton points out that the word has a "much broader meaning than the word 'family' does in English today. In Numbers 26, it is used of divisions of tribes, what might be better called clans."[174] In his analysis of *goy*, he concludes that it can be used of political, ethnic or territorial groups of people.[175]

In his work on the term *ethne* in Matthew 28:19, usually translated as nations, John Piper is concerned to show that the term is not limited to just geographic or political groupings. He points out that even in English the term nation can refer to a people with a unifying ethnic identity as when we speak of the Cherokee Nation or the Sioux Nation.[176] Piper shows that the singular, *ethnos*, in the New Testament never refers to an individual, but rather to a people group or nation, while the plural, *ethne*, can refer to Gentile individuals (Acts 13:48; I Cor. 12:2) it can also be used of people groups (Acts 13:19; Rom. 4:17-18). He concludes, "This means that we cannot be certain which meaning

---

172 Ibid.

173 Richard Showalter, "All the Clans, All the Peoples," *International Journal of Frontier Missions* 13, no. 1 (1996): 12.

174 Stanley Horton, "Blessing for All," *Enrichment* Summer (1999): 93.

175 Ibid.

176 Piper, 17.

is intended in Matthew 28:19."[177] However, Piper amasses a weight of biblical evidence to support his view that the term as used in Matthew 28:19 does indeed support the view that people groups are in mind. He bases this conclusion on the following arguments:[178]

- The 18 references to *panta ta ethne* (all the nations) in the New Testament favor a people groups view.

- The term appears 100 times in the Septuagint, all of which refer to people groups outside of Israel.

- The blessing of Genesis 12:3, reiterated in Genesis 18:18; 22:18; 26:4; 28:14, as translated by the Septuagint uses the term *phulai* (tribes) while *mishpahot* itself can be used to refer to grouping even smaller than a tribe.

- The New Testament references to the Genesis promise in Acts 3:25 and Galatians 3:6-8 support an ethnic group's viewpoint.

- There is an abundance of Old Testament texts which he puts in the categories of exhortations, prayers, promises and plans which demonstrate "that the blessing of forgiveness and salvation that God had granted to Israel was meant also to reach all the people groups of the world. Israel was blessed in order to be a blessing among the nations."[179]

- Paul's conception of the missionary task, particularly as is seen in Romans 15:18-21, shows that he was not concerned just to "win more individual people to Christ (which he could have done very efficiently in these familiar

---

177 Ibid.

178 Ibid., 18-22.

179 Ibid., 20.

regions), but the reaching of more and more peoples or nations."[180]

- John's vision of the missionary task as seen in Revelation 5:9-10 with his use of peoples, tongues, tribes and nations is supportive a people group viewpoint.

Piper concludes on the basis of this broader contextual witness that it would "go entirely against the flow of the evidence to interpret the phrase *panta ta ethne* as 'all Gentile individuals' (or 'all countries'). Rather the focus of the command is the discipling of all the people groups of the world."[181]

However, there are dissenting voices to the exegetical views that have been presented here. In his article, Showalter points out that Hesselgrave argues that although his understanding of the Great Commission allows for the methodology of approaching peoples as peoples rather than as individuals, it is not required by it.[182] Frank Severn, though accepting the vision of Revelation 5 and 7 which shows the Gospel will reach all the divisions of mankind, cites Kittle to show that *ethne* is used non-sociologically and refers generally to individuals who do not belong to the chosen people.[183] He also points out that most commentators do not read ethnicity into *panta ta ethne*, and cites Bosch to show that Paul's methodology, as depicted in Romans 15:20, is illustrative of regional and not ethnic thinking.[184]

---

180 Ibid., 21.

181 Ibid., 22.

182 Showalter, 12.

183 Frank Severn, "Some Thoughts on the Meaning of 'All the Nations,'" *Evangelical Missions Quarterly*, (1997): 415.

184 Ibid., 416.

It is apparent that there are two conflicting views of how to understand these key words in the commission passages of Genesis 12:3 and Matthew 28:19. What I want to suggest here is that both sides of this issue are actually very close to each other, having at their heart the best interests of those who have never heard and who have not believed. Where they differ is in emphasis and in how the biblical data is implemented into actual mission strategy. The frontier mission movement with its emphasis on unreached people wants to redress the imbalance that has occurred in the mission world and trumpet the need for reaching into every group, clan, culture, and subculture to plant a beachhead of Gospel witness. They admit that this frontier mission work is not the only work and use the biblical example of Paul leaving Timothy, as a foreigner, in Ephesus, to continue a work that he began.[185]

Those who feel uncomfortable with the emphasis on peoples are not rejecting the need to reach all the peoples of the earth (as Severn notes in his understanding of Revelation 5:9 and 7:9). Rather, they harbor a deep concern for "passing over multitudes of 'Gentiles/people' who live in neighborhoods, cities, regions, and nations where the church does not yet exist or where there are so few believers the Gospel has yet to be fully preached there."[186] Severn also cites the same text concerning Timothy to show that Paul's missionary team was involved not only in pioneering stages, but in the strengthening stage of church planting as well.[187]

Although I personally feel that the weight of the linguistic and contextual evidence favors a people group focus in Scripture, I want to suggest here that the peoples/people debate is virtually a moot point. First, the

---

185 Piper, 22.
186 Severn, 416.
187 Ibid., 414.

polarization that appears in the literature is actually only apparent and not real. It has created the impression of conflicting agendas when in reality the agendas of both "peoples" and "people" thinkers are identical. Everyone wants to see people come to know Christ personally and to reach the whole world. Second, as Hesselgrave points out:

> Almost all agree that whether the Great Commission requires it or not, the best way to plan for world evangelization is go divide its population up into some kind of identifiable and homogeneous groupings for which sound strategy can be devised and implemented.[188]

Even if no case could be made for *ethne* relating to people in their "groupness" and if the Great Commission referred explicitly to discrete individuals, an empirical examination of our world today would reveal large blocks of humanity that have no church movement present among them.

THE TASK REMAINING IN TERMS OF PEOPLES

Winter's third point dealt with the scope of the task remaining in terms of the need for E-2 and E-3 efforts. He pointed out that the task remaining was immense in two dimensions. The first was in sheer size. His data and the preliminary data produced for Lausanne revealed that about 4/5ths of the non-Christian world were beyond the reach of Christian's E-1 evangelism. Second, it was immense in the sense of the complexity of the task of E-2 and E-3 evangelism across cultural boundaries. In his 1974 address, Winter estimated that there were 16,750 people groups that still needed initial pioneer breakthrough. Interestingly, this was not the most important part of his presentation, which was the missiological concepts of his first two points. In retrospect it may

---

188 David Hesselgrave, *Today's Choices for Tomorrow's Mission: An Evangelical Perspective on Trends and Issues in Missions* (Grand Rapids: Academie Books, 1988), 52.

have been the quantifiability that thinking in terms of people groups and all that implies that sparked interest and set off vigorous debate. In any case, it was the notion of people groups and the demographic quest combined with the later hype surrounding involvement with unreached people groups that created feelings of ambivalence, even to the point of opposition among some involved in missions.

Johnstone says that although Winter's challenge and the 16,750 group number "motivated many Christians, churches and agencies to do something for the forgotten peoples with no exposure to the Gospel, . . . because the definitions of people, people group and unreached and hidden were not clear and consistent, considerable confusion resulted."[189] The initial problem was that back in 1974 there was no actual list of these peoples; they were estimates based on the sources of research available at that time. Johnstone notes that although it was a "wonderful mobilizing concept . . . frustration grew without the checklist of peoples—how could they become targeted and reached?"[190] It was not long before researchers began to make their own definitions of people and unreached/reached based on the type of ministry they were involved in, which started the process of eroding the very specific and technical use that those inside the frontier mission movement used. Because some of these terms became the focal point for debate and achieved buzzword status, I will trace in some detail their history and development in this section.

Defining and Counting People Groups

The Lausanne Strategy Working Group initially defined a people group as "a significantly large sociological grouping of individuals

---

189 Patrick Johnstone, "People Groups: How Many Unreached?," *International Journal of Frontier Missions* 7, no. 2 (1990): 36.

190 Ibid.

who perceive themselves to have a common affinity for one another."[191] In order to bring further clarity to the idea, a meeting was convened March 25-26, 1982 in Chicago by the Lausanne Committee in order to help settle a standardized terminology. A number of mission agencies and organizations involved in people group research attended. They agreed on the following definition:

> A people group is a significantly large sociological grouping of individuals who perceive themselves to have a common affinity for one another because of their shared language, religion, ethnicity, residence, occupation, class or caste, situation etc. or combinations of these. From the viewpoint of evangelization this is the largest possible group within which the gospel can spread as a church planting movement without encountering barriers of understanding or acceptance.[192]

Johnstone notes several variations from the original definition have been suggested.[193] It was Ralph Winter who argued for the addition of the terms "viable, indigenous" to the definition, while Barbara Grimes felt that the words "significantly large" were dangerous because it may cause people to overlook small language groups. Later in that same year, the Lausanne Strategy Working Committee dropped the phrase "as a viable, indigenous church planting movement" so that the idea of sociological groups could be added to the concept. Johnstone suggests that within this very definition there were two perspectives, that of ethnolinguistic peoples and sociological people groups.[194] This uncertainty as to whether or not to count sociological groups (such as prisoners, taxi drivers, drug addicts, etc.) along with ethnolinguistic groups has

---

191 Winter, "Frontier Mission Perspectives," 60.

192 Johnstone, "People Groups: How Many Unreached?," 36-37.

193 Ibid., 37.

194 Ibid.

been at the heart of the controversy over how many unreached groups actually remain.[195]

Refinement regarding the concept of people groups continues as mission leaders wrestle with how to measure progress toward the task of completing the Great Commission. Winter and Koch provide a very helpful summary of four major streams of people group thinking, each of which shines light on a different dimension of the task.[196]

Blocs of peoples

Blocs of people refers to a grouping of peoples along major cultural lines or clustering people into affinity blocs based on language, history and culture. This view is helpful for global level perspectives and assists missions agencies in developing strategic partnerships for related peoples.

Ethnolinguistic peoples

This is the view based on the idea of the ethnic group where self-identity is established on the notions of shared descent, history, customs, language and religion. They see strength of this view in terms of viewing the total task and helping the larger body of Christ be aware of their existence and spiritual need.

Sociopeoples

These are smaller associations of peers who group together around sharing interest, activities, or occupations. This view is helpful to church planters on the ground who may be able to reach a sociopeople as a sub-set of a larger society in order to plant churches among the broader group in the future.

---

195 Ibid., 36.

196 Winter and Koch, 17-19.

Unimax peoples

> This is the *maxi*mum sized group sufficiently *uni*fied to be the target
> of a single people movement to Christ. The idea of unified here is
> that within this group there are no significant barriers of acceptance
> or understanding to the spread of the gospel.

Winter and Koch point out that the 1982 definition of people group, which I have quoted above, described a unimax people. However, today most people think in terms of ethnolinguistic peoples when they talk about "unreached peoples."[197] They note that while generally small, geographically remote peoples are almost always unimax people in terms of the planting of churches, "discovering unimax realities within larger ethnolinguistic peoples in complex societies is a bit more challenging."[198]

Defining Unreached and Reached

The whole point of defining peoples, which is controversial enough in its own right, is to be better able to evaluate where church planting movements exist and where they do not. Thus, after defining people, the next step is to clarify terminology as to who has adequately responded to the Gospel and who has not. The terms chosen to express these ideas were "unreached" and "reached." By the 1982 definition, an unreached people group is

> a people or people group among which there is no indigenous
> community of believing Christians with adequate numbers and
> resources to evangelize the rest of its members without outside
> (cross-cultural) assistance.[199]

---

197 Ibid., 18.

198 Ibid., 18-19.

199 Johnstone, "People Groups: How Many Unreached?," 37.

A reached people group is

> a people group with adequate indigenous believers and re-
> sources to evangelize this group without outside (cross-cultural)
> assistance.[200]

The intent of those hammering out the definitions of peoples and unreached/reached people was to help clarify the task remaining before God's people in order to fulfill the Great Commission. The problem inherent in all of this, as with other disciplines, is that those in the missiological discipline had to draw upon terms that were already in common use. Once the idea of people groups and the need to reach unreached people groups caught the imagination of the Christian world, there was the immediate problem of people co-opting these technical terms to use in a popular sense because of their marketability, so to speak, in terms of raising both interest and funds. Thus, the very powerful idea of an unreached people in the unimax sense was often hijacked to justify efforts or programs that were not even close to the technical missiological use of the terms.[201]

---

200 Edward Dayton, "Reaching Unreached Peoples: Guidelines and Definitions for Those Concerned with World Evangelization," *International Journal of Frontier Missions* 2, no. 1 (1985): 33.

201 A good illustration of how ambiguous and confusing the concepts of unreached and reached people groups was is seen in a 1990 Evangelical Missions Quarterly survey of mission leaders on what "reached" means; "What Does "Reached" Mean? An EMQ Survey," *Evangelical Missions Quarterly* (July 1990): 316-321. There was very little agreement among the eight respondents, it depended primarily on their type of work. Those involved in church planting type ministries tend to conceive of reached in terms of a viable church present in that people, while others with ministries focusing more on evangelism tend toward a definition that speaks of having given people the opportunity to hear and respond to the Gospel.

It may be that the misappropriation of these terms was aided or at least facilitated by the fairly lengthy process that it took before there was a broader consensus in the mission community about exactly what they meant.[202]

In the early stages the Lausanne Committee Strategy Working Group defined an unreached group as one in which there less than 20% practicing Christians.[203] This number was chosen because sociological diffusion of innovation theory indicated that "when an innovation is proposed to a given society, the 'early adapters' will constitute somewhere between ten and twenty percent of the people. Until they adopt it the innovation spreads very slowly."[204] Hesselgrave says that it was predictable that such a definition would produce criticism.[205] There were two primary objections to the use of 20% benchmark. First, it meant that even places in the world where some of the most successful evangelism had occurred (like South Korea) would not be considered reached. Second, the definition said nothing about the state of the

---

202 Jaffarian, writing in 1994, documents some of the confusion that had occurred up to that time in trying to make estimates of the number of unreached people groups; E. Michael Jaffarian, "World Evangelization by A.D. 2000: Will We Make It?," *Evangelical Missions Quarterly* January (1994): 20, 26 footnote 9. He points out that Winter's first estimate of 16,750 was first changed up to 17,000 to show its imprecise character and then in 1989 after an agreement among researchers to look at larger segments was reached it was revised down to 12,000. Later it was dropped to 11,000 in 1991 to show progress. Adopt-a People Clearinghouse came up with a figure of 6,000 that was unconnected to the process used to determine the other lists. He concludes, "Those who produced the changed estimates are not claiming the changes are due to sudden progress"; Ibid., 20. The changes were due to the methodology used in doing the counting rather than in verifiable statistical studies among these groups.

203 C. Peter Wagner and Edward Dayton, eds. *Unreached Peoples '80* (Elgin: David C. Cook Publishing, 1980), 8.

204 Ibid., eds., 8-9.

205 Hesselgrave, *Today's Choices for Tomorrow's Mission: An Evangelical Perspective on Trends and Issues in Missions*, 53.

churches in such a culture and their ability to proclaim the Gospel.[206] Later, a breakdown of this percentage was proposed so that 0-1% represented initially reached, 1-10% minimally reached and 10-20% possibly reached.[207]

Another approach to quantify reachedness was that of David Barrett in the *World Christian Encyclopedia*. He uses 'reached' and 'evangelized' synonymously and "defined both in terms of the state of having had the Gospel made available or offered to a person or people."[208] In his efforts to chart out missiological reality, Barrett divided the world into what he calls Worlds A, B, and C. World C is evangelized and primarily Christian; World A is the unevangelized and non-Christian, while World B is the evangelized non-Christian. By this term, he means those who are not Christians; they are aware of Christianity, Christ and the Gospel, but have not yet responded positively.[209] As with the other sociological definitions, this has not been very satisfying since it appears to leave such a huge part of the non-Christian world as a lesser strategic target since it is already "evangelized" in this very narrow sense. In a 1993 article in *Mission Frontiers Bulletin*, Frank Kaleb Jansen points out that Barrett's use of the term "evangelized" is seeking to measure exposure to the Gospel, while the idea of "unreached" focuses on response.[210] It is a comparison of apples and oranges.

---

206 Ibid.

207 Winter, "Frontier Mission Perspectives," 60.

208 Hesselgrave, *Today's Choices for Tomorrow's Mission: An Evangelical Perspective on Trends and Issues in Missions*, 53.

209 David Barrett and Todd Johnson, *Our Globe and How to Reach It: Seeing the World Evangelized by A. D. 2000 and Beyond* (Birmingham: New Hope, 1990), 25; see Todd Johnson and Peter F. Crossing, "Which Peoples Need Priority Attention: Those with the Least Christian Resources," *Mission Frontiers*, (2002) for an introduction to the kinds of factors taken into account in the development of this tripartite division of the world.

210 Frank Kaleb Jansen, *Four Decisive Moves Forward* (*Mission Frontiers*, 1993, accessed 11 June 2007); available from http://www.missionfrontiers.org/1993/0102/jf935.htm.

Barrett and Johnson's work is one example of the way in which more sophisticated methods were used that looked at multiple factors in order to rank the states of unreachedness and reachedness.[211] The founding of the Joshua Project database in 1995 brought the whole enterprise of people group counting and unreached status ranking to a new and more comprehensive level. The significance of the Joshua Project list was that it brought together four major streams of research in a cooperative effort in order to identify and prioritize least evangelized peoples.[212] The creation of a master database brought the ability to put in one place information and systems ranking that were difficult to compare before.[213] A single database also made it possible to begin to develop some standardized definitions that are available to the mission community at large and which help create a shared nomenclature about people groups and the status of Christianity among them.[214] From my perspective one of the greatest services that the Joshua Project database

---

211 Another example is the proposal to use five independent criteria, any one of which would mean that a specific people group was unreached: the people have not heard the Gospel in an understandable way or form, not responded to the Gospel, they have no growing church or fellowship of believers, the Bible has not been translated in their mother tongue, or the Bible is not available (due to illiteracy or legal restrictions of the country); Terry Riley, "Intercession and World Evangelization," *International Journal of Frontier Missions* January-March (1995): 18-19.

212 Joshua Project, *Joshua Project: Bringing Definition to the Unfinished Task* (Joshua Project, 2007, accessed 11 June 2007); available from http://www.joshuaproject. net/index.php. For a brief history of the background and development of the Joshua project database see Johnson, "Analyzing the Frontier Mission Movement and Unreached People Group Thinking Part II: Major Concepts of the Frontier Mission Movement," 96.

213 For an example of how the various rankings were incorporated into one view in the database see Dan Scribner, "A Model for Determining the Most Needy Unreached or Least-Reached Peoples," *Mission Frontiers*, (2004).

214 From the homepage at http://www.joshuaproject.net you can navigate to places that provide information about the database. The overview tab has links that explain what the database is, some background on people group counting, and a section on how they define people groups. Under the help tab there is a set of frequently asked questions and the definitions link, which is the key to understanding the information presented.

has given to the mission community is a standardized four-fold classification of the world in terms of the status of Christianity and the ability to track that status among every people group on earth.[215]

Unreached / Least-Reached
Located where the Gospel is not generally available.
1.0   Status data unavailable.
1.1   Very few, if any, known believers. Adherents <=5%
1.2   Evangelicals > 0.01%, but <=2%. Adherents <=5%.

Formative or Nominal Church
Located where the Gospel is generally available.
2.0   Status data unavailable.
2.1   Very few, if any, known believers. Adherents >5%
2.2   Evangelicals > 0.01%, but <=2%. Adherents >5%.

Emerging Church
Probable group of Evangelical fellowships.
3.1   Evangelicals >2% but <=5%.
3.2   Evangelicals >5%.

Growing Church
Accelerating rate of new fellowships.
4.1   Evangelicals >10% or one Evangelical fellowship per 10,000 individuals.
4.2   Evangelicals >15% or one Evangelical fellowship per 5,000 individuals.

This typology keyed to a simple baseline of the percentage of Evangelicals makes it possible for the first time for the world mission community to know the status of Christianity not only in the countries that they are working in, but among each ethnolinguistic people. The decision to use

---

215 http://www.joshuaproject.net/definitions.php#jpscale

two percent Evangelical as the break point was based on the sociological reality that groups greater than two percent in a larger society have a significant level of influence.[216] This becomes a powerful tool that highlights the needs of those who have the least exposure to the Gospel, and the least numbers of Christians and church movements.

SUMMARY AND CONCLUSIONS

Thinking about the mission task in terms of peoples is fraught with difficulties. It is the kind of exercise where if you get too caught up in the details and the problems associated with making distinctions you lose the power of the principles and tools. The point has never been to count simply for the sake of counting, but rather to help humans grasp what remains to be done. It is God's people wrestling with the implications of the Great Commission and seeking how to best carry out that mandate. I believe that our stance to the five commissions left with us as God's people in Matthew-Acts needs to be one of awe, fear, trembling, and humility. It is best to admit that as humans we are not precisely sure of what those commissions mean and how to measure them, only God knows. When the missions community talks about planting churches among all the peoples and languages of the earth, it is because of our limited human understanding of God's revelations that this appears to be the best way of fulfilling those commissions. Certainly other ways have been construed (which is Bosch's observation on the varying mission paradigms through history) and are being construed today (not everyone sees finishing the task in terms of planting the church).

Winter's observation needs always to be kept in mind when thinking about people groups, "The unimax peoples definition was never intended to quantify precisely the total task. Instead, it helps us recognize when the unreached peoples task is finished and identify where that

---

216 Scribner.

task is not yet begun." You can never know how many peoples there are until you are on the ground and discover barriers of acceptance or understanding that require a separate church planting effort. One thing is for certain: you can agree or disagree with the concepts of frontier mission, you can debate its merits in terms of the understanding of Scripture and the assumptions it operates on, and you can reject its view of strategy, but like it or not, it was this form of mission thinking that led people to look at the world and produce the detailed information now available regarding the status of the Christian movement in every corner of our globe. That information cannot be argued with; God's people cannot say they did not know there were people and places where Christ has not yet been proclaimed and His Church planted.

6

PROBLEMS AND CONTRIBUTIONS FROM FRONTIER MISSION MISSIOLOGY

In chapter three I made the point that missiological paradigms act like a magnifying glass. In the center of the lens, they make the central biblical commitment they are looking at very clear. However, if you go to the edge of the lens, things become fuzzy. This chapter examines what is clear in the lens of frontier missiology and how it contributes to our understanding and practice of mission and where things become distorted or fuzzy when not balanced with other perspectives. The analysis here is not meant to be comprehensive, but highlights the problems and contributions that are most important when looking at frontier mission missiology.

PROBLEMS

The Problem of a Minimalist Conception of the Great Commission

One of the driving forces of the frontier mission movement is the laudable goal of closure, seeking to bring the Great Commission to completion. While this desire to come up with precise measures of the status of world evangelization is one of the strengths of the movement, the practical result is (for those who misunderstand intermediate for final goals) the creation of a minimalist conception of the meaning of the Great Commission. The burning desire to be able to say that we have in some sense finished the task has led to a very limited definition of what the task means so that it becomes possible to finish.

Gary Corwin feels that this truncated conception of the Great Commission has led to a minimizing of both the missiological task and foundational theology.[217] Missiologically, in order to maximize closure, the task has been minimized from "making disciples" to "evangelizing." Robertson McQuilkin points out that when we try to measure where we are in terms of completion of the Great Commission, it simply depends on how we choose to define the issues.[218] If inclusivistic numbers for "Christians" are used, the sense is that we are nearing completion. On the other hand, if we look at absolute numbers of people who do not know Christ personally on the planet, then we are far from finished. McQuilkin believes that the A. D. 2000 movement has redefined the task around the establishment of a witnessing church group in each people. "But such an approach should not be used to lull us into thinking the task is completed in any people group where we have a beachhead. . . .the Great Commission speaks of discipling the nations, not implanting a nucleus."[219]

Theologically, the doctrine of justification by faith has been minimized in order to maximize the missionary task force by defining major parts of the world as "Christian" which has the effect of lessening the number of people and groups that need to be reached. Corwin argues that neither Great Commission Christianity nor biblical Christianity can exist where the principle of justification by faith has not been

---

217 Gary Corwin, "Just Where Are the Frontiers," *International Journal of Frontier Missions* 9, no. 1 (1992): 4.

218 Robertson McQuilkin, "Six Inflammatory Questions," *Evangelical Missions Quarterly* April (1994): 130-131.

219 Ibid., 132.

embraced.[220] He points out "that in significant parts of the so-called 'Christian' world, the percentage of true believers is so small that a lack of focused missionary endeavor would constitute nothing short of practical heresy."[221]

There are also strategic problems that arise out of a minimalist conception of the Great Commission. When the focus is placed on initial goals of minimal church planting in order to reach the whole world as quickly as possible, there is the risk of turning over the work of evangelization within a people group to a church that is not yet capable of carrying on that task. There is the very real possibility of the premature death or weakening of young church planting movements where the work would virtually need to be redone at another point in time.

The missiological, theological and strategic problems inherent in a minimizing of the task of the Great Commission represent a change within the frontier mission movement itself and are, in large part, driven by a "closure fixation." This change can be tracked by comparing definitions given at the 1980 Edinburgh World Consultation on Frontier Missions with those connected with the unveiling of the Joshua Project 2000 in 1995. The concepts as outlined by Ralph Winter in his lecture on frontier mission terminology show that the idea of reaching a people group, far from being minimalist, was a very ambitious project. At Edinburgh, Winter defined the task of the penetration of a people for missiological breakthrough as the development of an evangelizing church capable of continuing the evangelization of their group without E-2 or E-3 help.[222] He notes that, "this kind of breakthrough is a more profoundly difficult task than is the task of evangelistic church planting

---

220 Corwin, 5.

221 Ibid.

222 Winter, "Frontier Mission Perspectives," 64.

in a culture once such a breakthrough has taken place.[223] Commenting on the stated goal of "A Church for Every People by the Year 2000," Winter points out that the term church "must mean a viable church, . . . [which means] "at least that minimum yet sufficiently developed indigenous Christian tradition to be capable of evangelizing its own people without E-2 or E-3 help."[224] For Winter, this lofty goal is just the minimum for missiological breakthrough.

It is true that trying to operationalize the goal of a "viable indigenous church" in order to measure it has been an elusive task. Although it has been hard to reach consensus on the precise indicators used to quantify viability, Ted Elder believes that in spite of these difficulties there is value in measuring, since "definitions help us to look at what's left to do."[225] We need to realize that any time we attempt to define the Great Commission in order to measure its completion we are of necessity developing a human construct to do so. The whole idea of "reachedness" and concepts like missiological breakthrough are human attempts at quantifying what the Great Commission would look like if it were completed.

Difficulties with measurement notwithstanding, what Ralph Winter articulated in 1980 appears to me to be a rather different concept than McQuilkin's criticism of the A. D. 2000 movement for merely implanting a nucleus. Viability, as Winter defines it, which is both quantity and quality, is the means which best insures that the people of a given culture will have an opportunity to hear the Gospel message in a way that is understandable. However, when we come to 1995 and the unveiling of Joshua Project 2000 in the *Mission Frontiers Bulletin* there is a tangible change in approach to definitions and terminology.

---

223 Ibid., 65.

224 Ibid.

225 Ted Elder, "Where Are the Frontiers?," *International Journal of Frontier Missions* 9, no. 1 (1992): 8.

The sense of precision is gone, with the goal being variously described as "at minimum, a pioneer church-planting movement among every people (or *ethne*),"[226] "a minimum of 50 believers in reproducing fellowships,"[227] or to "ultimately plant a biblical congregation of believers within practical and cultural distance of every person in every class and kind of people in the nation and beyond."[228] In a photocopied update on the Joshua Project 2000 peoples list that I received dated June 6, 1996, the initial minimum goal is stated as the establishment of a pioneer church-planting movement, which is then defined as 100 or more believing Christians in one or more churches by December 31, 2000.[229]

There is a great gulf between the minimum missiological breakthrough that Winter outlined in 1980 and a pioneer church planting movement of 100 believers. Winter, writing in 1990, believed that unreached people thinking made realistic the goal of making initial missionary penetration of all the unimax groups by the year 2000. For him the proper focus is not how many people are won but how many have been given a chance to respond. He points out that the Bible does not talk about winning a certain percentage, but rather it speaks of ethnic groups being discipled. "To plant 'a viable, indigenous, evangelizing church movement' (a paraphrase of the 1982 definition) only requires some minimum, vital, incarnational response within a group."[230] I think it is important that Winter's use of the term minimum be understood in the

---

226 Luis Bush, "What Is Joshua Project 2000?," *Mission Frontiers* November-December (1995): 7.

227 Varuchi Davalai, "South Asia Rises to Play Its Role in Joshua Project 2000," *Mission Frontiers* November-December (1995): 24.

228 Ross Campbell, "National A. D. 2000 Initiative," *Mission Frontiers* November-December (1995): 49-50.

229 Joshua Project 2000 Unreached Peoples List (A. D. 2000 and Beyond Movement 6/4/96), n.p.

230 Winter, "Mission in the 1990's," 100.

context that he defined it in during the 1980 Edinburgh consultation. The ideas of minimal and initial breakthrough have been picked up and used by others without the same depth of meaning that Winter gives them.

It would seem that this is a case of what Gary Corwin calls, "sound-bite missiology" that majors in catchy slogans, but minimizes the realities of the task for the sake of short-term mobilization goals."[231] The erosion away from the more robust concept of viability to a minimalist definition of reachedness seems to be connected to the issues of the race for closure by the year 2000 and the accompanying need for promoting this goal. In the next section, I will examine some of the strategic difficulties that arise from this concept of closure.

Strategic Problems Arising From the Human Construct of Closure

The idea of closure is based on the biblical idea found in Matthew 24:14 that after the Gospel is preached to all the nations (*ethne*) then the end would come. However, just as with the concept of reachedness, once we begin to attempt to operationalize closure so that it becomes measurable in our terms, we have moved beyond the biblical idea to a human construct. Advocates of frontier mission are careful to say that they do not understand precisely what closure is and when the Lord will return, rather they are trying to come up with a clear definition that provides some common ground for evaluating progress on the Great Commission. The intent of developing such a construct is good. However, the implication that comes across is that "reaching" every group in this minimalist way opens the door to the return of the Lord since the Gospel will indeed have been preached in this narrow, restricted sense to every ethnic group in the world.

---

231 Corwin, 5.

What this means is that an entire strategy of mission is being developed around a limited human construct designed to quantify for our benefit the sense of progress we are making on the Great Commission. This is problematic in my mind for several reasons. First, eschatological systems abound; the extreme complexity of the texts and the wide variation of opinion among scholars would seem to recommend caution for anyone trying to track progress towards the goal of bringing the Lord back. Jesus himself told the disciples that these matters the Father has fixed by his own authority (Acts 1:6), and that it is our role to be his witnesses to the ends of the earth (Acts 1:8). What makes us think that we will understand the details of the second coming of the Lord any better than the Jews of the first century understood the prophetic words of the Old Testament about the first coming? It seems wisdom to me to realize that in such matters we see through a glass darkly and that our time is best spent aggressively trying to reach both those who have never heard and those who have not yet responded.

Second, the push for closure seems to be more of a promotional tool to get people excited about a tangible goal than as a reasoned program for completing the Great Commission. It seems there could be a danger of developing a truncated strategy where a potentially responsive "reached" group is neglected in order to pursue a breakthrough in an unreached one. Also, it opens the door for neglecting discipleship and leadership training issues as new groups are "reached" because we are rushing to the next unreached group to usher in the return of the Lord.

Another problem that occurs when closure is linked to the reaching of all the people groups in the world is that inherent in the very definition employed by the frontier mission movement for the term "people" is the inability to finally quantify the number of groups. Since a people is the largest possible group where the Gospel can spread without encountering barriers of understanding or acceptance, this means that by definition until the Gospel is really spread to the fringes of every current "people" we cannot know if such barriers have been encountered. When they are, a "people" is born and there is a need for cross-cultural mission work to start a new church planting movement. Ralph Winter points out that "it is inevitable that this number [of unreached people groups] can only be estimated until all clusters of such groups are actually penetrated and the necessary homogeneity is confirmed."[232] Therefore, it seems somewhat dangerous to postulate closure and develop strategies based on that construct when the very nature of quantifying the task is an emerging and changing one.

Strategic Problems with the Reached/Unreached Distinction

In my opinion, the paradigm of looking at the world in terms of peoples is a very powerful tool that helps in many ways to clarify the missionary task. It does have limitations however, and when the concept is stretched to its outer limits it can result in some strategic missiological weaknesses. Thinking about peoples in terms of being reached or unreached highlights the critical need for cross-cultural evangelism. However, to begin to draw conclusions much beyond this and base strategic decisions on them is problematic.

One such area is the development of mission strategy based on an extreme literalistic view of the concept of reached. Part of the scriptural basis for pursuing church planting among all people groups is the need for having representatives from every tribe, tongue, people and nation around the throne (Revelation 5:9; 7:9). If this idea were pursued literally, and implemented into strategy, it would mean that once a particular people has enough representatives to gather around the throne (again the problem of defining how many that would be arises), then further work among that people is not necessary. It seems to me that within the ranks of the unreached peoples movement that there is a lack of consistency in the application of this principle. On

---

232 Winter, "Mission in the 1990's," 100.

one hand, it appears that in some circumstances the frontier mission movement falls back to standard Evangelical missiology rather than adhering to a strict "people group representation" viewpoint. For instance, although the North and South Koreans are a single people in the ethnolinguistic sense, North Korea is listed as unreached, even though there is a very adequate representation of Koreans in the Kingdom already. Another case would be where a people was "reached" during the early centuries of Christianity but is now "unreached," as it is with some groups in North Africa that had strong churches until the coming of Islam. Today they are still counted as unreached, even though technically as an ethnic group they have representatives around the throne. On the other hand, when considering European peoples with a long history of Christianity and large numbers of nominal Christian adherents with only small current Evangelical populations, such groups are considered adequately reached.

Two observations need to be made here. First, when the unreached/ reached distinction is pushed to it logical limits it becomes less helpful in understanding missiological reality because it designates large blocks of people who are nominally exposed to Christianity as "reached." Secondly, the concept makes a naïve distinction between those who are in other religions and those who live in nominal Christian, postmodern cultures. One group becomes a target for mission because it has no chance to hear, while the other is passed over as a target since they are considered to possess within their culture the chance to hear if they want to take it. This kind of view is naïve for three reasons. First, it does not take seriously enough the reality of spiritual blindness in any system that rejects a personal knowledge of Jesus Christ. It makes an assumption that a lost person in a nominal Christian culture has a chance to "hear" the message or seek it out. Second, this view does not take into account the kind of prejudices that can make a person look for answers everywhere but Christianity that arise from being exposed to a nominal Christian setting. In such cases the weakened form of Christianity that people have been exposed to acts almost as a vaccine to keep them from hearing the Good News. Finally, it does not take into consideration the health of the Evangelical church movement in such lands. If the Evangelical church is not vibrant in its passion to reach the lost, the opportunity for someone to truly hear the Gospel in an understandable way is very small. Thus, to make a distinction in evangelistic priority between peoples that have virtually the same small percentage of evangelical Christians in their cultures simply because they are geographically inside or outside the 10/40 window and historically have little Christian background is to ignore some critical spiritual realities.

Another difficulty posed by an over pressing of the reached/unreached distinction is the extreme emphasis on the 10/40 window as the most important target of mission efforts. McQuilkin comments that while "a far greater proportion of our task force should be going to the neediest and most neglected areas of the world. . . . the church must not use the 10/40 window to deflect us from our responsibility to the rest of the world."[233] While the 10/40 window is a very helpful targeting tool, and highlights the least-reached parts of the world, as a principle for devising strategy, it is too limited. The reached/unreached distinction focused on the 10/40 window emphasis has been made the center of promotion for the final great mission thrust, and has led to a popular understanding that the only place for valid missionary work is there. (This problem will be discussed in more detail in a section below). However, Ralph Winter himself has declared in writing that very strategic missionary effort that benefits the unreached can and must take place outside of 10/40 window countries. He points out that there have been two classic responses to the fact of the imbalance that has existed in the missionary world with" most missionaries laboring among already existing church movements. He says:

---

233 Robertson McQuilkin, "Six Inflammatory Questions-Part 2," *Evangelical Missions Quarterly* July (1994): 263.

One response to this unfinished task is that we must drag all or most of our missionaries off the well-established fields and send them to the frontier peoples. Another response is that we ought to channel all our new missionaries to the frontiers and consider all other missionary mere international church workers. I have never agreed with either of these ideas, however well-intentioned they may be.... these proposals give the wrong answer I believe, or at least they surely do not give the best answer to the unfinished task.[234]

He believes instead that missionaries need to catch a new vision where they are at, to help the church movements they live and work among to develop and implement a mission vision of their own.[235] Such a view is much more helpful for the further development of a mission paradigm that embraces the entire world and all of the missionary task force, rather than just a part of it.

Another strategic problem that arises from overstressing the reached/unreached concept is the fact that responsive populations can be neglected. McQuilkin warns that we must always be prepared to "flood newly opened windows of opportunity whether or not they are '10/40.'"[236] In his response to Ralph Winter's Lausanne paper on cross-cultural evangelism, J. Philip Hogan anticipated this very difficulty that was implied in the notion of a focus on reaching unreached peoples. He appeals for recognition of the sovereignty of the Holy Spirit in mission and notes that "we are witnessing worldwide, an outpouring of the Spirit of God upon persons and places for which there is no human design and in which there is not one shred of human planning."[237]

---

234 Ralph Winter, "Are 90% of Our Missionaries Serving in the Wrong Places?," *Mission Frontiers*, (1991): 34.

235 Ibid., 35.

236 McQuilkin, "Six Inflammatory Questions-Part 2," 263.

237 J. Philip Hogan, "Response to Dr. Ralph Winter's Paper," in *Let the Earth Hear His Voice*, ed. J. D. Douglas (Minneapolis: World Wide Publications, 1975).

Finally, taking the reached/unreached distinctions too far creates a focus on "peoples" to the neglect of "people." Trent Rowland points out that what is at issue when we talk about unreached peoples is access to the Good News of Jesus Christ's victory on the cross.[238] Although all people are lost, not all have equal access to the Gospel message. The heart cry of the frontier mission movement is that all peoples have a chance to hear, that every group be given a chance to respond to that Good News. Yet in the emphasis to reach peoples there has been a subtle devaluing of the need to reach lost people, wherever they are. It is interesting that the biblical understanding about peoples was not the initiating point of the unreached peoples paradigm. Rather it was the experience of missiological reality, of barriers rooted in "peopleness," that led to a closer examination of Scripture and the refined understanding of God's desire to have some from every people around his throne. However, it appears that over time, and particularly with the drive in the 1990s to reach every people by the year 2000, a selectiveness of understanding to support this "peoples group thinking" paradigm has grown. Within the movement, the Bible is understood only through the peoples lens, and other themes such as God's love for the world are understated. While the peoples emphasis lends urgency to the task to penetrate all the ethnic groups, the global emphasis brings urgency to reaching anyone who is lost. God loves the whole world (John 3:16) and Jesus died for the sins of the whole world (I John 2:2). Our Lord is not willing that any should perish (II Peter 3:9) and He is still calling the ends of the earth to turn to Him and be saved (Is. 45:22-23).

When it comes to peoples and people it is not a case of either/or with the Lord of the harvest, but both/and. We cannot play one emphasis of Scripture against another in order to justify either a peoples only approach or a "lost people anywhere" approach. Missiologists and missionaries need to remind themselves that our reached/unreached

---

238 Elder, 8.

distinctions are merely human criteria that have been constructed to aid in our thinking about the task that remains, not to obscure the fact or de-emphasize the need to reach lost people wherever they are. Ted Elder argues that since we cannot share with everyone at once, "we have to decide where to start and how to proceed. By default we will prioritize. Definitions help us make these priority decisions."[239] This is true, and the beauty of the frontier mission movement has been its call to address the imbalance in our world in order to reach every people. But when efforts to address this imbalance create neglect of other lost people that God loves, it is indicative that the paradigm needs to be adjusted. We do not want to create a new generation of "hidden peoples," should the Lord tarry, by missing opportunities and continuing to sow seeds in such cultures.

Problems with the Notion Of "People Groups"

I have already noted in the previous chapter some of the controversy that has surrounded the idea of "people groups" in terms of the attempt to arrive at a definition of the concept and to quantify their numbers. Here I want to look at anthropological critiques of the whole notion of discrete "peoples." Taber sees the endeavor to enumerate the number of discrete people groups in the world in the work of Winter and Barrett as an offshoot of the homogenous unit principle propounded by McGavran.[240] He feels that the numerical quantification engaged in by Winter and Barrett "suggest an altogether spurious sense of precision"[241] and that the thinking on which these ideas are based fall into the weaknesses of Maliknowskian functionalism and are on sociocultural grounds too "simplistic and inaccurate [a] conceptual tool to describe modern societies, or for that matter societies of any degree

---

239 Ibid.
240 Taber, 144-45.
241 Ibid., 145.

of inner complexity."[242] Taber sees the homogeneous unit principle and people group thinking as recent reincarnations of nineteenth-century German missiology[243] that was in part based on Warneck's novel reading of the Great Commission's use of *ethne* as "all the peoples, each as a unit" rather than its primary use in the Septuagint to refer to Gentiles collectively.[244] He concludes that these missiological formulations "failed to give the weight to the New Testament vision of a church which would incorporate people from all human groups, relativizing and transcending but not homogenizing their differences."[245]

Taber lists the problems associated with Maliknowskian functionalism as the assumption that each culture is a discrete, bounded and self contained unit; that ideal culture is pure and untainted by outside contaminating influences and thus should be stable, harmonious and theoretically unchanging; its dualism that leads to the erroneous conclusion that what is in people's heads is separate from their material existence; and its relativism that "led in missions to an overreaction against the older ethnocentric judgmentalism and to an excessive readiness to approve of almost anything and everything."[246] More current views of sociocultural theory help us see that often it is the relationship between bounded groups in a complex society that is the critical issue for that society; that people often participate in many groups whose membership does not coincide; that human personality resists closure; and that anthropology, as a discipline, has moved beyond functionalism to see the importance of diffusion, acculturation, the permeability of

---

242 Ibid., 143-44.

243 Ibid., 77-9.

244 Ibid., 78.

245 Ibid., 79.

246 Ibid., 141-42.

cultural boundaries, culture change, migration, urbanization, and the importance of material conditions.[247]

In a similar vein, critiquing from the anthropologist's viewpoint, Len Bartlotti charges the A. D. 2000 movement with a kind of people group fixation that assumes "neat solid line boundaries around people groups—what could be called a primordial view—rather than fluid and overlapping dotted line identities."[248] Bartlotti believes that this ignorance of complex ethnographic realities can lead to ecclesiastical apartheid, processes of evangelism that are insensitive to social change, a minimizing of bridge building similarities between peoples and the impeding of church growth "where ethnic realities and multiple identities may more fruitfully contribute to the formation of multi-ethnic (heterogeneous) or 'urban conglomerate' church movements."[249]

There is no doubt that refinements in sociocultural theory provide challenges that need to be addressed by proponents of people group thinking. However, there is nothing in the critique that negates the power of the original conceptions; rather it can be seen as helping to strengthen and improve the way in which the principles are applied in real-life contexts. This should serve as a warning to those who would use this anthropological critique to dismiss the ideas as outmoded. Ralph Winter's original core concept was that people groups who do not have a church movement present such that E-1 near neighbor evangelism is being done require a cross-cultural missionary to penetrate and plant the Gospel. Here Taber's own caveats to his arguments are very telling. He admits that it is indeed possible to divide the world into regions that have not been evangelized and those that have, that "hu-

---

247 Ibid., 144.

248 Lawrence Radcliffe [Len Bartlotti], "Part-2: A Field Worker Speaks out About the Rush to Reach All Peoples," *Mission Frontiers* January-February (1998).

249 Ibid.

man social groups, as distinct from cultures, can be bounded"[250] and that "on the balance, there is no doubt that people in general gravitate toward their 'own kind.'"[251] Winter's point is not simply to enumerate groups as an academic exercise, but recognizing the human propensity for groupness, to seek to evangelize within a particular group as widely as possible. Then, when due to this human propensity to group together and share identity barriers to acceptance or understanding are encountered, a new cross-cultural effort must be started. The emphasis is not upon people groups as a concept, but upon evangelizing people in their groupness and not requiring them to cross out of their groupness and sense of identity in order to hear the Gospel. It seems to be backwards thinking and to doom the process of reaching lost people if we end up requiring non-Christian people to break down walls and barriers they have erected in their human fallenness in order to hear the Gospel message which alone can help them to see the fact of their fallenness and human unity via God's physical creation and spiritual recreation of humans.

The original concept of reaching people groups is unassailed by contemporary views of anthropology and sociocultural theory which see relations between groups and cultural permeability with much more precision than in the past. If there are no barriers of acceptance and understanding then, from Winter's broad unimax definition, you are still operating with the bounds of a single people for the sake of the purposes of evangelization even though that unimax people may be made up of multiple ethnolinguistic groups when categorized through different filters. The problem that Bartlotti perceptively points out has to do not with the original principle, but the application in a narrow operationalization leading to a popular and unsophisticated missiology

---

250 Taber, 145.

251 Ibid., 144.

that may sacrifice quality of ministry and effectiveness among individual peoples in order to make sure that every group is engaged.

A theological issue is at stake here as well. While theological critique of the homogeneous unit principle and by extension people group thinking often draws on Paul's passage about the creation of the one new man out of two in Ephesians 2:11-22, there are other perspectives to consider. Taber questions whether the descriptive observation of human behavior gravitating to their own kind should be made a normative principle for the church's practice.[252] In such a view, Paul's argument in Ephesians 2 is another example of the indicative/imperative divide that we so often see in his letters, where a theological reality (the potential for human unification in Christ) needs to be worked out in human relations where the opposite is the norm. But there are other ways to understand the passage.

An alternative to the imperative/indicative account is provided by Andrew Walls in his examination of the model in which the early Christians conceived and practiced faith in Jesus. Although limitations of space do not allow me to reproduce his detailed argument, I will share some of his conclusions as a stimulant for further research and exegesis on this important subject. Walls understands the language and metaphors of Ephesians 2 in light of the record that we find in Acts and Paul's writings that legitimate two forms of converted life, what he calls Old Believers (Jewish background Christians who continue in a Jewish lifestyle) and New Believers from Gentile backgrounds.[253] He notes how in Acts 15 the Jerusalem elders saw in the New Believers the work of the Spirit promised for the messianic age and affirmed

---

252 Ibid.

253 Andrew F. Walls, "Evangelical and Ecumenical," *Evangelical, Ecumenical, and Anabaptist Missiologies in Conversation: Essays in Honor of Wilbert Shenk*, ed. James R. Krabill, Walter Sawatsky, and Charles Van Engen (Maryknoll: Orbis Books, 2006), 29-33.

that they were indeed the people of God, but they were not required to practice Jewish culture.[254] Paul goes even further in Galatians and says that there is no need for Gentiles to enter Jewish culture; that "under the guidance of the Holy Spirit they were not to find a Hellenistic way of being Christian, to demonstrate Hellenistic life turned toward Christ, to translate the life of Christ into a new segment of social reality."[255] He concludes from this overview that cultural diversity is built into the very fabric of Christian faith:

> Two diverse systems of Christian living—one might almost say two parallel Christianities—existed side by side in a single church. Each depended on conversion; the difference between lay in what was being converted, as devout traditional Judaism and eastern Mediterranean Hellenistic civilization were alike turned toward Jesus Christ. And the two systems, each based on cultural conversion, were interdependent, co-inhering.[256]

This understanding then controls the reading of the Ephesians passage so that "the two converted lifestyles . . . are building blocks in the construction of a new Temple. Each is needed in the construction (Eph. 2:20-22)."[257] He points out that these are not seen as two modes of faith that are equally valid choices, but rather they "are necessary to each other and to the church. In itself, each is only partial, neither can build the Temple alone."[258]

A final point here from Walls reminds us that theologically there may indeed be a rationale for reaching people in their groupness:

---

254 Ibid., 31.
255 Ibid., 32.
256 Ibid., 33.
257 Ibid.
258 Ibid., 34.

We are back to the paradox of incarnation. Humanity is one, but we never meet it in generalized form. We know humanity only in culture-specific segments of social reality. . . . [the triumph of the cross] breaks down the wall around culture and ethnicity that separate the segments of humanity, but it does not annihilate culture and ethnicity. The cross brings reconciliation of culture, not unification; and reconciliation reveals a co-inherence of the various cultural segments that opens up the possibility of a fuller, richer humanity.[259]

The Implication that Frontier Mission is the Only Valid Form of Mission

I think that is important to make a distinction between the actual concepts that make up frontier mission missiology and the ways in which it has been promoted, particularly from the late 1980s through the decade of the 90s. Beginning with his 1974 Lausanne address, Ralph Winter has been advocating a very specific type of missionary task, the pioneer task of breaking into a previously unreached culture with the Gospel. Yet even in that address he recognized at least four levels of valid ministry: the work of nurturing Christians, renewal of nominal Christians, ordinary E-1 near neighbor evangelism and the critical task of cross-cultural evangelism.[260] His position is that although frontier mission is not more legitimate than other forms of mission, "it may, in a given situation in history, be more neglected."[261] In a sense, his work since the founding of the U.S. Center for World Mission has been to highlight this neglect and plead that the mission world take seriously the challenge that people groups represent. Focusing on the core concept, that people groups who do not have within them a church movement capable of providing E-1 near neighbor evangelism need a cross-cultural

---

259 Ibid.

260 Winter, "The Highest Priority: Cross-Cultural Evangelism," 229-31.

261 Ralph Winter, "Defining the Frontiers," *International Journal of Frontier Missions* 9, no. 1 (1992): 9.

missionary effort from the outside, there would be little debate as to the validity of this point. There is very little controversy here as this is consonant both with missiological reality and biblical reality.

However, what has created a great deal of controversy and sense of uneasiness among mission agencies has been the impression conveyed by the broader frontier mission movement through its publications that frontier mission is the only truly valid form of mission in these days. In a presentation to the 1991 meeting of the International Society for Frontier Missiology Gary Corwin said:

> The question is then posed, 'If reaching unreached peoples is the essence of mission, and if all but the stragglers among the unreached peoples are to be found within this [10/40] window, then what in the world are mission agencies doing in the rest of the world? And aren't they almost criminal in not deploying their resources more effectively?' While the argument may not always be stated so bluntly, the message permeates almost everything published on the subject. . . . the problem is that many fine mission organizations today feel they have been all but written out of the 'frontier' missions script, and that their efforts are viewed as second-class at best.[262]

In 1992, Frank Severn wrote, "I am very uneasy abut some applications of the principle of reaching the unreached that call into question the validity or importance of missions to people where there are churches, albeit those churches may make up less than 1 percent of the total population."[263] Five years later, he writes:

> My concern is that 'people group' theology so dominates mission thinking in North American churches that 'true and valid' mission

---

262 Corwin, 4.

263 Frank Severn, "The Critical Context of Today's World Mission," *Evangelical Missions Quarterly*, (1992): 177.

only occurs when we focus on the unrelated people groups that have 'no significant missiological breakthrough" (no Bible, no church, no missionaries). The rest of the world is considered 'reached,' even though the church may be very small and many towns, villages and even large urban areas have no gospel witness.[264]

The thoughts of these two mission leaders, who are in basic agreement with the fundamental concepts of unreached people group thinking, are no doubt representative of the concerns of many others. This represents to me a weakness in the presentation of the broader frontier mission movement. The major advocates of the movement themselves are careful to say that other forms of mission are important and valid, yet those brief comments are overwhelmed by the powerful promotion of reaching the unreached as the most critical need. I believe that the push for closure has been a contributor to this phenomenon in that it has created a somewhat short-term viewpoint with a limited focus that discourages looking at the broader issues of developing vibrant churches.

Bypassing Mission Agencies and Amateurism in Mission

One of the byproducts of the promotion driven mobilization that happened in the decade of the 1990s in the push to reach all peoples by the year 2000 has been the phenomenon of local churches becoming directly involved in mission activities. This has created two serious problems that may actually impede progress in the penetration of all people groups and the development of church planting movements among them. One of the manifestations of this interest in mission has been the bypassing of mission agencies to send workers directly to field situations. Len Bartlotti points out that originally the idea behind the adopt-a-people program was that local congregations interested in adoption should consult a mission agency rather than

---

264 Severn, "Some Thoughts on the Meaning of 'All the Nations'," 415.

consulting a list and choosing, so that they could be supportive of frontier work already begun or about to begin.[265] The lack of expertise single congregations have in the complexities of mission means not only ineffective ministry, but also the possibility of costly mistakes in sensitive areas of the world.[266]

The second manifestation grows out of the first, an increasing amateurism in mission. It is a great irony that Ralph Winter, 20 years after his Lausanne presentation that launched the frontier missions into full swing, feels compelled to issue a warning that real damage to the movement is possible due to a lack of knowledge upon the part of a newly mobilized generation of short-term workers.[267] In another place he says, "I fear that much of this frontier enthusiasm is ill-prepared and doomed to failure and damage to the cause...."[268] It seems that Winter's continual plea for understanding the complexity of the frontier task of penetrating an unreached culture has gone unheeded by the very movement that he had a major part in founding.

From the beginning, Winter advocated that the business of frontier mission is one of great complexity, far more difficult than near neighbor evangelism. He points out that, "Missions—in contrast to evangelistic organizations—are in the lock picking business. They are the only organizations whose unique skill is pioneering—'getting inside of' a culture that is bafflingly strange."[269] Winter also proposed in 1978 in the lead article in the first edition of the MARC Unreached Peoples series that one of the first necessary strategic

---

265 Radcliffe.

266 Ibid.

267 Ralph Winter, "Editorial Comment," *Mission Frontiers*, (1995): 2.

268 Ralph Winter, "Three Types of Ministry," *Evangelical Missions Quarterly*, (1997): 420. Len Bartlotti points out the irony of a millennial movement with a time-date stamp in its title using an a-historical approach to missions; Radcliffe.

269 Winter, "Are 90% of Our Missionaries Serving in the Wrong Places?," 34.

steps is to reevaluate all previous approaches to the reaching of a group.[270] Winter's writings and comments stand in stark contrast to some of the promotional material that came from places like the A. D. 2000 and Beyond Movement. In a May 1999 letter I received from their missions mobilization network, a new concept called Acts 13 Breakthrough was announced, with a goal of generating 200,000 new missionaries from 100,000 churches. Many of these were expected to go to the 10/40 window with their support coming from tentmaking. A single sentence counsels near the end of the brochure that good missionary training is important and advises contacting a mission agency.[271] The trend towards amateurization and the bypassing of mission agencies goes hand in hand. Again, this seems to be an example of promotional driven mobilization that is in part connected to a particular view of closure. By ignoring history, and downplaying the complexity of the task, there is a real danger of producing a great deal of action with little overall impact on the least-reached.

CONTRIBUTIONS

It is quite natural that in a vibrant and emerging movement like that of frontier missions and unreached people group thinking that there should be conceptual and strategic problems like those that have been discussed in the section above. With a recognition of some of the difficulties inherent or implied in the missiology that has grown from this movement, it is now appropriate to offer some assessment as to its core contributions to the broader framework of Evangelical/Pentecostal/Charismatic (EPC) stream of missions. I will be using this lens of frontier missions to focus light upon contemporary issues in the mission world to see how this paradigm can help clarify real-life situations and sharpen our practice.

---

270 Ralph Winter, "Penetrating the New Frontiers," in *Unreached Peoples '79*, ed. C. Peter Wagner and Edward Dayton (Elgin: David C. Cook, 1978), 51.

271 George Verwer and Chacko Thomas, letter to missions mobilizers, May 1999.

The Importance of Cross-Cultural Evangelism

In my opinion the most important contribution to missiology from the frontier mission movement is found in the theme of Ralph Winter's 1974 paper at Lausanne: the importance of cross-cultural evangelism. Using both biblical and missiological reality Winter hammered home the point that in order to finish the Great Commission there must be the penetration of peoples which were not capable of being reached by near-neighbor E-1 evangelism. By its very definition, since there were either no Christians or not enough of a Christian movement in such cultures to carry out vibrant E-1 work, it necessitated a believer crossing out of their own culture to enter another and seek to root the Gospel there.

Winter made a further refinement of this concept by not only con-ceptualizing the cultural distance of the evangelist from the hearer with the E-0 to E-3 scale, but also the distance of that people from a culturally relevant church in the P-0 to P-3 scale. Peoples that are P-2 and P-3 are far from a church movement that is understandable or relevant to them and Winter called them Hidden Peoples. The E-Scale and the P-Scale remain a challenge to EPC missions to make a course correction to insure that every people has a chance to hear and respond to the Gospel. This is an incredibly powerful concept that has forever changed the way that we view the missionary task. The call, not just to do cross-cultural evangelism, but to do so among a people that is culturally distant from a relevant church movement reveals the critical cutting edge of missions. It becomes much too easy for efforts that began as pioneer church planting to move towards maintenance relationships with the resulting national church, and for that church to have its own people blindness. Taking seriously the insights of the E and P-Scales means that the needs of those who have never heard are not forgotten.

Addressing the Imbalance in Missionary Placement

At Lausanne in 1974 Winter asked the question, "Are there any tribal tongues and linguistic units which have not yet been penetrated by the Gospel? If so, where? How many? Who can reach them?"[272] Those questions now have answers. As I noted in my discussion of the issues surrounding the definition of peoples, reached, and unreached, there are difficulties and complexities, but these issues and uncertainties cannot obscure the fact that the mission world now has access to information on the people groups with little or no Gospel presence among them. It is also an undeniable fact that among these unreached and least-reached peoples there is a minority portion of the world missionary force and financial resources present. The call to cross-cultural evangelism is a call to address this tragic imbalance that grieves the Spirit of harvest. This increasing clarity of information about both the harvest field and harvest force cries out as an indictment against the Christian world as to why we collectively in the body of Christ worldwide have been so slow to bring the message of the Gospel to these groups. While there have indeed been excesses and much that is unwise and short-sighted propagated in the name of reaching the least-reached, we need to tread carefully lest our assertion of being led by the Spirit does not end up to be mere rhetoric in the face of all the places we have manifestly not gone. It is inconceivable that the Holy Spirit, who loves all people and is not willing that any should perish, would not be calling laborers into the harvest fields of the least-reached. The imbalance in the world today reflects more our inability to hear, and our hardness of heart, than God the Father, Son, and Spirit overlooking millions of people who have no one in their sociocultural setting to tell them the story of salvation.

---

272 Winter, "The New Macedonia: A Revolutionary New Era in Mission Begins," 346.

The Passion to Reach the Lost

The frontier mission movement provides a clarion call to all involved in mission that we must reach the lost. Those who have never heard must have the chance to hear the saving message of Jesus Christ. This was the heartbeat of every new pioneering thrust in mission. However, as the missiological landscape changes, what were once pioneer fields are now the home of powerful national churches. It is too easy for missionaries to become caught up in the maintenance of mechanisms designed to assist emerging church movements, rather than staying on cutting edge evangelism among the least-reached. Jim Plueddemann points out that a major weakness of standard mission agencies is the tendency to lose vision and focus in the midst of being engaged in hundreds of strategic activities.[273] Those of us who work in standard mission agencies should beware of the ease in which our own successes now threaten us with the possibility of having a large proportion of our staff doing primarily support work.

Unreached people group thinking reminds us that no matter where we are working, there is a people somewhere that is unreached and we are bound to labor in our context to see that God's global purpose to reach all the peoples is fulfilled. This passion provides a powerful reorientation to the work of every missionary no matter where they are located to make sure that the least-reached both near and far are given the chance to hear the message.

The Changing Role and Strategic Nature of Every Missionary

The reorientation that a passion to reach the lost provides means that every missionary has a critical role to play in reaching the frontiers, even if they themselves are not located in an unreached people group. The challenge of cross-cultural evangelism means that the missionary

---

273 Winter, "Six Spheres of Mission Overseas," 17.

role is a changing one. Cross-cultural workers do not simply employ their spiritual gifts in another social setting, they catalyze and facilitate near neighbor evangelism as well as helping to bring new church movements full cycle to initiate their own cross-cultural evangelistic efforts. This means that the missionary role, while changing as the new church movement grows, can always be strategic. In my thinking, one of the most overlooked and yet powerful contributions that frontier mission missiology makes is in assigning a vital role to every missionary. It is a great misfortune that Ralph Winter's thinking on this very point has not been picked up and articulated with more vigor during the decade of the 1990s with its extreme emphasis on the 10/40 window. If we can set aside for a moment some of the rhetoric and promotion that went on the good intent of addressing the imbalance of the world missionary force, the essence of frontier mission thinking for every missionary regardless of location becomes the power of a new perspective. This perspective, moving a national church movement towards participation in a frontier effort, makes whatever kind of work we are engaged in strategic.

Majority of World Churches

We are now more aware than ever that "missions" is not just the province of cross-cultural workers from the Western world. Fifteen years ago Winter made the point that "the most exciting reality in missions today is the gradual discovery of the vast unrealized potential of our precious sister churches as the source of new missionaries to go further out."[274] If existing western missionaries in these emerging and younger

---

274 Winter, "Are 90% of Our Missionaries Serving in the Wrong Places?," 35. A *Christianity Today* web article from 2006 says that in 1973 the magazine reported 3411 non-western cross-cultural missionaries and currently reliable estimates are around 103,000, which is nearly equal to the 112,000 missionaries sent out of the USA and Canada; Rob Moll, "Missions Incredible" (*Christianity Today*, March 1, 2006, accessed 11 October 2007); available from http://www.christianitytoday.com/38168.

movements can play a strategic role in training pioneer missionaries, then it is the role of these churches to come full cycle and begin to send their own laborers to the unreached. Frontier mission thinking provides a framework for embracing and directing the work of these majority world missionaries by highlighting the urgency of cross-cultural evangelism among the unreached. In this way, while recognizing the sovereignty of the Spirit of harvest in calling laborers to various fields, whether among the so called reached or unreached, there is a natural and strategic connection for majority world laborers to start in new ground among those who have had the least access to the Gospel.

For both practical and missiological reasons, as it concerns the focus of mission and the placement of missionaries, the majority world missions movement should major upon the pioneer penetration of least-reached groups. The practical reason can be framed in this way: for Western-based organizations, their long standing relationships with existing national churches constrains their work so that it is primarily facilitative and supportive of those churches. Those who come to such agencies with a Spirit led burden to work among the least-reached will be sent, but for the most part their system will produce new candidates for their already developed fields of labor. In contrast, missions coming out of the majority world do not have the same long-standing relationships and commitments with already existing mature national churches. This means that the focus of mission and the placement of missionaries can much more easily be directed to the least-reached peoples.

The missiological reason is even more compelling than the practical one. It has to do with the E and P scales. The original application of these concepts was to churches in the West. However, if we change the center of mission from the West to somewhere in the majority world it becomes clear that there is strategic significance in sending missionaries to people groups where the Christian movement is smaller than among the sending people. It makes no sense for majority world missions to send a missionary into an E-2 or 3 situation that is P-1 for that people, and where there are most likely already Western missions working. So to avoid reduplicating efforts and to keep from sending missionaries to places where a national church is already capable of doing near neighbor evangelism, majority world mission agencies can focus on founding beachheads of the Gospel among the least-reached.

Sharpening the Focus of Mission Agencies

A large part of what mission agencies do is involved in the placement of cross-cultural workers. No matter how they choose to handle that process, from being highly directive to sending people where the Spirit calls them, there is always a "where" component. Frontier missions is a paradigm that explicitly deals with the "where" question in missions. The people group lens continually asks the question, "Who has not yet had access to the Good News?" This simple question brings a tremendous amount of focus to a mission agency. Any agency that chooses to address that question will be unable to continue on with the status quo and work merely on maintaining and supporting their already existing work. To ask the question does not at all imply that they must stop what they are doing, redeploy, or even shift and major in sending new personnel to the unreached. What it does mean is a radical reorientation of every aspect of their work so that the goal of all efforts becomes the discipling of the *ethne*.

It Breaks Down the Home/Foreign Distinction by Focusing on Cultural Boundaries and Can Reinvigorate All Kinds of Evangelism

For many mission agencies connected to denominations, it is common that they use the terms home and foreign to distinguish between work done within their home country and outside of it. Often times these represent two completely separate departments. The distinction between monocultural and cross-cultural evangelism shows that the home/foreign split is a misguided focus on geography, when the real issues are in fact cultural. The peoples lens and the ideas of reached/unreached add an additional dimension that it is not just crossing a cultural boundary per se, but rather crossing a boundary to plant the church among a people that has no significant near neighbor witness.

It is often the case that when a local church movement is in decline (as in North America) that Jerusalem needs (that of the local church) are pitted against the needs of the uttermost parts of the earth (foreign missions). It can even be the case that missions outside of the home base can be seen as competing with and eating up valuable resources that could be used for the home base. Let me illustrate for a moment from my own home base, which is North America. There are times when missiological technical terms are misappropriated and misapplied to North America in order to stimulate the sense of urgency for evangelism. My point is that rather than trying to argue for the importance of outreach in America using "unreached" as a buzzword and missing its technical definition in missiology, it would be more effective in the long run to embrace the distinction between the evangelistic outreach of a local church within its sociocultural setting and the essential missionary task of cross-cultural evangelism planting the church in sociocultural settings without a church movement.

This has the benefit of challenging local churches to be lighthouses within their own Jerusalem, and to challenge these same churches to the truly immense cross-cultural task wherever it confronts us, whether it is with Muslims in Dearborn or Khartoum, or Buddhists in Denver or Mongolia. This preserves evangelistic passion for outreach to Americans without attempting to pit it against the truly critical cross-cultural evangelistic task of bringing pioneer breakthrough where there is no church movement. While 200 million Americans are lost theologically and are unreached in the sense of not yet belonging to Christ, their potential access to the Gospel is a completely different issue compared to the large blocks of ethnolinguistic peoples that have either no church movements or exist as small and embattled minorities.

The Concept of Cultural Distance in Evangelism Challenges All Churches to be Missional at All Points in the E-Scale

The notion of cultural distance and evangelism that Winter articulated in the E-Scale has now found application to churches in the West in terms of the necessity of bridging the increasing cultural distance between Christians in the post-Christian environment of Europe and North America. It is outside the scope and purpose of this monograph to address issues of what is now called "missional church" thinking in the West. However, I do want to address potential areas of misunderstanding that church leaders in Western, postmodern social settings, may have about the missional terminology, cross-cultural evangelism, and how it impacts the least-reached and unreached of the world. I also want to illustrate the power of E-Scale thinking for application within Western societies and indicate a couple of points where additional study and debate is needed to stake out a more sharply defined terminology and methodology.

It is becoming more common in the EPC streams of Christianity to use three distinct terms when talking about mission in its broader sense. The singular "mission" or *missio dei* refers to everything God the Father, Son, and Spirit desire to do with our world. This includes human redemption but goes beyond it.[275] Missional, as an adjective, is

---

275 Bosch defines *missio dei* as God's self-revelation as the one who loves the world, his involvement in both the world and the church, and that *missio dei* declares the good news that God is a God-for-people; Bosch, 10. Verkuyl sees the ultimate goal of *missio dei* as the restoration of the liberating domain of God's authority, bringing the Kingdom of God to expression; Verkuyl, 197-98. For background on the shift from a church-centered to a theocentric focus of mission rooted in the Trinity see Thomas' overview in his chapter "Mission as Missio Dei" and the associated excerpts in *Classic Texts in Mission and World Christianity* 21 vols., American Society of Missiology Series, vol. 20 (Maryknoll: Orbis Books, 1995),

used to describe people and churches that embrace the mission of God and want to put it at the center (or spiritual DNA) level of what they are about. Missions, the plural, is then used to describe the mission of the church, our participation in the *missio dei* worked out in specific places and times.

It is important to understand that the term "missional," in its current context, was drawn upon to help Western Christians think about their task in the face of the massive decline of influence of the institutional church in the West.[276] The reason for the need of churches to become "missional" and to adopt a missionary stance towards their culture is two-fold but is wrapped up in the culture change that has happened in the west in the wake of the breakup of the modern period. In the Christendom period, which Hirsch sees as paradigmatic from the rise of Constantine to the present,[277] the Church had dominance over the prevailing culture, state, and society. The problem for the church of the West in a nutshell is that the world changed and the operational mode of the church did not. Hirsch summarizes:

> The problem we face is that while as a sociopolitical-cultural force Christendom is dead, and we now live in what has been aptly called the post-Christendom era, the *church still operates in exactly the*

101-121; and Bevans and Schroeder's tracing of the history back through Barth, Hartenstein, and the IMC conference at Willingen, Germany in 1952; Bevans and Schroeder, 290-91.

276 Guder et al. defines a missional ecclesiology as one that emphasizes the "essential nature and vocation of the church as God's called and sent people"; Darrel L. Guder and others, eds. *Missional Church: A Vision of the Sending of the Church in North America*, The Gospel and Our Culture Series (Grand Rapids: William B. Eerdmans Publishing Company, 1998), 11. The rise of the term "missional" can be traced back to the work of the Gospel and Our Culture Network (GOCN) that started in Great Britain out of discussions generated from the work of Lesslie Newbigin in a 1984 publication *The Other Side of 1984: Questions for the Churches*, Ibid., 3-7; see also Hirsch, 81.

277 Hirsch, 60.

same mode. In terms of how we understand and 'do' church, little has changed for seventeen centuries.[278]

Christendom-based assumptions of outreach are based wholly in attractional models where we go out and try to bring people into our buildings to be exposed to the Gospel. A sidelight here is that missional has also now achieved buzzword status and is often used synonymously for anything that "reinvents" church to make it more attractive to people in the post-Christian environment.[279] This is a helpful distinguishing mark in that any model that is primarily based on attracting and bringing people to a building is not missional in the sense as it was originally conceived and applied to the Western church.

The culture shift in the west that rendered the Christendom attractional model ineffective and irrelevant is the postmodern rejection of hegemonic ideologies and grand narratives that has resulted in the "flourishing of subcultures, and what sociologists call the *heterogenization,* or simply the *tribalization,* of Western culture."[280] What this cultural shift means is that the church of the west is on missional ground because the attractional models appeal to only a small slice of the population. Whereas crossing cultural boundaries by crossing a geographic boundary was the iconic understanding of the occupation of the missionary, it is now mandated for churches to do the same in the West. Again, Hirsch's summary is appropriate here:

---

278 Ibid., 61.

279 Ibid., 82.

280 Ibid., 61. This tribalization means that "people now identify themselves less by grand ideologies, national identities, or political allegiances, and by much less grand stories: those of interest groups, new religious movements (New Age), sexual identity (gays, lesbians, transsexuals, etc.), sports activities, competing ideologies (neo-Marxist, neofascist, eco-rats, etc.), class, conspicuous consumption (metrosexuals, urban grunge, etc.), work types (computer geeks, hackers, designers, etc.), and so forth"; 61.

> To reach beyond significant cultural barriers we are going to have to adopt a missionary stance in relation to the culture. And partly that will mean adopting a *sending* approach rather than an *attractional* one, and partly it will mean that we have to adopt best practices in cross-cultural missionary methodology.[281]

So far so good. Aside from the problem of the latest hot term being co-opted and used without holding to its original meaning, which I alluded to above, a more pressing problem is the potential for misunderstanding around the ideas of cultural distance and "peopleness." The misunderstanding is often expressed in terms like this: if we now have to cross cultural barriers to share the Gospel with post-Christian North Americans, and traditional missionaries cross-cultural boundaries to share the Gospel with people in other parts of the world, what is the difference? At least in the Christendom mindset there was a need to proclaim the gospel in the foreign fields far away; now, however, with the missional mindset it becomes easy to conflate the crossing of a cultural boundary of virtually any "size" or complexity as being of equal importance. Thus, we are back to everything is mission and everyone is a missionary again. The final result is that the 40 percent of the world that lacks near neighbor witness is again neglected because the "need" to cross cultural boundaries in the North American base is so great.

In people group thinking, the key issue that defines when a new cross-cultural church planting effort is needed is when "barriers of acceptance or understanding are encountered." The importance of the missional church movement's insight that the North American church needs to recognize and take a missionary stance toward the post-Christian is critical, but it cannot be at the expense of the truly unreached and least-reached in the frontier mission sense. The issues in North American society with its massive Christian resources and disaffected people

---

281 Ibid., 62-63.

due to the models of existing churches is a completely different world where there is no access to near neighbor witness and scant resources. To confuse crossing the cultural gap from Christians to post-Christians in the North American setting with the situation of the 40 percent who lack near neighbor witness is tragic.

The question becomes how can we preserve distinctions that will keep us on a missionary stance and sending orientation in North America while not missing the needs of the unreached and least-reached? I want to suggest that it is at this point that we need to keep in clear focus the definition of people group, the distinction between individual churches and church movements, and work towards refinements in our understanding and explication of the notions of cultural distance between the Gospel messenger and the recipient. Using the ideas of the E-Scale and the definition of people group, I want to suggest some ideas that I think help to avoid the merging of all cultural distances and the corresponding lack of clarity that brings to the task. Using Winter's E-0 to E-3 scale, the insight of the missional church movement is that in the E-1 environment of North America there is an increasing cultural distance present here between Christians and the post-Christian culture. What practitioners in North America meet as they try to share the Gospel is barriers of acceptance and understanding. What was not hammered out in the initial phrasing of the E-Scale and the idea of barriers is the precise nature of those barriers.

I believe that the cultural distances that practitioners are meeting are still broadly within the E-1 non-Christian zone of a *single* people group as defined by the frontier mission movement. The tribalization of American culture with its subgroups and sub identities will now require different evangelistic strategies for these varying sociopeoples. This will even require different flavors of individual churches, but it still is within the bounds of the broader movement of churches within generic American culture. Inside of this E-1 zone, the cultural distances that must be bridged relate to style (the music, dress), subculture identity (skate boarders), impression (ranging from mildly unfavorable to extreme dislike of institutional Christianity), and overall religious orientation (New Age, atheist and so forth). The key issue here is that these are often temporary orientations, they shift naturally over time, can be molded by exposure (a negative opinion can be changed by a positive experience with a Christian), and they are chosen rather than given at birth. An evangelistic strategy to reach Goth youth is not likely to require a Goth church that becomes intergenerational. It is a subculture and people will not be marrying and having children and raising little Goths. These converts will likely shift their subculture identity and fit easily into any number of types of church styles.

By way of contrast, when we are talking about E-2 and E-3 cultural distances, these often relate to language and identity differences. It is not just a matter of planting churches of different styles that are all part of a broader movement within a larger pluralistic culture, but planting churches within that setting that will make disciples who retain their identity to their group as faithful disciples of Jesus. While people may stop skate boarding, or dressing Goth, or playing a sport, you cannot shed being Thai, or a Banjar or Turk so easily. If we want to actually reach a people group it is not enough to simply pick off a few converts from the fringes who are willing to trade in their identity for a new one. What is required is the complex work of rooting the Gospel in a sociocultural setting so that the good news can become good news for them as a people.

What then does it mean to be missional in a North American setting? To embrace the mission of God, from whatever starting point I am in, means to be sent into my own E-1 culture, not simply attempting to attract people to the program and building, but taking the message to people and demonstrating the good news in the society. At the same

FIGURE 6
Modified E-Scale to Represent Cultural Distance
Within a Single Sociocultural Setting

E-0 and E-1 represent a single social cultural setting for the purpose of planting church movements among a unimax people group

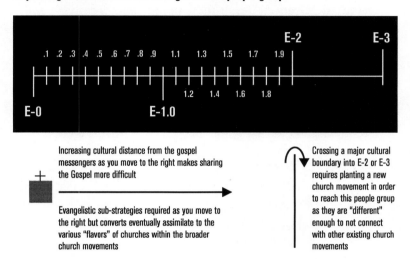

Increasing cultural distance from the gospel messengers as you move to the right makes sharing the Gospel more difficult

Evangelistic sub-strategies required as you move to the right but converts eventually assimilate to the various "flavors" of churches within the broader church movements

Crossing a major cultural boundary into E-2 or E-3 requires planting a new church movement in order to reach this people group as they are "different" enough to not connect with other existing church movements

time, it means that as the community of God's people emerges there is the awareness of linguistic and cultural barriers need to be crossed in order to tell those who have no access to the Gospel the saving message. The church that is truly missional in its own context will mobilize its people to connect with all the people of their social setting (not simply those who fit their local church style) and build new local congregations of every kind for the converts that come. It will also seek to mobilize mission sodalities to cross E-2 and E-3 barriers to plant the church in social settings where Christ is not known.

Clarifies the National Missionary Question

Some would argue on two counts that expatriate cross-cultural workers from the western world should be replaced by workers that are "national" or "native." The first count is that westerners are much too expensive, and many tens of nationals can be supported for the price of one expatriate westerner. The second is that nationals can do evangelism much better than outsiders. Again, frontier mission missiology with its notion of evangelism and cultural distance brings a helpful perspective here. Since both of these points have been dealt with in detail elsewhere I will only briefly touch on the second one to illustrate how this paradigm brings clarity to practical problems like this.[282]

When people say that nationals do things like evangelism better than missionaries, the E-Scale reminds us that that there are different *kinds* of evangelism. If we are talking about evangelism in their own sociocultural setting to people who are like them, then that is an absolutely correct concept. However, you cannot make the same statement when it is dealing with true cross-cultural evangelism. The point is this, once you truly cross a cultural boundary you are no longer "national" even if it is within your own nation-state.

When an American, Korean, Brazilian, Angolan, or Indian crosses a cultural boundary to proclaim Christ the advantages derived from being "national" and thus a near-neighbor E-1 witness disappears for all of them. In a cross-cultural evangelism situation the ground becomes quite level. In this sense you cannot be "national" or "native" and be a missionary. From a practical point of view, organizations that encourage westerners to support the efforts of national missionaries are usually in reality supporting the efforts of Christian workers who are ministering to their own people as near neighbor E-1 witnesses.

---

282 See the entire issues of *Mission Frontier* magazine September-October 1994 and November-December 2005.

Challenges Us to a Theology of Success: What Do We Do If It Works?

I noted in the last chapter that a foundational underlying assumption of frontier mission thinking is that missiological reality changes over time. Basic to this idea is that it is the responsibility of local churches to reach people in their sociocultural setting, while mission sodalities carry a different priority, that of establishing missiological breakthrough where the church does not exist. This notion of breakthrough, expressed as a viable indigenous church means that it is possible to measure when the primary task in a given setting is finished. This of course does not mean that everyone is a Christian, but rather that the social setting has the potential for access to the Gospel because of the presence of an indigenous church movement. All of this implies that mission agencies need to have a theology of success that defines for them what to do when their efforts have worked and an indigenous church exists among a people. Normally missions and cross-cultural workers do not think in terms of developing an exit strategy, in part because the development of a truly viable church is no simple thing and often stretch beyond the time horizon of a person or teams career. A viable church movement is not a single church or even a cluster of them or even a successful single denomination. It means that within that people group they have enough resources to evangelize their own people without any outside help. Difficulty aside, it is not hard to produce examples where the Gospel has truly taken root and flourished and there are multiple church movements that are fully able to successfully carry on the task of near neighbor evangelism as well as to initiate their own cross-cultural work. This kind of success should push mission agencies to delineate their own theology of success and develop a strategy of exiting and moving their resources elsewhere.

Beats the Trap of Double-Blindness

I have observed over my years of working as a cross-cultural missionary in an organization committed to developing indigenous national church movements that there are times when our commitment to the national church unwittingly makes us blind to other groups that are often right within the borders of the nation-state where we are working. I have already noted Winter's idea of "people blindness;" this is not something that is unique to people in the West or North America. The result is what I call the trap of double-blindness where there is a people blindness on the part of the national church and a strategic people blindness on the part of the mission because of their commitment to work with the national church (see figure 7).

FIGURE 7
Two Kinds of "People Blindness"

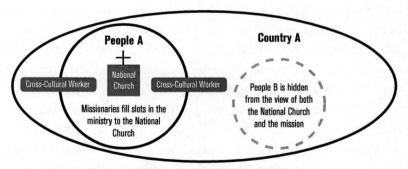

*The National Church is blind to people B because they naturally "see" their own people
*The mission is blind to people B because of their commitment to work with the national church among people A

What can happen is that when a mission agency has as its primary lenses for placement a sense of call and its commitment to the national church, the trend becomes to feed called people (who often have a broader generic sense of being called to cross-cultural work and do not have a specific place that they feel they must go to) into already existing slots in ministry with a national church that they are working with. As I have already noted, any national church no matter what size is inherently needy, there are never enough workers.

The national church (people A) itself, as we all do, has its own people blindness for a variety of reasons. Because they do not "see" other peoples, who may even be significant minority groups with the nation-state or close to it (people B), they will not automatically attempt to bring the Gospel to them. The mission agency working with people A, without meaning to, ends up participating in a practical sense in people A's people blindness with the result that there are two levels of blindness now separating people B from the Gospel.

Frontier mission thinking confronts this situation by reminding all the participants of the people group lens and its importance for developing strategy. The people group lens challenges people A's blindness to people B, and it challenges the mission agencies *de facto* dropping of people B from their strategic planning horizon. Here is a real life scenario where people group thinking combined with the self-identity of a mission team committed to apostolic function can have a major impact. The ethos of apostolic function on the part of the mission team means that they address the people blindness of the national church not simply by asserting their values as a mission sodality to reach such a group unilaterally, but that they seek to build this vision (apostolic genius, missional DNA, full cycle mentality, whatever you choose to call it) into the national church. The people group lens linked with a sense of the apostolic function of the mission team does not take an either/or approach (unilateral work with people B or working only within the frame of people A's vision) but seeks instead to insure that people B hears the Gospel and that the church in people A fully embraces the mission of God and develops its participation both within and outside of its own sociocultural setting.[283]

---

283 There are numerous other real life scenarios that could be expanded out of the situation that I have used for my illustration. What I try to get across in discussions

Clarifies the Task so that We are Not Forced to Use Language that Pits One Part of the World Against Another

I think that it is important to keep separate the major ideas that are the core of frontier mission thinking from some of the issues and causes of organizations and movements that have grown out of this kind of missiological orientation. One of the unfortunate and unintended consequences of the A. D. 2000 and Beyond movement and the rush to engage the unreached in what became known as the 10/40 window during the 1990s was the sense that somehow ministry to the unreached in that area was in some way *more* strategically important than in other places. The result has been that, for some, the close association of these very useful missiological ideas with such movements meant that people ended up rejecting or feeling very uncomfortable with both. The critical "baby" of frontier mission concepts got tossed with the "bath water" of movements and promotional hype.

The rush to the window meant that places like Europe or Latin America were looked down upon, and the language of strategic importance could very easily pit one place against another. As time has gone on, the data has become more sophisticated and the four-fold classification system of the Joshua Project now allows for a view of the world that does not require pitting any place or people against anywhere else. Knowing roughly the status of the Christian movement in any people

---

that focus on the practical application of these principles is that there is not a single vector answer to reaching the least-reached and unreached. For instance, in reaching a group like people B in my illustration above, a newer mission agency could choose to simply work directly with them and not connect at all with the church in people A. Another route would be to try to reach people B by exclusively mobilizing the church in people A. Questions arise as to what to do if the church in people A refuses to work with people B. Should a mission agency with a historic relationship with that national church strike out on their own? There are no fixed answers. The frameworks supplied by the people group lens, cross-cultural evangelism and apostolic function help to clarify what needs to be done without specifying how.

group helps to clarify the kinds of tasks that should be and need to be done, and the type of workers needed. It helps newer missions to determine if they should focus there or not, and helps older missions with longstanding relationships with national churches to see what kind of emphases should inform their work.

One of the most important consequences of the decision to use the less than two percent Evangelical as a primary line of demarcation was that it immediately put the spiritual need of Europe back in focus. The only distinction between the unreached/least-reached and formative or nominal church classification is the presence or absence of a historic Christian population of more than 5 percent. The only difference is whether the person hearing the Gospel has a historic presence of Christianity in the broader culture, or is an adherent of a non-Christian world religion like Hinduism, Islam, or Buddhism. In both instances the Evangelical church movements are very small and are minorities in a world that is often hostile to them. While the issues are different and the social identity issues of Christianity are much more intense in the Hindu, Muslim, and Buddhist world, it is still very much a task that requires the pioneer planting of new communities of faith. Peter Kuzmic, citing a 1989 Lausanne conference workshop on nominalism, notes that nominal Christians make up nearly one billion people.[284] These four major types of nominals, those whose faith is bound to their ethnic religious identity, second generation nominals, ritualists, and syncretists, present a great evangelistic challenge to Christians in the EPC streams. The presence of this block of people is a reminder that there are spiritually lost people in every religious system, and that the Gospel call to be born again and enter the kingdom is for all those far from the Father whether their sociocultural system has a history of the presence of the Christian faith or not.

---

284 Peter Kuzmic, "Europe," in *Toward the Twenty-First Century in Christian Mission: Essays in Honor of Gerald H. Anderson*, ed. James M. Phillips and Robert T. Coote (Grand Rapids: Eerdmans, 1993), 153.

The standardization that the Joshua Project data allows for a dispassionate appraisal and reminds us not to pit one part of the world against another. There is no need to do that as the information in hand indicates clearly the places and peoples that are most in need of cross-cultural efforts to win new disciples and plant new churches because of their lack of an adequate E-1 witness within their social setting.

SUMMARY AND CONCLUSION

Despite the problems I have enumerated, the frontier mission perspective is a powerful missiological paradigm that gives the mission community a number of tools that help clarify real life situations and sharpen the focus of cross-cultural work. The contributions I have discussed certainly do not exhaust the value of frontier mission missiology. They do, however, illustrate how a missions lens can focus light on missions issues that are not of small consequence and have immense ramifications as they are played out in practice. In the next chapter, I move back to the broad persepctive of the four mid-level paradigms I have identified and illustrate how integrating insights from all four paradigms at the same time can help mission practitioners in their work.

7

THE POWER OF INTEGRATING
PARADIGMS

In this chapter I am now returning to a theme I proposed in chapter 3. Before I pick up that thread, I will review the flow of thought and argument up to this point. In the first chapter, I argue that we, collectively in the various streams of missions and missiologies that are broadly represented by Evangelicals, Pentecostals, and Charismatics (EPC), have a problem with our understanding of missions. There are two primary ways that this problem is expressed. The first is that everything has become missions; we lack conceptual clarity so that mission has become a catchment for virtually any Christian activity done in any place. The second is that this pan-missionism takes place primarily in places that have the most Christians so that mission is becoming increasingly disconnected from the idea of planting the church in societies where it does not exist.

I then suggested in Chapter 3 that one way of dealing with this crisis regarding the meaning of mission is to draw upon the biblical and practical insights of major missions paradigms in an integrative fashion. I noted at that point three major orienting mission frameworks. In Chapter 4, I argued for a fourth framework, which serves as the paradigm of missionary identity which I call apostolic function.

In Chapters 5 and 6, I focused on the "where" question in mission and examined in detail the frontier mission paradigm. My reason for focusing on this frame and not others is two-fold. The first is that the others represent major paradigms that had extensive literature and critique while frontier missions does not to the same degree. The second is that the "where" question of missions, despite the growth of major mission centers and a turn of the millennium burst of energy, presents a great challenge to the Christian community.

This is the backdrop to the argument I will develop here. Although it is an oversimplification, it is constructive to think about our task in terms of four interrogatives: why we do mission, what we do in terms of content and methods employed, how we carry out our work and where we engage in it. The why question is that of motives for mission and is drawn from Scripture. Our areas of divergence, both in philosophy and practice, tend to concern the what, how and where questions. By asserting a lack of clarity in our understanding about mission, I am also arguing that we need to seek solutions to the dilemmas posed by our current situation.

There are two points here that need to be made. First, the three major paradigms of church planting/growth, Christian social concern, and frontier mission individually are unable to help us because they cannot account for all that is happening in the world and they are often seen as competing with one another. The second point is that we cannot turn the clock back and attempt to operate in a pristine environment; the fact of the existence of churches and cross-cultural workers in many places has to be recognized. Any solution has to take these factors into account as a baseline.

A COMPREHENSIVE AND INTEGRATIVE
APPROACH TO MISSION PRACTICE

My proposal to address the current scene is that we look for an approach that is comprehensive and integrative. It needs to be comprehensive because we need to find a way to embrace all that God is doing and wants to do. This means that people both as individuals and as groups are in view. It also includes all cross-cultural workers right where they are at, affirms the importance of their role, and challenges them to a reorientation around seeing God's glory among the whole earth and all peoples. To seek an integrative approach means that we explore the way in which the "where" paradigm speaks into other frames. The philosophical and strategic clarity that this framework brings to the practice of missions has forever changed the way that we look at the world. It is no longer enough to see a monolithic world of spiritually lost individuals; instead we are sensitized to the reality of their "people-ness" or "groupness" and the biting fact that after nearly 2000 years of mission history many such groups have never had a chance to hear the Gospel. Confronted with the reality of equal lostness and unequal access to the saving message, every missionary and organization must be stirred by the urgency of harvest fields awaiting harvesters. The notion of having a priority of going where the church does not exist is very powerful; it cuts across the major frames of mission and, if allowed, can help them sharpen their focus. Integration also means taking all four of the paradigms and looking through them at the same time in order to inform our practice rather than operating primarily out of only one perspective. The paradigms represent biblical commitments and integration is an exercise of increasing the coverage of biblical insights into our understanding and praxis of mission. Our current realities are showing us that even though these varying paradigms are very powerful, taken individually they are inadequate to the task of dealing with mission in the whole world. They are unable to account for the complexities that we find at the ground level of missions. The exercise of integration that seeks synthesis of the best thinking offered by the major paradigms does not create a new paradigm, but rather sharpens and refines our focus by shining the light of Scriptural commitments on particular places and settings.

In this chapter, I will develop in more detail what it means to approach missions in a comprehensive and integrative fashion. I begin by illustrating what a comprehensive approach looks like at the field level with a mission team and at the agency level. I then introduce a methodology whereby practitioners can work intentionally at integrating all four mission paradigms into their practice.

A Comprehensive Approach

I have already noted the problem that arose during the final decade of the 1990s and the media-driven push for the laudable goal of a church for every people. It left many missionaries and their agencies feeling as if they were at best second class citizens in the missions world if they were not directly working among an unreached people group. As I pointed out, this was unfortunate because within the movement itself there was a clear understanding of the strategic importance of cross-cultural workers at every location. It was not an issue of placement, but of purpose and direction of the work that connected it to the larger goal of seeing churches planted among peoples where there were no Gospel movements. This notion was severely downplayed with the result that many in the mission community were left with a bad taste in their mouth regarding the frontier mission movement. In my opinion, the foundation of a comprehensive approach for a church, agency, or cross-cultural workers and teams is rooted in affirming and developing the strategic importance of every worker and their ministry and their role in bringing the Gospel to both people as individuals and to people in their groupness and particularly those who do not as ethnolinguistic groups have an adequate witness of the Gospel.

This sense of the importance of all forms of ministry is a conviction that comes from Scripture where all ministries come from the working of the Spirit (I Cor. 12:4-6) and where gifts are given to all individuals (Eph. 4:7). You cannot read the New Testament and find any ammunition to support the idea that some kinds of service are "better" than others. When thinking about missions through the frontier missions lens we must always take care to remind ourselves that the concepts and ideas are human generated constructs that are based in Scriptural commitments and human observation of missiological reality. As such, they are tools to help cross-cultural workers, but as is the case with all kinds of tools, they can be misused and misapplied.

The starting point for a comprehensive approach is found within Winter's Lausanne address and his E-0 to E-3 continuum. While the focus of his argument was on the need for cross-cultural evangelism, the continuum itself clearly acknowledges there is the ministry of nurture to believers, the renewal of nominal Christians, near-neighbor evangelism of non-Christians and finally the critical and complex task of cross-cultural evangelism. Similarly, in the work of David Barrett and Todd Johnson there is recognition of the need for ministry across a seven-point continuum. To help highlight the need of the least-reached, they developed a three-fold categorization of the world into zone A (unreached, no witness of the Gospel), B (evangelized non-Christians), and C (the Christian world). In light of this categorization they then ask the question, "Where shall we put our resources? Where should the churches 300,000 foreign missionaries be asked to work?"[285] Their answer is in the 7-fold typology moving from most reached and most exposed to the Gospel to the least.[286] Their point in developing the

---

285 Todd Johnson and David Barrett, eds., *A. D. 2000 Global Monitor* 33(July 1993): 2.

286 Ibid. Their terminology is as follows: World C (Christians) 7-Great Commission Christians, providing nurture, pastoral care and support, 6-non-practicing church members, 5-nominal Christians, World B (Evangelized non-Christians) 4-Heavily evangelized non-Christians, 3-partially evangelized non-Christians,

trichotomy is to show the church that current placement and evangelistic effort is lopsided and unbalanced with most missionaries being engaged in heavily evangelized places. The plea is for more workers in World A, and not less anywhere else. They are quick to add that any of the 7 levels is an honorable vocation if that is the calling of the Lord. They note, "Our categories Worlds A, B, and C must not be taken as describing anybody's relative importance in God's eyes. Individuals in A, B, or C are all equally important to Him. Our God yearns for the salvation of a nominal Christian in World C just as earnestly as for an unevangelized, untargeted [group] in World A."[287]

Another model of thinking comprehensively comes from the work of Jon Haley, who suggests that a unified theory of the mission task is needed. Haley points out that the missionary task is usually defined in terms of either need, approach or timing, each of which currently has dichotomous poles of theory.[288] Need theories are either based on those who are lost everywhere, or those who have had least opportunity to hear. Approach theories are based on either reaching people groups or urban centers. Timing theories focus on either responsive peoples or creative access, going about the task to the degree God opens the doors.

Haley's criticism is that all of these theories are situation driven rather than objective driven from the mandate of the Great Commission.[289] He believes that the crux of the matter has to do with the definition of reaching the world with the Gospel. He suggests that there has been the failure to distinguish between different levels of reaching, and the

---

World A-Unevangelized non-Christians 2-unreached non-Christians, 1-untargeted non-Christians.

287 Ibid.

288 Jon Haley, "Seeing the Big Picture: A Unified Theory of Our Task," *Evangelical Missions Quarterly* (October 1996): 424-425.

289 Ibid., 425-26.

failure to keep all of those levels in focus at the same time.[290] He then proposes four levels and integrates the role of the missionary and the emerging church movement with each one.[291]

- Frontier Mission—the objective is penetration of a culture, cross-cultural missionaries are involved in church planting.

- Critical Mass—missionaries are involved in church planting, leadership training and mobilization so that a strong viable church movement emerges that is able to evangelize its own group and touch its society.

- Real Access—at this point the church movement takes the lead in seeking to give every person in their culture access to the Gospel. The missionary works in leadership development and mobilization as needed.

- Real Hearing—the church movement attempts to present the Gospel to everyone in their culture in an understandable way. Missionaries are no longer needed.

Haley correctly identifies the most difficult concept in his unified theory, trying to quantify and measure when critical mass is reached. In my opinion, the strength of his model lies in the way that he handles this point. He wants not only to look at the statistical presence of a church and numbers of church attendees, but also the overall health and vibrancy of that movement. He suggests criterion such as percentage of Christians who can and will reach their own people, ownership of the task, sufficient resources to complete the task, how "radioactive" the raw material of the church is in terms of its ability to reproduce, its fervor and the presence of strong leaders. He concludes that when we

---

290 Ibid., 426.

291 Ibid., 426-29.

look at criterion such as these "critical mass will vary from grouping to grouping, depending on social structures, receptivity and so on."[292]

Stan Nussbaum of Global Mapping International offers another model that seeks a comprehensive view based on what he calls the mission matrix that takes into account both knowledge of God and the zeal to serve Him.[293] This matrix is composed of five frontiers of mission, which he believes is a more holistic view. In the matrix, God's ultimate goal is high knowledge and high zeal. Frontier 1 represents no knowledge of God or zeal to serve, these are the unreached peoples. The second Frontier is people who are nominal Christians, who know about God, but do not really serve Him. The task here is the renewal of these believers. Nussbaum criticizes the traditional Evangelical approach to such groups, which is to either ignore them or treat them as unreached. Frontier 3 consists of those with great zeal, but little knowledge, such as the house church Christians in China, and independent churches in Africa. Such movements need help in grounding their movements in God's Word. Frontier 4 extends the scale into negative numbers for both knowledge and zeal and represents those who are anti-Christians. Such groups either have wrong knowledge of the Gospel, or oppose everyone who believes, or have both problems. Nussbaum suggest such groups require special strategies to help overcome the negative bias so the Gospel can be heard. Frontier 5 consists of Evangelical believers who take the Great Commission seriously. The task here is to deepen believers so that they put love in action.

Taken together, the conceptual models from Winter, Barrett, Haley, and Nussbaum put to rest any notion that the only important kind of cross-cultural work is among the least-reached and unreached. A comprehensive approach recognizes the necessity and validity of different

---

292 Ibid., 429.

293 Stan Nussbaum, "The Five Frontiers of Mission," *GMI Info* (Winter/Spring 1999): 1.

kinds of mono-cultural and cross-cultural ministry that work towards God's ultimate purpose. Whether it is framed in terms of Winters E-0 to E-3, Nussbaum's concept of frontiers, Barrett and Johnson's typology or Haley's levels, it is clear that important and strategic ministry needs to take place outside of classically unreached groups. It also accepts the changing role of the missionary through time as a church movement emerges. Haley's concept of levels shows clearly that missionary labors must change as the church grows. Thus, cross-cultural missionary work is dynamic rather than static and requires sensitivity to the contextual factors of the people group and the emerging church movement. Finally, it sees the value of using qualitative factors in the life of church movement in order to assess viability so that the critical mass stage can be reached. It is not enough to have an initial penetration and then abandon a fledgling movement.

Illustrating a comprehensive approach at the field level

It is easy to talk hypothetically about being comprehensive in our approach to missions, but it is often hard to see what this would actually look like. I have developed a diagram that helps illustrate how these principles would apply in the specific situation of a particular "field" of labor. The diagram represents cross-cultural workers, local Christians and churches within one single sociocultural setting.

I have overlaid two elements in this diagram. Over the top are terms that some use to describe four stages of missionary labor:[294] the pioneering stage, when initial church planting takes place; the paternal

---

294 Winter credits the work of Henry Venn, Harold Fuller of Sudan Interior Mission and Geoffrey Dearsley of S.U.M. Fellowship; Winter, "Four Men, Three Eras," 20; Ralph Winter, "Frontier Mission Perspectives," in *Seeds of Promise: World Consultation on Frontier Missions*, Edinburgh '80, ed. Allan Starling (Pasadena,: William Carey Library, 1981), 59; and Ralph Winter, "The Long Look: Eras of Mission History," in *Perspectives on the World Christian Movement: A Reader*, ed. Ralph Winter and Steven Hawthorne (Pasadena,: William Carey Library, 1981), 170.

stage, where expatiate workers train local leaders as a church movement emerges and they still play an important role in overall leadership; the partnering stage, where the missionary and the national church work together; and the participation stage, where missionaries work at the invitation of the national church. The line represents the status of the Christian movement within the people group, moving potentially from zero percent on the left where there are no believers to 100 percent on the right where everyone is a believer

FIGURE 8
The Changing Missionary Role

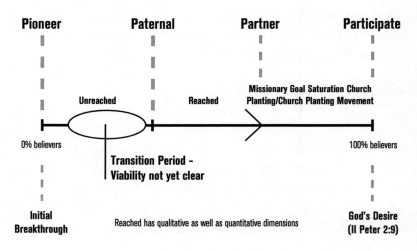

From the point of view of a mission agency, they would be involved in multiple social settings where the status of Christianity was varied in each place. The issue for many in the mission community is that recognition of the imbalance of missionary placement in the world (where most cross-cultural workers are in social settings where there are lots of Christians, and there are many peoples and places with little or no Christians and churches) problematized their presence in places with growing and maturing Christian movements. Mission agencies and their workers were faced with the question of what to do with their current staff in places where the church exists in light of the tremendous need for workers among people groups without church movements.

If I were to summarize what some of the responses have been in this environment, I would characterize it by two poles. Standard mission agencies with historic commitments to national churches across a broad geographic spectrum have tended to answer the "what to do" question by continuing to do the same thing. They feel uncomfortable with the implications of the call to go where the church does not exist and resent the implication that they are in some sense second class citizens in the mission community because they are not working among the unreached. The other pole is represented by those in the frontier mission stream. At the most radical level, the message is stop going where the church exists, redeploy current staff to do new church planting among the unreached and mobilize all resources for such labor.

I have oversimplified and overdrawn the picture here for purposes of illustrating my point. Both of these poles have strengths in their commitments and approaches, but they have trouble hearing the contributions of the other side. What I particularly want to do with this diagram is to help mission agencies with broad historic commitments to see that a comprehensive approach that values and utilizes existing staff in their current locations is possible. Being comprehensive means that agencies, workers and teams intentionally orient themselves to seeing God's will worked out among all people who are not reconciled to God and people in their groupness as well. This entails not only helping individuals find personal salvation, but seeing church movements rooted within whole sociocultural systems where the Gospel previously was unknown. What follows here are some of the hallmarks of what a comprehensive approach looks like when played out by a mission team in a single social setting and its sending agency.

1. In the past, the issue has been framed in terms of whether or not a people group is "reached." The corollary is that mission agencies need to move their resources towards groups that are "unreached." The problem is that this approach ignores the realities of cross-cultural workers already located in places where the church exists. My suggestion is that we reframe the problem by moving past the reached/unreached distinction. Acknowledging that these technical terms are helpful human constructs, it is quite clear that the problem area is not reached and unreached, since it is relatively easy to determine if there are no Christians present or if there are large and very powerful church movements. The critical issue lies in the transition zone I have noted in the diagram where the church is small and is approaching the arbitrary limits that define "reachedness" (which is two percent Evangelical Christian). Much of the world's distinct ethnolinguistic peoples fall somewhere on either side of this number. The reality is that within those social settings there are vast numbers of people who have not experienced salvation and are not part of a fellowship of believers.

2. I propose that we make "reachedness" a moot point, since the arbitrary assignment of two percent Evangelical does not anywhere near embrace what God wants to see happen inside a given social system. The statistical view of the status of Christianity among the ethnolinguistic peoples of the world, as represented in the Joshua Project database, is a phenomenal tool that challenges us in many dimensions, but if used as the only criterion for macro decisions regarding cross-cultural worker placement, it is misleading and inadequate to the task.

3. If we have a mission team on the ground with expertise in a given cultural setting, they should be pursuing the goal of making disciples to the farthest fringes of that culture and inserting the vision of that movement moving full cycle to send out its own cross-cultural workers to participate in God's global vision

for this world. The work of saturation church planting, seeking to plant a living witness within an accessible distance of every person in that culture, is not just a stage, but a goal and strategy from the very beginning.

4. What should the church do when cross-cultural workers are in place where the church already exists? A comprehensive view affirms the value of these workers and at the same time reorients them to a global view and apostolic identity rather than seeing themselves only in a supportive role. Veteran workers, who in some cases have played a role in "picking the lock" to bring the Gospel into that culture or who have extensive language and culture skills, are key people who can help the emerging church to develop a Scriptural vision for reaching all peoples and people. Often they bring the unique "outsider" vision to see areas within an emerging church that need to be strengthened in light of the New Testament vision of the church. The challenge of laboring shoulder to shoulder in saturation church planting with emerging leaders, modeling evangelistic passion, training a new generation of leaders and bringing a missionary vision, structure and strategy to a church movement is of vital strategic importance.

5. One of the foundations of a comprehensive approach is the dynamic rather than static view of the missionary role. The pioneer, paternal, partner, and participant in this view are not just seen as happening in a sequence, although there is a sense in which they are sequential, but rather they are re-happening all the time. They become the driving spirit to the work of the missionary. For instance, in a strong existing church planting movement, the missionary who keeps in mind the dynamic of these four stages will always be looking for ways to lead fresh pioneering initiatives to the least-reached, both inside and outside that particular group. This pioneering may take the form of working together with Christians of that culture,

and it may represent their own first forays into cross-cultural mission, but the pioneering spirit remains the driving force of the missionary. The stages are recreated as new outreaches and mission ventures are initiated. In this new framework, the missionary carries in his heart a local and global perspective, so that everything done locally has an impact on God's global purpose to see all peoples reached. This means that every current missionary no matter, where they are located, can play a strategic role both for that single people group and those who are least-reached in the world.

A comprehensive approach and mission agencies

In attempting to demonstrate how a comprehensive approach can work in real-world missions, I used an illustration that focused primarily on the contribution of individual missionaries. When the premise that "reached" is not the terminal point of mission is accepted, this opens the door for a radical reorientation of missionary labor in all cultures whether they are reached or unreached in the technical sense of these terms. This reorientation, however, goes beyond the labors of cross-cultural workers in a single setting to impact the work of mission agencies as a whole. In this section I want to explore some of the implications of the challenge delivered by the core message of the frontier mission movement concerning the urgency to reach the least-reached.

1. One of the potentially powerful contributions that the "where" framework can have upon a mission agency is to recast all of their work into a global framework. Rather than seeing their work as fulfilling the Great Commission in discrete units, such as countries, the frontier mission perspective raises the horizon to a truly global level to challenge every church movement, at whatever stage of growth, to participate in taking the Gospel to

those who have never heard. It is precisely this reframing that brings a strategic dimension to cross-cultural work regardless of the status of Christianity among that particular group. This means that agencies of all stripes can forsake either/or thinking, and begin to move into a both/and mode that accepts the tensions between the poles of reached/unreached and peoples/people.

2. A large part of what made the frontier mission movement necessary was the fact that successful mission work inherently carries the seeds of people blindness and the temptation to become caught up in maintaining what has been started. A comprehensive approach means that mission agency leadership sees one of its roles as fighting the natural spiritual entropy that leads away from a pioneering passion to reach the least-reached. In a practical sense, this means that every agency needs to continually work to see that all mission staff operates upon three focal points:

   A. What is currently being done, both personally and as a mission in this culture, to reach those who have never heard and are geographically and culturally near or far?

   B. What is being done to disciple this people to the very edges of the society and to plant the church so that every person has an opportunity to be confronted with a relevant witness of the Gospel?

   C. What is being done to bring the national church organization to full participation in world mission and to reach the least-reached?

3. Being comprehensive means that agencies have to read both Scripture and the increasingly available empirical data concerning the status of Christianity among all the peoples of the world. Studying the information on the unreached and least-reached

does not in any way hinder agencies or their staff from being guided by the Holy Spirit. Agencies can use this information to analyze their current work and seek to mobilize their mission teams and the national church entities they are in partnership with to penetrate truly unreached groups that are within their sphere of ministry. Many times, church movements and mission efforts literally exist right next to a people group that is totally cut off from the Gospel. The natural tendency toward people-blindness means that one can easily overlook these God-given opportunities. By prayerfully considering the current data on the least-reached, mission agencies can prepare themselves to hear the voice of the Spirit to find ways to touch these groups.

4. A commitment to a comprehensive approach means that the issue of imbalance in personnel is taken seriously. As I have noted above, citing Ralph Winter, redeployment and sending all new staff to the unreached are not the answers. But the fact is the majority of existing personnel are among groups that do have existing church movements. We know too much today in terms of hard data to be complacent about this issue. It is time for agencies to fast and pray over this data and corporately seek God's agenda for them as an organization. They also need to find creative ways to share this information with new potential personnel so that they have the spiritual need of the entire world before them, and not simply the parts with the most Christians, as they seek to hear God's voice and direction for their lives. Agency leadership would do well to keep in tension the recognition of the sovereign calling of the Spirit in people's lives coupled with the acknowledgment that perhaps we have not always understood the cry of the Holy Spirit to reach those in the least-reached places, areas of difficult access, severe resistance, and often grinding poverty.

5. Finally, agencies need to view themselves as service agents to their constituents. Agencies have expertise to offer in cross-

cultural mission. The trend towards hands-on involvement and the corresponding amateurization of mission that it leads to cannot be controlled, but it can be influenced at the training level. Penetrating new cultures and working to plant churches as widely as possible is not a work to be undertaken lightly. It cannot be accomplished by a kind of brief foray into a new place with a sincerity of heart, but lack of expertise and longevity. Agencies have long-term experience and can play a vital role in shaping the new energy being released by the challenge of the last mission frontiers.

Integrating the Four Paradigms

In the previous section I developed the theme of seeking a comprehensive approach in mission practice. I now want to examine the notion of integrating the insights of the various paradigms. As I noted in chapter 1, the streams of missions concerned with church growth, Christian social concern, and unreached peoples are often seen as being competing forms or at least somewhat incompatible. While there is a great deal of overlap and shared values among all three of these, the fact remains that many cross-cultural workers and agencies see themselves and their work primarily within the framework of one of these major streams.

I would suggest that all the participants in mission (see figure 3, page 32) would benefit from bringing more Scriptural insight into their thinking and practice by intentionally seeking to integrate the biblical commitments and key concepts of all these paradigms, rather than just one. I believe that it would be beneficial to examine and evaluate present work as well as for planning future labor to look through all of the lenses that these frameworks provide as figure 9 illustrates.[295]

---

295 It was in a conversation with DeLonn Rance about paradigm integration that the idea came for turning the "lenses" I was using to illustrate this procedure to the side to highlight looking "through" them rather than just "at" them.

FIGURE 9
Integrating Mission Paradigms

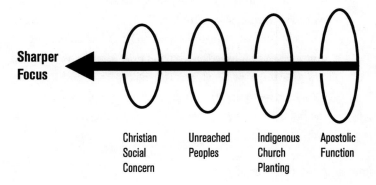

Sharper Focus

| Christian Social Concern | Unreached Peoples | Indigenous Church Planting | Apostolic Function |

The process of utilizing multiple lenses is helpful because it brings a greater breadth of scriptural insight to bear upon one's work. Rather than seeing things in just one frame, it allows for multiple views and challenges and critiques of what one does. The process of integration can be carried out by any of the participants in God's mission with benefit, but it is an exercise that is particularly fruitful at the level of the mission agency and field team. I see it as a corporate exercise that involves reflection on the biblical commitments central to each paradigm and seeking the Spirit's guidance on how these insights are to be worked out in particular contexts.

I envision this process involving the following components. The four paradigms are apostolic function, which is the paradigm of missionary identity, church planting and growth, frontier mission and pioneering work among the unreached and least-reached, and Christian social concern. Taken together the biblical ideas and related concepts function as tools that help us in working out the mission of God. It is important that we keep in mind the distinctions between the actual biblical texts, the history of exegesis and interpretations of those texts, and the concepts and applications that have grown from this body of interpretation. The first is divine in origin, while the second and third are human endeavors. We need to continually remind ourselves that our human attempts at developing conceptual tools is a process done while "seeing through a glass darkly" and we need to be open to ongoing critique and refinement as we grow in our understanding of Scripture.

In terms of process, the first step is to locate the core concepts of each framework. As I have noted, each of these paradigms has a set of key ideas that are very clear. When pressed too far, or made the single lens through which we work, they can become "fuzzy" at the edge. Once we have settled on these major ideas, the second step is to develop a set of questions that grow out of these concepts. Step three is to use these questions for both prayer and reflection in order to discern how they will be worked out in the particular context under consideration. Thus, this is not in any way a mechanical exercise, but rather a demanding one where we lay our agendas down and seek the guidance of the Holy Spirit as we reflect on God's Word. One of the explicit values of this exercise is the belief that the mission team cannot fully discern what needs to be done until they are aware of the status of the Christian movement within the specific context under consideration. A second is that we have a human tendency to do what we have always done, and the process of posing questions and thoughtfully working through them challenges the status quo of our normal ministry patterns.

In the remainder of this section, I want to illustrate steps one and two of this integration process. I am not attempting to be exhaustive; I simply want to provide an example of what the process of building questions out of a key concept can look like.

Apostolic function

KEY CONCEPT:

A mission team that coheres around the focus to insure that the Gospel is preached and churches planted in places and peoples where Christ is not known and that uses the synergy of its giftings to work towards seeing apostolic genius and missional DNA imparted to the church movement they are working in no matter what its size.

QUESTIONS:

1. In the church movement that our team is working among, at what points does it need to be strengthened in its missional understanding?

2. How is our team currently contributing to the evangelization and discipling of a unreached or least-reached people?

3. In what ways do our present activities as a team contribute to seeing a New Testament church established?

4. Are we periodically revaluating the work in our setting and our roles in it?

5. Is any of our work redundant with what is being done by the local church?

Church planting/growth

KEY CONCEPT:

Planting indigenous churches and a church movement that is self-supporting, governing, propagating, theologizing, and missionizing.

QUESTIONS:

1. How is the church movement we are involved in doing in regards to the five marks of indigeneity?

2. Is the work we are doing helping to contribute to a responsible New Testament church?

3. Are we scanning the environment to see what is in the best interest of this church movement?

Christian social concern

KEY CONCEPT:

God's Kingdom rule has been inaugurated in the life, death, and resurrection of Jesus and the Spirit has been poured out to carry out God's mission to create new communities of faith that live under his rule.

QUESTIONS:

1. What would the setting we are working in look like if God's will were being done?

2. What are the social implications of the coming of God's rule among the people of God and the greater community?

3. Who needs to be shown the compassion of Jesus in this social setting?

Frontier mission to the unreached/least-reached

KEY CONCEPT:

Plant the church across cultural boundaries among people groups that do not have an existing church movement capable of evangelizing and discipling their own people without outside assistance.

QUESTIONS:

1. How are our efforts in our current setting contributing to the planting of the church among the unreached/least-reached?

2. Who are the people groups that are geographically within our reach that do not have church planting movements?

3. Are we studying, promoting, engaging, or contacting an unreached people group?

What is important about this exercise is that it intentionally seeks to link together concerns that are often separated within mission agencies or teams into departments or that are not even part of the normal ethos of the organization. Examining our specific work, in a particular time and social setting by shining the light through all four of these paradigms brings a sharpness of focus and biblical critique. When questions of our identity as a team, where we work, and what and how we do it are brought into focus all at the same time, it can protect us from our own preferred interests and biases and tendency to move towards a maintenance mode rather than staying tuned to the specific guidance of the Holy Spirit. A sincere attempt at integrating all four of these paradigms means that we cannot simply plant churches and ignore the social implications of the good news in that society; nor can we care for physical needs without seeking to plant new communities of people reconciled to God. We cannot plan to go to the least-reached without considering the health and viability of church movements that are emerging; and at the same time we are challenged to see those who do not have church movements even while working in traditional fields where the church already exists.

8

ISSUES RELATED TO THE "WHERE" QUESTION IN MISSIONS

A simple summary of the thinking behind this book looks something like this:

1. An understanding of the Bible: God's mission is to see all of humanity reconciled to him. His people in every age are the vessels through whom he works to accomplish this plan. Jesus asked his followers to make disciples throughout the entire world.

2. An observation of the world: when we look at the world today from the perspective of God's mission we find that there are vast areas and peoples who are not aware of the reconciling work of his Son neither do they have a living expression of God's people among them.

3. An observation of the church: the places that have the most believers and churches are continuing to work with each other and ignore for the most part these areas that have the fewest believers and churches.

The bulk of this book deals with how God's people can grapple with this imbalance in where there is access to the message of reconciliation. The concepts and ideas that I have interacted with and introduced are powerful tools that help focus our attention on places and peoples who have had very limited opportunity to hear and respond to the message about redemption through Jesus Christ.

But these ideas are controversial and contested. It is not by accident that the current configuration and frontiers of faith/unbelief exist in the world; thus ideas that challenge the status quo create discomfort. In this final chapter I take a look at some of the issues that are generated from thinking about bringing the Gospel to places where Christ is not known. I structure this chapter around a cluster of three major issues: those relating to the placement of cross-cultural workers, questions of terminology, and problems growing out of our human constructs.

ISSUES RELATING TO THE PLACEMENT OF CROSS-CULTURAL WORKERS

At some point when you look at the task of taking the Gospel to the world and making disciples of the *ethne* you have to broach the issue of deciding where cross-cultural workers will go. No matter what form the mission enterprise takes, from apostolic bands, to workers sent from local churches, or full blown mission agencies; somewhere in the process decisions will be made on where the work will be done.[296] If you take the three observations that I have opened this chapter with, it might appear that the obvious solution is to simply move all existing personnel and material resources to the places where there are the

---

296 McGavran argues that it is the role of missionary statesmanship to assign priorities about where the work should be pursued; Donald Anderson McGavran, *The Bridges of God: A Study in the Strategy of Missions* (New York: Friendship Press, 1955), 114-17. Even in mission agencies where personal calling is the primary determinant of where a worker goes, the reality is that mission leadership still wields a great deal of influence. This occurs both at the broader level in terms of the kind of information that is communicated to the supporting constituency where workers come from, and in the kind of information and opportunities that are shared with potential candidates who feel a call or burden to cross-cultural work but who do not have a specific place in mind as they come to the agency.

fewest Christians. In fact, this kind of suggestion has been made and I have argued that it is a misunderstanding and misappropriation of principles. However, the response generated to these three observations has created a great deal of unease among parts of the church involved in missions. Both Evangelicals and Pentecostals have expressed misgivings with some of the methodologies that have arisen to address the unreached world.

One of the leading critics has been Samuel Escobar who levels the charges of an excessive reliance on a quantitative approach, pragmatism, reducing missionary action to a linear task and logical steps to be managed by objectives, turning the evangelistic task into a process based on marketing principles, and the problems associated with American functionalist social science and its limited view of social change.[297] Much of the substance of the managerial critique has been also leveled at church growth practices. Yoder points out that church growth theory had its origin in observing mission churches, some of which grew rapidly and others that did not.[298] From these observations theories and methods were developed which aimed at helping people to become followers of Christ and members of local churches. The problem, as Yoder points out, is that this seemed to focus on managing and engineering social and cultural factors to get people into church and to start new ones.[299] He also notes a lack of theological reflection on the nature of the church and its mission and

---

297 Samuel Escobar, "Evangelical Missiology: Peering in the Future," in *Global Missiology for the 21st Century: The Iguassu Dialogue*, ed. William D. Taylor (Grand Rapids: Baker Academic, 2000), pp. 109-112; for a specific response to Escobar's criticisms see Levi T. DeCarvalho, "What's Wrong with the Label "Managerial Missiology"," *International Journal of Frontier Missions* 18, no. 3 (2001):141-46.

298 Lawrence M. Yoder, "Church Growth Theories in Indonesia," in *Evangelical, Ecumenical, and Anabaptist Missiologies in Conversation: Essays in Honor of Wilbert Shenk*, ed. James R. Krabill, Walter Sawatsky, and Charles Van Engen (Maryknoll: Orbis Books, 2006), 110.

299 Ibid., 110-111.

the transformation of life that turning to Christ should produce.[300] Engel and Dryness go back even further to the late 1800s and note that dominant Evangelicals called for accelerated evangelism with the return of Christ being a primary motivating theme.[301] In their opinion, "it would almost seem as if the future of the world and the ultimate victory of Christ had become dependent on human initiative."[302] In their view, method-driven missions has a number of undesirable and unintended consequences: an uncritical adoption of strategic planning, a preoccupation with numerical success, an unhealthy relationship between numerical success and funding, and reducing the Gospel to presenting the plan of salvation so that it becomes a mass-marketed consumer product that is a manageable enterprise.[303] The Pentecostal critique has focused on how the push to reach all peoples has been approached in a mechanistic fashion that ignores the role of the Holy Spirit in leading and directing missionary efforts.[304]

---

300 Ibid., 111.

301 James F. Engel and William A. Dryness, *Changing the Mind of Missions: Where Have We Gone Wrong?* (Downers Grove: InterVarsity Press, 2000), 64.

302 Ibid., 64-65.

303 Ibid., 68-69. For a general overview of the values of American missiology, see Miriam Adeney, "Telling Stories: Contextualization and American Missiology," in *Global Missiology for the 21st Century: The Iguassu Dialogue*, ed. William D. Taylor (Grand Rapids: Baker Academic, 2000), 377-388.

304 Everett Wilson notes that while Hogan was personal friends with mission theorists like McGavran, Nida, and Glasser, he felt that as a whole church growth theory had severe limitations; Wilson, 63. Wilson observes that "he especially parted company with what he believed to be a reductionist view of missions as mechanics. Some extremes of church growth theory, he protested, made the guiding principles of missionary deployment into mere abstract coefficients of need—the relative per capita Christian population of a given country or the proportion of the total missionary force allocated to a given field"; Ibid., 64. In an address that Hogan gave to the EFMA in 1970, he makes clear his contrasting view of the work of the Spirit versus human management: "I have long since ceased to be interested in meetings where mission leaders are called together to a room filled with charts, maps, graphs, and statistics. All one needs to do to find plenteous harvest is simply to follow the leading of the Spirit"; Ibid., 136.

The points raised are well taken and are needed to help advocates of unreached people group thinking to refine their views and to guard against the pitfalls of pragmatism. In the final section I will address the problem of pragmatism as it relates to EPC streams of mission in general. Here, however, I want to offer a perspective that is mindful of the critique, but moves past it. It is important to keep in mind that the critique offered does not assail the core concept, which is the need to take the message of the Gospel to all people. While the observations are sound, the problem is that the critique can be used by some as a reason to dismiss the whole enterprise of frontier missions rather than grappling with its' central thesis and seeking a way to fulfill the heart cry of those who advocate for the need of the unreached without falling into the traps they have enumerated. In this section, I want to acknowledge the critique, but seek a more constructive path towards the task of church planting that deals with the issues surfaced by those critical of the frontier mission movement.

First, we need to be careful in distinguishing between a problem with a concept in and of itself and with its application. Simply because some have taken a managerial or mechanical approach to addressing the reality of people groups without church movements does not invalidate the idea in and of itself. It would be easier to hear the critique if there was a clear effort on the part of those involved to concretely provide better ways to conduct mission so as to bring the Gospel to unreached people groups rather than dismissing it as a mistaken missiology. The empirical reality of large blocks of people without a witness of the Gospel and viable, culturally relevant church movements demands a response, but it is not required to be a mechanistic one.

A second consideration is the relationship between known information and the guidance of the Holy Spirit. Once we know something, it is not wise or reasonable to attempt to act as if we do not know that thing.

This is the weakness in both the Evangelical and Pentecostal critique. It is not enough to say that one should not be managerial or mechanical without providing a means for addressing the issue at hand. Neither Evangelical nor Pentecostal critiques are able to argue the non-existence of large blocks of humanity that have fewer Christians and churches present among them. All they have been able to do is to assert that they do not like the current suggested approaches for the mission world to address this issue. The presence of information does not negate the working of the Holy Spirit or of necessity destroy spiritual dynamics.

Think of the difference between the role of a pastor and that of a guest speaker. A pastor has knowledge of the people in a way that the outside speaker does not have. However, that knowledge does not ruin the pastor's ability to be led by the Spirit; rather it is a matter that the guidance of the Spirit will be different in terms of what to do in light of that information. It is, however, still possible to be led by the Spirit even when knowing information. The rule of thumb is that the guest speaker prepares in light of the knowledge she has, and the pastor does the same. The fact of more detailed knowledge does not deprive pastors of the ability or necessity of being guided by the Spirit in their work. In the same way, just because we know about ethnolinguistic groups that do not have church movements, that knowledge does not take away our ability or necessity to be led by the Holy Spirit as we seek a response.

A related issue is that of receptivity. Both church growth theorists and Pentecostals affirm that it is important to take the Gospel to the receptive. They arrive at this conclusion by coming at the issue from opposite sides of the issue. For church growth theorists, a decision about placement can be based on a detailed study of the situation such that the place of labor is determined by where there are the most factors that would indicate receptivity to the message. Pentecostals would reject such a notion and hold that one should go where there is evidence of the moving of the Spirit in terms of response. From both of these positions, the difficulty with going to places where there are the fewest Christians and church movements is that, on the whole, they are the least receptive and have the least happening among them in terms of harvest.

My response to this is two-fold. First, one of the values of a comprehensive and integrative approach is both/and rather than either/or thinking. To advocate for the unreached is to plead for new church planting where the church does not exist and is not in any way to argue against putting workers among receptive populations. A balanced view that takes into consideration the Bible's evidence about God's concern for both people as individuals and as groups rejects any approach that will pit one against the other. I also believe that we need a theology of preparation and seed planting to work in tandem with our thinking about receptivity. It would be a mistake to allow the concept of receptivity to become the analog to the hyper-Calvinism of Carey's day where we argue that God will make these groups receptive in his own time and way. In John 4:38, in the context of well-known passage about the fields being ripe for harvest, Jesus tells the disciples that they will reap what they have not worked for, that others have done the hard work and they will reap the benefits of their labor. A "theology of the hard work" is needed so that the seed of the Gospel can be planted among many peoples and settings that will one day bring about a receptivity that will require many laborers putting their hands to the harvest.

A final issue related to worker placement is that of calling. Many missions communities place a great emphasis on a sense of calling for determining where cross-cultural workers serve. The issue for mission agencies becomes how to handle the role that information plays in calling. While acknowledging the sovereignty of God in directing his servants, both practical and empirical evidence show that, in general, information plays some kind of role in people determining their sense of call to missionary service.[305] It is the exception and not the rule to find that people have had some level of exposure to a place or people that is involved in their sense of being called to work among them, rather than hearing from God something that was completely new information to them. If this is the case, the question becomes what to do with people who say that they are called to go to places with large numbers of Christians and churches who have never had any exposure to the world that does not have this. Is it truly fair and reasonable to say that such a person is specifically "called" to that place, which in this new era they have generally visited on a short-term trip, when they have never received clear information on the world where the church does not exist? I have now come back around to my original point in this section dealing with information. Our knowledge of the status of Christianity among the world's peoples cannot be erased from our minds, nor can it force us to not be led by the Spirit. What this knowledge does do is to collectively make us responsible to share it. It becomes incumbent on those who value the guidance of the Holy Spirit and the role of calling in missions to make this information known to their constituency of potential missionary candidates so that they can pray for the guidance of the Spirit in how to respond.

---

305 See DeLonn Lynn Rance, "The Empowered Call: The Activity of the Holy Spirit in Salvadoran Assemblies of God Missionaries" (Ph.D., Fuller, 2004). In examining the call of Salvadoran missionaries, Rance found numerous factors, many of which relate directly to some kind of information conveyed either through first hand personal experience, a personal relationship with another person, or some form of communication media. In looking at the issue of calling, Rance observes that "the interviews clearly indicated that the Spirit uses a diversity of forms, manners or means by which the missionary call is communicated and confirmed"; Ibid., 197. Spiritual disciplines such as prayer and Scripture reading and supernatural spiritual experiences like dreams, visions, prophetic words play an important role, but a number of factors emerged in the interviews that clearly are oriented to some kind of information. Ibid. This includes missions conventions, conferences, retreats, the influence of mentors, encounters with missionaries, personal relationships, short-term trips and other cross-cultural experiences, missionary training centers, institutes and Bible schools, reading missionary biography and listening to missionary testimonies; Ibid., 197, 206, 211, 219, 253.

ISSUES RELATING TO TERMINOLOGY

I touched on this briefly in the chapter on apostolic function. I noted there in the discussion of the relationship between the terms apostle and missionary that the two were tied together and could be construed in a wider or more narrow sense. The final determination was dependent on which elements were emphasized. Here I want to delve into a related area, that of coming to terms with the meaning and use of "missionary." While it is the use of this word in English that is my main focus, the influence of the Western missionary movement means that the word is often borrowed and taken wholesale into other languages along with the conceptual difficulties that I will talk about here.

Let me summarize first what I perceive is the kernel of the terminological problem. While "missionary" has a lot of negative baggage in some contexts, for many in the EPC streams, the missionary epitomizes the ultimate values of the Christian life. It stands for sacrifice, obedience, and above all, is connected with the sharing of the Gospel message. Thus, for many Christians, the word "missionary" has outgrown its original connection to the idea of cross-cultural and geographic boundaries to plant the church and become a motivating symbol for witnessing, mobilizing for ministry and fundraising. Many Christians find it very helpful to consider themselves as a "missionary" in their everyday life, thus tapping into the vision of sharing the Gospel within the context of their daily routine. They can be a "missionary to their neighbors" and "everyone is a missionary." Thinking of themselves in terms of missionary symbolism helps to lead them towards obedience in sharing the good news of Jesus Christ, which is the heart of missionary endeavor. In terms of mobilizing and fundraising, the symbol of the missionary is much more powerful than other forms of service. Thus, to attach "missionary" to an activity is to endue it with a higher level of commitment, sacrifice and spiritual value. A trip to visit a rural church takes on a whole new image when cast as a "mission" trip. The use of the phrase "mission of God" and the use of "missional" have served to heighten the importance of everyone taking part in the mission and thus being "missionary."

It is not hard to see from the discussion above that we are right back where we started with the observation of Stephen Neill that when everything is mission nothing is mission. People who find the use of the term "missionary" a motivational tool to help them in seeing their role of sharing the Gospel in their everyday life contexts have told me that they find it very disempowering when they hear me argue for a narrow definition of mission. Seeing what they are doing as evangelism does not carry the same freight as thinking of it as mission. In the current climate in North American Christianity, I have heard some younger leaders express resentment at the seeming hegemonic control that foreign missions has over the term missionary. Their reasoning is that there has been a huge emphasis on "missionary" work "overseas" such that local Christians are willing to give money to help reach people outside their own borders, but will not make any effort to share the good news with their neighbors. Consequently, the cross-cultural mission enterprise is seen as competing for space with the missionality of local churches. This kind of thinking leads to a flattening where we are all missionaries, doing the work of God in sharing the Gospel.

One day I was teaching a class of leaders and we had been talking in detail about the distinctions between evangelism, cross-cultural evangelism, and people groups that have no church movements. I kept fielding questions about whether or not a certain form of ministry was "missionary?" In my answers I consistently drove the students back to use the concepts we had talked about relating to the E and P scales and asked them to answer their own questions within those frameworks. The issue that caused the most consternation was sending people from their ethnolinguistic group to another geographic location in the world to gather Christians and win non-Christians of that particular group.

They wanted to call that "missionary" work because it was happening in another country even though it was among their own people. They found that there were various benefits in terms of raising support and workers around the idea of this being missionary activity.

In working through these questions, I ended up drawing the following schematic:

FIGURE 10
Three Distinct Kinds of Ministry

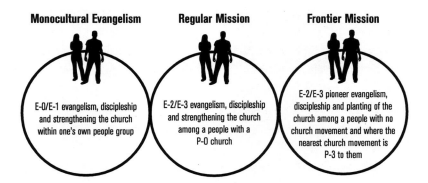

Monocultural Evangelism	Regular Mission	Frontier Mission
E-0/E-1 evangelism, discipleship and strengthening the church within one's own people group	E-2/E-3 evangelism, discipleship and strengthening the church among a people with a P-0 church	E-2/E-3 pioneer evangelism, discipleship and planting of the church among a people with no church movement and where the nearest church movement is P-3 to them

You can call Christian workers whatever you want. If you want to call people who are evangelizing their own people missionaries, that is fine, but please realize that if you do, you have to find some kind of terminology to distinguish between that activity, and those who go to another culture to work among Christians, and those who go to pioneer the church where it does not exist or is very small. The problem with applying the term missionary to every form of ministry sharing the Gospel is that by making everything the same, the reality of people blindness will mean that those different than us will be left out.[306]

---

306 I later discovered an article by Winter that addresses a similar problem with the term missiology and suggests that there are three distinct kinds of missiology that parallel the three kinds of distinct ministry I am describing here. Winter notes that words do gain expanded meaning, that no one owns the words "mis-

In terms of the E and P scale, there are three distinct kinds of workers that we need to have acceptable terms for, and that need to remain separable. Workers doing evangelism within their own sociocultural setting which is E-0 and E-1; cross-cultural workers who connect with existing church movements, thus they are E-2 or 3 among a P-0/P-1 people group, meaning that it has a cultural relevant church present among that group; and finally, cross-cultural workers where the church does not exist or is very small, which is E-2 or 3 among a P3 people. If you call the first missionary, then you must have some kind of added adjective for the next two. If you call the first evangelism and the next two mission, then as Winter has done you must add adjectives (such as "regular" and "frontier") to distinguish between the next two. A more precise alternative would be to discard the term missionary altogether and talk only about forms of evangelism and use the terminology of the E and P Scale. But that is hardly realistic as there is very little motivational or fundraising power in trying to encourage people to do E-1 outreach to their neighbors or go on an E-3/P-0 mission trip.

Terminology would not be an issue were it not for our natural tendency to see people who are like us and remain blind to those who are different. It could be that the study of light in physics gives us a rubric

---

sion" or "missiology," and "that the *purposeful* element in the meaning of the word *mission* allows us to describe any purposeful activity as mission"; Ralph Winter, "Missiological Education for Lay People," In *Missiological Education for the Twenty-First Century: The Book, the Circle, and the Sandals,* ed. J. Dudley Woodberry, Charles Van Engen and Edgar J. Elliston (Maryknoll: Orbis, 1996), 177-178. The three kinds of missiology that are talked about and practiced today are: intracultural or the missiology of church growth which includes growth in internal quality and planting churches within the same people group; interchurch missiology, the "activity of believers in one part of the world who are working among other believers at a distance, across significant cultural barriers," thus interchurch missiology is *cross-cultural intracultural missiology* (178); and classical or frontier missiology, which is the Pauline kind of missiology which is "believers reaching out from their own culture to begin work in *new groups in which Christ is not yet named,* or at least within those peoples where there is not yet a 'viable, indigenous, evangelizing church movement'" (179).

for interpreting Scripture on the theme of mission. Just as light has the characteristics of both a wave and particle, so mission inseparably has both narrow and broad dimensions. When you look through one framework at the mission of God, everyone is a part of that mission. However, from another perspective missionary work can be seen in a narrow fashion, consisting of those who specifically plant the church among peoples where Jesus is not known. As light is one, so mission is one; as light has both particle and wave properties, the work of mission embraces all of God's people in its broadest sense, and yet also has properties where it is the task of a few working cross-culturally to pioneer the church in a social setting where Christ is not known.

ISSUES RELATING TO OUR USE OF HUMAN CONSTRUCTS

I never pick up a book on the history of Christianity or church history without feeling moved towards tears and laughter by practices and beliefs that were at one time a part of our history in church life and mission. From the perspective of one's own age, you wonder how they could have ever understood Christianity and the Christian mission in that way. This experience however, also makes me wonder what others will want to laugh and cry at in the years ahead as they look back at our practice of mission.

In fact, even among our contemporaries, the notion of mission and missionaries can be unpopular. People who do not share our view of the authority of God's Word, whether inside or outside of institutional Christianity, find the proclamation of the good news of Jesus Christ among the peoples of the world to be an exercise in intolerance and arrogance. While there is always value in listening to critique from whatever source, I am interested not in the views of those who do not share our assumptions about the Scripture, but rather in critique that is generated from within the EPC missions movements themselves. It is a healthy exercise to put what we are doing under the light and judgment of God's Word. I am making these remarks here not as a trained theologian, but as a practitioner who draws on a number of sources both written and via personal conversations. My goal is to put mission in the EPC streams in a theological context that needs to shape our practice, rather than the other way around.

My first observation is that we do mission in response to God who speaks. He has revealed his plan and our role in it. Yet I want to assert that finding and understanding God's will as to how it should be worked out in specific settings is not an easy thing.[307] It becomes too tempting for us to identify our constructs and practices with the truth, as if we had it all right. There is an ongoing need to stand back and look at our understandings and practices from other angles. Thus, the proper attitude towards our missiologies should be one of humility.

With humility as a baseline attitude for our reflection, I think that we need to remember that the "where" question of missions today has grown out of an observation about the state of our world in light of the Great Commission. The question then becomes, having made that observation, what are we going to do about it? There is no way to get around the fact that some places and peoples of our world have the presence of church movements and many Christians while others do not. To either ignore it or act as if we can simply roll up our shirt sleeves, divide up the task and get the job done is to respond with a lack of

---

307 Sawatsky's observation is relevant here: "All the most common biblical texts for mission motivation manifest the vision that the gospel is for all. Yet our telling of the story, and hence our appropriating it theologically, particularly ecclesiologically, is even now less than 'for all the nations.' Like Israel of old, the frequent bias has been toward separate parts of the *missio dei* that we claim for our denomination, our confessional tradition, or our civilization. That is, the historically shaped vision of God's church we carry has been insufficiently true to the evangel of God's intent for the *oikumene*." Walter Sawatsky, "What If the Three Worlds of Christian History Converged?," in *Evangelical, Ecumenical, and Anabaptist Missiologies in Conversation: Essays in Honor of Wilbert Shenk*, ed. James R. Krabill, Walter Sawatsky, and Charles Van Engen (Maryknoll: Orbis Books, 2006), 38.

humility. Although these positions appear to be polar opposites, they have at their core the hubris that thinks we have somehow understood God's heart completely and, thus, know how to proceed.

What I am advocating here is that all of us collectively approach our participation in God's mission with a sense of awe and wonder, reverent fear, a willingness to self-critique and openness to learn from others in the Body of Christ. There is a danger in the whole enterprise of writing with its false sense of finality that comes from the completed copy to think that what I have discussed, argued, and advocated here is the right way to pursue mission. These are human constructs, forged around our attempts at understanding the Word of God and powerful for that reason, but they do not exhaust what God wants to do in our world.

How then do we approach our human missiological constructs? A humble heart would have us seek to uncover our own brands of syncretism and idolatries. It is easy to forget that the Old Testament passages condemning idolatry among Israel were written to a people who were happily mixing the worship of Yahweh with Baalism to insure agricultural success. Glasser points out that a bifurcation developed in popular thought where the worship of Yahweh focused on national and heavenly matters and Baal worship was used to guarantee fertility both for people and the land.[308] Taber reminds us that in the compartmentalization of modernity, where religion is but one among several "quite distinct, specialized, and autonomous institutions" it becomes possible for the "ultimate allegiance of people to be elsewhere, in quite other domains."[309] He reminds us that whatever is ultimate becomes an idol; and it is precisely here where it becomes possible for us to slip into syncretism with the unseen idols that are

---

308 Glasser, et al., *Announcing the Kingdom*, 115.
309 Taber, 187.

the gods of our age. In John Seel's stinging critique of modernity and Evangelicals, he argues that:

> modernity is for all modern people an unconscious and therefore an invisible reality, lived on the basis of recipe knowledge. It is analogous to what the New Testament refers to as *kosmos*, the human sociological reality that exists in estrangement from God. Modernity defines what is 'real' for modern people. It represents today what the medieval world represented in the years prior to the Reformation . . . simply, the way things are.[310]

In his essay he argues that Evangelicals are particularly blind to the dangers of modernity;[311] while "intellectually defiant they have also been prone to practical accommodation. They carefully maintain theological orthodoxy while simultaneously uncritically accommodating to the tools of modernity . . . ."[312] These tools include the dangers of unchecked consumerism and capitalism's reduction of "all reality to its commodity form,"[313] the values of "market totalitarianism," the values of efficiency, calculability, predictability, and control involved in the process of rationalization[314] and the idolatry of images.[315]

What this means, if Seel is correct in his analysis, is that all the EPC streams are influenced at the deepest level by the double-edged sword of

---

310 Seel, 292.

311 Ibid.

312 Ibid., 295.

313 Ibid., 297.

314 Ibid., 301-302. Ritzer sees the fast-food restaurant as the paradigm of a process he calls McDonaldization, with its emphasis on efficiency, calculability, predictability, and control; George Ritzer, *The McDonaldization of Society*, New Century Edition. (Thousand Oaks: Pine Forge Press, 2000), 12-15, 23. In his view, McDonaldization is "an amplification and extension of Weber's theory of rationalization" where the model was bureaucracy; Ibid., 23.

315 Seel, 304.

modernity. When we scratch beneath the surface of our rhetoric about the leading of the Spirit and spiritual dynamics we find ourselves to be part of a system, and committed to a highly rationalistic organization of everyday life that informs our practice of mission with is emphasis on technical solutions to our problems.[316] Thus, we believe that more money and better technology will solve our problems; our trust in the tenets of rationalization makes us pragmatists who seek efficiency and control as the highest goal, leading us to ask sociological rather than theological questions. As we pursue the efficient production of results based on our market driven indicators of success our agendas supersede all else, while those we purportedly come to serve become the tools that we utilize to achieve our ends.[317]

What would it mean to repent of our pragmatism, linear pursuit of goals, commodification of the Gospel, and market values? It is complicated to forsake the idolatries of our age, precisely because they are so unseen. It is also an exercise that must be done privately and corporately in our various expressions of the body of Christ on an ongoing basis, not a single act; it is our work together to see that we love not the world system nor the things that are in it. Trying to conduct ourselves in mission with an awareness of these dangers means that

---

316 "Technology, on which we now depend in almost all departments of life, is itself the encapsulation of rational principles. Technology is the attempt to provide the most efficient means for certain given ends, and in the acceptance of new scientific techniques for so many social purposes we have become committed to a highly rationalistic organization of everyday life. One implication of this development is that increasingly we come to look for technical solutions to our problems . . . ."; Bryan Wilson, *Religion in Sociological Perspective* (Oxford: Oxford University Press, 1982), 42.

317 A friend of mine who is also an Assemblies of God missionary is finishing up his thesis with the Oxford Centre for Mission Studies on the subject of faith-based organizations and children at risk in Eastern Europe. He has a great line about the pragmatic approaches of Christian organizations that emerged very clearly in his interview data. He says that many of these organizations "put a child in their midst" and then proceeded to run right by the child in pursuit of their own agendas.

we would acknowledge that our missiologies and concepts are human constructs and treat them accordingly; not as final answers but as part of our grappling with Scripture to understand what we should be doing in this present moment. There would be less triumphalist language and more about the Crucified One who came not to be served but to serve and give his life a ransom for many. It would involve learning from others who come at mission from a different paradigm rather than vilifying or rejecting outright their insights into the mission of God. Mission that rejects pragmatism asks more questions, reflects on its assumptions, and admits that you cannot mobilize believers to go to the least-reached based on the canons of rational use of resources. Bang for the buck thinking does not work in the pioneer settings that remain in our world. Such mission also admits that you cannot simply divide up the task, check off the boxes and wait for the results to roll in on a pre-set time line. Mission that follows the Crucified One sets itself up to be vigilant against the power of mammon and the spirit of the world system that encroaches upon all organizations and institutions. Whether we are building up existing churches, caring for physical needs, or pioneering among the unreached, we are wound into systems that involve raising money and managing personnel and material resources. It is too easy for those systems to take on a life of their own, and despite our rhetoric of relying on the Spirit, we become caught up in commitments, institutional habits, and fads that inhibit our ability to hear from God and his Word.

SOME CONCLUDING THOUGHTS

Thinking about mission is a discipline that is done on the fly. As I noted in the introduction of this monograph, it is a dynamic and not static exercise, as the terrain changes with the spread of the Gospel so does the work of those the Lord of the Harvest has commissioned to go out into his world. The argument of this book can be condensed into a single sentence: Go where the church does not exist. That this is not a simple or uncomplicated thing to do is justification for the many pages devoted to arguing various points related to that theme in this book. It is my hope that one day soon, the argument of this book expressed in that single sentence will be a moot point, and a new challenge will have to be made. If it happens that every tribe and tongue on this globe does have a witness and still our Lord has not returned, there will be the need for new reflection on that state of affairs for the church in the world.

What will tie this reflection into any new thinking in future days as the missiological terrain shifts is the necessity of trying to adhere as closely as possible to the heart of the Gospel. In Fee's reconstruction of the setting that is behind Paul's argument in I Corinthians 1:10-4:21 he looks at the issue of the "quarreling" and "divisions" and notes how this theme tends to become the dominant idea that influences people's interpretation of the rest of the letter.[318] He argues that more likely it is not the existence of parties within the church that is the issue, but rather the Corinthian construal of their newfound faith as a form of wisdom.[319] The division caused by boasting in their various teachers is thus only a symptom of a greater problem which is the threat that this false theology posed to the Gospel, the nature of the church and apostolic ministry.[320] Quarrels were not the most significant error, rather "the nature of this particular strife had as its root cause their false theology, which had exchanged the theology of the cross for a false triumphalism that went beyond, or excluded the cross."[321]

The issue of planting the church among peoples where it does not currently exist is not simply fodder for missiological debate. It is not

---

318 Fee, *Corinthians*, 47.
319 Ibid., 49.
320 Ibid., 50.
321 Ibid.

a small side-issue in the greater life of the church to be engaged in by missionaries and missiologists while the church at large goes about its business. In a more profound way it has to do with the very nature of the Gospel and the work of the cross. Is this good news really for everyone? Is the cross just a defining symbol or does it have the power to turn us from the pursuit of our own agendas to follow Jesus as he seeks and saves the lost? People who write on the biblical theology of mission tell us that God is the God of mission and the Bible is a missiological book. The good news really is for all the peoples and is still the power of God unto salvation. It is my hope that this small book will help us to contend for the Gospel of the crucified and risen Jesus that embraces all of the peoples of this earth. May the Spirit help us as we read and listen to his voice.

WORKS CITED

ADENEY, MIRIAM. "Telling Stories: Contextualization and American Missiology." *Global Missiology for the 21st Century: The Iguassu Dialogue,* Edited by William D. Taylor, 377-88. Grand Rapids: Baker Academic, 2000.

AGNEW, FRANCIS H. "The Origin of the NT Apostle-Concept: A Review Research." *Journal of Biblical Literature* 105, no. 1 (1985): 75-96.

ANDERSON, JUSTICE. "An Overview of Missiology." *Missiology,* Edited by John Mark Terry, Ebbie Smith and Justice Anderson, 1-17. Nashville: Broadmann & Holman, 1998.

BARRETT, DAVID B., TODD M. JOHNSON, CHRISTOPHER R. GUIDRY, AND PETER F. Crossing, eds. *World Christian Trends AD 30-AD 2200: Interpreting the Annual Christian Megacensus.* Pasadena: William Carey Library, 2001.

BARRETT, DAVID, AND TODD JOHNSON. *Our Globe and How to Reach It: Seeing the World Evangelized by AD 2000 and Beyond.* Birmingham: New Hope, 1990.

BEVANS, STEPHEN B. AND ROGER P. SCHROEDER. *Constants in Context: A Theology of Missions for Today.* Maryknoll: Orbis, 2004.

BOSCH, DAVID J. *Transforming Mission: Paradigm Shifts in Theology of Mission.* Maryknoll: Orbis Books, 1991.

_____. "Reflections on Biblical Models of Mission." *Toward the Twenty-First Century in Christian Mission: Essays in Honor of Gerald H. Anderson,* Edited by James M. Phillips and Robert T. Coote, 175-92. Grand Rapids: Eerdmans, 1993.

BRADSHAW, B. *Bridging the Gap: Evangelism, Development and Shalom.* Monrovia: MARC, 1993.

BUSH, LUIS. "What Is Joshua Project 2000?" *Mission Frontiers* November-December (1995): 6-11.

CAMPBELL, ROSS. "National AD 2000 Initiative." *Mission Frontiers* November-December (1995): 49-50.

CORWIN, GARY. "Just Where Are the Frontiers." *International Journal of Frontier Missions* 9, no. 1 (1992): 3-6.

_____. "Sociology and Missiology: Reflection on Mission Research." *Missiology and the Social Sciences: Contributions, Cautions and Conclusions*, Edited by Edward Rommen and Gary Corwin. Pasadena: William Carey Library, 1996.

DAIN, A. J. "International Congress on World Evangelization." *In Let the Earth Hear His Voice: International Congress on World Evangelization Lausanne, Switzerland*, Edited by J. D. Douglas Minneapolis: World Wide Publications, 1975.

DAVALAI, VARUCHI. "South Asia Rises to Play Its Role in Joshua Project 2000." *Mission Frontiers* November-December (1995): 24.

DAYTON, EDWARD. "Reaching Unreached Peoples: Guidelines and Definitions for Those Concerned with World Evangelization." *International Journal of Frontier Missions* 2, no. 1 (1985): 31-38.

DOLLAR, HAROLD. "The Twelve Apostles: Models for Frontier Missions?" *International Journal of Frontier Missions* 10, no. 2 (1993): 59-63.

ELDER, TED. "Where Are the Frontiers?" *International Journal of Frontier Missions* 9, no. 1 (1992): 7-8.

ENGEL, JAMES F. AND WILLIAM A. DRYNESS. *Changing the Mind of Missions: Where Have We Gone Wrong?* Downers Grove: InterVarsity Press, 2000.

ESCOBAR, SAMUEL. "Evangelical Missiology: Peering in the Future." *Global Missiology for the 21st Century: The Iguassu Dialogue*, Edited by William D. Taylor, 101-122. Grand Rapids: Baker Academic, 2000.

FEE, GORDON D. *The First Epistle to the Corinthians*. Grand Rapids: Eerdmans, 1987.

GLASSER, ARTHUR. "Evangelical Missions." *Toward the Twenty-First Century in Christian Mission: Essays in Honor of Gerald H. Anderson*, Edited by James M. Phillips and Robert T. Coote, 9-20. Grand Rapids: Eerdmans Publishing Company, 1993.

GLASSER, ARTHUR F., CHARLES VAN ENGEN, DEAN S. GILLILAND, AND SHAWN B. REDFORD. *Announcing the Kingdom: The Story of God's Mission in the Bible.* Grand Rapids: Baker Academic, 2005.

GRAHAM, BILLY. "Let the Earth Hear His Voice." *Let the Earth Hear His Voice: International Congress on World Evangelization Lausanne, Switzerland,* Edited by J. D. Douglas, Minneapolis: World Wide Publications, 1975.

_____. "Why Lausanne?" In *Let the Earth Hear His Voice: International Congress on World Evangelization Lausanne, Switzerland,* Edited by J. D. Douglas, 22-36. Minneapolis: World Wide Publications, 1975.

GREENE, DAN. "Dusting Off the Apostolic Function." *International Journal of Frontier Missions,* 1984. Accessed 5 October 2007. Available from http:www.ijfm.org/PDFs_IJFM/01_3_PDFs/greene.pdf.

GUDER, DARREL L., LOIS BARRETT, INAGRACE T. DIETTERICH, GEORGE R. HUNSBERGER, ALAN J. ROXBURGH, AND CRAIG VAN GELDER, EDS. *Missional Church: A Vision of the Sending of the Church in North America,* The Gospel and Our Culture Series. Grand Rapids: William B. Eerdmans Publishing Company, 1998.

GUTHRIE, STAN. *Missions in the Third Millennium: 21 Key Trends for the 21st Century.* Carlisle, Cumbria, UK: Paternoster Press, 2000.

HARRIS, PAULA. "Calling Young People to Missionary Vocations in a 'Yahoo' World." *Missiology: An International Review* 30, no. 1 (2002): 33-50.

HESSELGRAVE, DAVID. *Today's Choices for Tomorrow's Mission: An Evangelical Perspective on Trends and Issues in Missions.* Grand Rapids: Academie Books, 1988.

_____. *Paradigms in Conflict: 10 Key Questions in Christian Missions Today.* Grand Rapids: Kregel Academic and Professional, 2005.

HIEBERT, PAUL. "Foreword." *Announcing the Kingdom: The Story of God's Mission in the Bible,* Edited by Arthur F. Glasser, Charles Van Engen, Dean S. Gilliland and Shawn B. Redford, 7-9. Grand Rapids: Baker Academic, 2005.

HIRSCH, ALAN. *The Forgotten Ways: Reactivating the Missional Church.* Grand Rapids: Brazos Press, 2006.

HOGAN, J. PHILIP. "Response to Dr. Ralph Winter's Paper." *Let the Earth Hear His Voice,* Edited by J. D. Douglas. Minneapolis: World Wide Publications, 1975.

HORTON, STANLEY. "Blessing for All." *Enrichment* Summer (1999): 93-95.

HURST, RANDY. "The Secret of Accelerating and Lasting Growth." *Today's Pentecostal Evangel,* (2006): 24-25.

JAFFARIAN, E. MICHAEL. "World Evangelization by A.D. 2000: Will We Make It?" *Evangelical Missions Quarterly* January (1994): 18-26.

_____. "The Statistical State of the Missionary Enterprise." *Missiology: An International Review* 30, no. 1 (2002): 15-29.

JANSEN, FRANK KALEB. "Four Decisive Moves Forward." *Mission Frontiers,* 1993. Accessed 11 June 2007. Available from http://www.missionfrontiers. org/1993/0102/jf935.htm.

JENKINS, PHILIP. *The Next Christendom: The Coming of Global Christianity.* Oxford: Oxford Press, 2002.

JOHNSON, ALAN R. "Analyzing the Frontier Mission Movement and Unreached People Group Thinking Part I: The Frontier Mission Movement's Understanding of the Modern Mission Era." *International Journal of Frontier Missions* 18, no. 2 (2001): 81-88.

_____. "Analyzing the Frontier Mission Movement and Unreached People Group Thinking Part II: Major Concepts of the Frontier Mission Movement." *International Journal of Frontier Missions* 18, no. 2 (2001): 89-97.

JOHNSON, TODD, AND PETER F. CROSSING. "Which Peoples Need Priority Attention: Those with the Least Christian Resources." *Mission Frontiers,* (2002): 16-23.

JOHNSTONE, PATRICK. "People Groups: How Many Unreached?" *International Journal of Frontier Missions* 7, no. 2 (1990): 35-40.

JOHNSTONE, PATRICK, AND JASON MANDRYK. *Operation World: 21st Century Edition.* Carlisle, United Kingdom: Paternoster Lifestyle, 2001.

JONGENEEL, J. A. B. AND J. M. VAN ENGELEN. "Contemporary Currents in Missiology." In *Missiology: An Ecumenical Introduction: Texts and Contexts of Global Christianity,* ed. A. Camps, L. A. Hoedemaker, F. J. Verstraelen and J. D. Gort, 438-457. Grand Rapids: Eerdmans, 1995.

JOSHUA PROJECT. "Joshua Project: Bringing Definition to the Unfinished Task." *Joshua Project*, 2007. Accessed 11 June 2007. Available from http://www.joshuaproject.net /index.php.

KEESING, ROGER. "Theories of Culture." *Annual Review of Anthropology* 3 (1974): 73-98.

KLAUS, BYRON AND DOUGLAS PETERSEN, EDS. *The Essential J. Philip Hogan.* Vol. 1, The J. Philip Hogan World Missions Series. Springfield, Missouri: Assemblies of God Theological Seminary, 2006.

KUHN, THOMAS S. *The Structure of Scientific Revolutions.* Vol. II, No. 2, 2d ed., Enlarged ed. International Encyclopedia of Unified Science, Foundations of the Unity of Science, Edited by Otto Neurath, Rudolf Carnap and Charles Morris. Chicago: The University of Chicago Press, 1970.

KUZMIC, PETER. "Europe." *Toward the Twenty-First Century in Christian Mission: Essays in Honor of Gerald H. Anderson,* Edited by James M. Phillips and Robert T. Coote, 148-163. Grand Rapids: Eerdmans, 1993.

MCGAVRAN, DONALD. *Understanding Church Growth.* Fully rev. ed. Grand Rapids: Eerdmans, 1970.

MCGAVRAN, DONALD ANDERSON. *The Bridges of God: A Study in the Strategy of Missions.* New York: Friendship Press, 1955.

MCGAVRAN, DONALD ANDERSON, AND ARTHUR F. GLASSER. *Contemporary Theologies of Mission.* Grand Rapids: Baker, 1983.

MCGEE, GARY B. "Saving Souls or Saving Lives?" *Paraclete* 28, no. 4 (1994): 11-23.

MCQUILKIN, ROBERTSON. "Six Inflammatory Questions." *Evangelical Missions Quarterly* April (1994): 130-34.

_____. "Six Inflammatory Questions—Part 2." *Evangelical Missions Quarterly* July (1994): 258-64.

MOLL, ROB. "Missions Incredible." *Christianity Today,* March 1, 2006. Accessed 11 October 2007. Available from http://www.christianitytoday.com/38168.

MYERS, BRYANT L. *Walking with the Poor.* Maryknoll: Orbis, 1999.

NEILL, STEPHEN. *Creative Tension.* London: Edinburgh House Press, 1959.

NEWBIGIN, LESSLIE. *The Household of God: Lectures on the Nature of the Church.* London: SCM Press, 1953.

_____. "Preface." *Toward the Twenty-First Century in Christian Mission: Essays in Honor of Gerald H. Anderson*, Edited by James M. Phillips and Robert T. Coote, 1-6. Grand Rapids: Eerdmans Publishing Company, 1993.

PIERSON, PAUL. "Local Churches in Mission: What's Behind the Impatience with Traditional Mission Agencies?" *International Bulletin of Missionary Research*, (1998): 146-50.

PIPER, JOHN. "The Supremacy of God among 'All the Nations.'" *International Journal of Frontier Missions* 13, no. 1 (1996): 15-26.

POCOCK, MICHAEL, GAILYN VAN RHEENEN, AND DOUGLAS MCCONNELL. *The Changing Face of World Missions: Engaging Contemporary Issues and Trends*. Grand Rapids: Baker Academic, 2005.

PRIEST, ROBERT J., TERRY DISCHINGER, STEVE RASMUSSEN, AND C. M. BROWN. "Researching the Short-Term Mission Movement." *Missiology: An International Review* 34, no. 4 (2006): 431-450.

RADCLIFFE, LAWRENCE [LEN BARTLOTTI]. "Part-2: A Field Worker Speaks out About the Rush to Reach All Peoples." *Mission Frontiers* January-February (1998).

RANCE, DELONN LYNN. "The Empowered Call: The Activity of the Holy Spirit in Salvadoran Assemblies of God Missionaries." Ph.D. Dissertaton, Fuller Theological Seminary, 2004.

RILEY, TERRY. "Intercession and World Evangelization." *International Journal of Frontier Missions* January-March (1995): 18-19.

RITZER, GEORGE. *The McDonaldization of Society*. New Century Edition. Thousand Oaks, California: Pine Forge Press, 2000.

ROBERT, DANA L. "Encounter with Christ: Luke as Mission Historian for the Twenty-First Century." *Evangelical, Ecumenical, and Anabaptist Missiologies in Conversation: Essays in Honor of Wilbert Shenk*, Edited by James R. Krabill, Walter Sawatsky and Charles Van Engen, 19-27. Maryknoll: Orbis Books, 2006.

SAMUEL, VINAY, AND CHRIS SUGDEN, EDS. *Mission as Transformation: A Theology of the Whole Gospel*. Irvine, California: Regnum, 1999.

SAWATSKY, WALTER. "What If the Three Worlds of Christian History Converged?" *Evangelical, Ecumenical, and Anabaptist Missiologies in Conversation: Essays in Honor of Wilbert Shenk*, Edited by James R. Krabill, Walter

Sawatsky and Charles Van Engen, 38-48. Maryknoll, New York: Orbis Books, 2006.

SCHERER, JAMES A., AND STEPHEN B. BEVANS, EDS. *New Directions in Mission and Evangelization 1: Basic Statements 1974-1991.* Edited by James A. Scherer and Stephen B. Bevans. Vol. 1, New Directions in Mission and Evangelization. Maryknoll: Orbis Books, 1992.

SCOGGINS, DICK. "Nurturing a New Generation of 'Pauline' and 'Petrine' Apostles." *Mission Frontiers* July-August (2006): 11-12.

SCOTT, WALDRON. *Bring Forth Justice: A Contemporary Perspective on Mission.* Grand Rapids: Eerdmans, 1980.

SCRIBNER, DAN. "A Model for Determining the Most Needy Unreached or Least-Reached Peoples." *Mission Frontiers*, (2004): 6-13.

SEEL, JOHN. "Modernity and Evangelicals: American Evangelicalism as a Global Case Study." *Faith and Modernity*, Edited by Philip Sampson, Vinay Samuel and Chris Sugden, 287-313. Oxford: Regnum Books International, 1994.

SEVERN, FRANK. "The Critical Context of Today's World Mission." *Evangelical Missions Quarterly*, (1992): 176-79.

_____. "Some Thoughts on the Meaning of 'All the Nations.'" *Evangelical Missions Quarterly*, (1997): 412-419.

SHENK, WILBERT R. *Changing Frontiers of Mission.* Maryknoll: Orbis, 2001.

SHOWALTER, RICHARD. "All the Clans, All the Peoples." *International Journal of Frontier Missions* 13, no. 1 (1996): 11-13.

SIDER, RON. *Evangelism and Social Action: Uniting the Church to Heal a Lost and Broken World.* London: Hodder and Stoughton, 1993.

SINCLAIR, DAN AND DICK SCOGGINS. "Introducing the Apnet: A 21st Century Approach to Apostolic Ministry." *Mission Frontiers* November-December (2006): 13-16.

TABER, CHARLES R. *The World Is Too Much with Us: "Culture" in Modern Protestant Missions* The Modern Missions Era, 1792-1992: An Appraisal. Edited by Wilbert R. Shenk. Macon: Mercer University Press, 1991.

THOMAS, NORMAN E., ED. *Classic Texts in Mission and World Christianity.* Vol. 20, American Society of Missiology Series. Maryknoll: Orbis Books, 1995.

VAN ENGEN, Charles. *Mission on the Way: Issues in Mission Theology.* Grand Rapids: Baker Books, 1996.

VERKUYL, JOHANNES. *Contemporary Missiology: An Introduction.* Translated by Dale Cooper. Grand Rapids: Eerdmans, 1978.

WAGNER, C. PETER, AND EDWARD DAYTON, EDS. *Unreached Peoples '80.* Elgin: David C. Cook Publishing, 1980.

WALLS, ANDREW F. "Evangelical and Ecumenical." *Evangelical, Ecumenical, and Anabaptist Missiologies in Conversation: Essays in Honor of Wilbert Shenk*, Edited by James R. Krabill, Walter Sawatsky and Charles Van Engen, 28-37. Maryknoll: Orbis Books, 2006.

WILSON, BRYAN. *Religion in Sociological Perspective.* Oxford: Oxford University Press, 1982.

WILSON, EVERETT A. *Strategy of the Spirit: J. Philip Hogan and the Growth of the Assemblies of God Worldwide 1960-1990.* Carlisle, Cumbria: Regnum Books International, 1997.

WINTER, RALPH. "Introduction: Why an Evangelical Response to Bangkok?" *The Evangelical Response to Bangkok*, ed. Ralph Winter, 1-24. South Pasadena: William Carey Library, 1973.

_____. "The Highest Priority: Cross-Cultural Evangelism." *Let the Earth Hear His Voice.* Edited by. J. D. Douglas, 213-241. Minneapolis: World Wide Publications, 1975.

_____. "Penetrating the New Frontiers." *Unreached Peoples '79.* Edited by C. Peter Wagner and Edward Dayton, 37-77. Elgin: David C. Cook, 1978.

_____. "Frontier Mission Perspectives." *Seeds of Promise: World Consultation on Frontier Missions, Edinburgh '80.* Edited by Allan Starling, 45-99. Pasadena: William Carey Library, 1981.

_____. "Mission in the 1990s: I. Ralph D. Winter." *International Bulletin of Missionary Research*, (1990): 98-102.

_____. "Are 90% of Our Missionaries Serving in the Wrong Places?" *Mission Frontiers*, (1991): 34-35.

_____. "Defining the Frontiers." *International Journal of Frontier Missions* 9, no. 1 (1992): 9-11.

_____. "Editorial Comment." *Mission Frontiers*, (1995): 2, 4.

_____. "The Story of the Frontier Mission Movement." *Mission Frontiers*, (1995): 44-53.

_____. "Missiological Education for Lay People." *Missiological Education for the Twenty-First Century: The Book, the Circle, and the Sandals.* Edited by J. Dudley Woodberry, Charles Van Engen and Edgar J. Elliston, 169-85. Maryknoll: Orbis, 1996.

_____. "Four Men, Three Eras." *Mission Frontiers,* (1997): 18-23.

_____. "Three Types of Ministry." *Evangelical Missions Quarterly,* (1997): 420-421.

_____. "The Meaning of Mission: Understanding This Term Is Crucial to the Completion of the Missionary Task." *Mission Frontiers,* (1998): 15.

_____. "Six Spheres of Mission Overseas." *Mission Frontiers,* (1998): 16-45.

_____. "The New Macedonia: A Revolutionary New Era in Mission Begins." *Perspectives on the World Christian Movement: A Reader.* Edited by Ralph D. Winter and Steven C. Hawthorne, 339-53. Pasadena: William Carey Library, 1999.

_____. "Advancing Strategies of Closure: From Mission to Evangelism to Mission." *International Journal of Frontier Missions* 19, no. 4 (2002): 6-8.

WINTER, RALPH, AND BRUCE A. KOCH. "Finishing the Task: The Unreached People Challenge." *International Journal of Frontier Missions* 19, no. 4 (2002): 15-25.

WRIGHT, CHRIS. "Re-Affirming Holistic Mission: A Cross-Centered Approach in All Areas of Life." *Lausanne World Pulse,* 2005. Accessed 6 October 2007. Available from http://www.lausanneworldpulse.com/pdf/issues/LWP1005.pdf.

YODER, LAWRENCE M. "Church Growth Theories in Indonesia." *Evangelical, Ecumenical, and Anabaptist Missiologies in Conversation: Essays in Honor of Wilbert Shenk.* Edited by James R. Krabill, Walter Sawatsky and Charles Van Engen, 109-119. Maryknoll: Orbis Books, 2006.

INDEX

A

Johnstone, Patrick, 127–128
Joshua Project
 comprehensive mission approach, 194
 minimalist conception of the Great Commission, 141
 Progress Scale, 12
 purpose of, 134–135
 reminder not to pit one part of the world against another, 180–185
 website, 134, 135
 world classifications, 135
Joshua Project 2000, 142–143
Justification by faith, 140–141

K

Koch, Bruce A., 129–130
Kostenberger, Andreas J., 69–70
Kuhn, Thomas S., 37–41
Kung, paradigms and missions, 37–40
Kuzmic, Peter, 181

L

Language barrier, 119
Lausanne Committee Strategy Working Group, 132
Lausanne Congress. *See* International Congress on World Evangelization
Lausanne Strategy Working Group, 127–128
Lightfoot, Joseph Barber, 53–54
Luke, planting churches, 62–63

M

Macro-paradigms, 39–42
 divisions, 39–40
 normal missions, 41–42
 questions in Christian mission, 40–41
Magnifying glass illustration, 46–47
Maliknowskian functionalism, 151–153
MARC Unreached Peoples, 160–161
Matrix of apostolicity, 101
McDonaldization, 220
McGavran, Donald, 119–120
McQuilkin, Robertson, 140, 148–149
mDNA, 87–88
Medieval-Roman Catholic, 40
Meso paradigm, 41

O

P